Furthering Fair Housing

Edited by
JUSTIN P. STEIL, NICHOLAS F. KELLY,
LAWRENCE J. VALE, AND MAIA S. WOLUCHEM

Furthering Fair Housing

*Prospects for Racial Justice in
America's Neighborhoods*

TEMPLE UNIVERSITY PRESS
Philadelphia • Rome • Tokyo

TEMPLE UNIVERSITY PRESS
Philadelphia, Pennsylvania 19122
tupress.temple.edu

Library of Congress Cataloging-in-Publication Data

Names: Steil, Justin, editor. | Kelly, Nicholas F., 1987– editor. | Vale, Lawrence J.,
    1959– editor. | Woluchem, Maia S., 1991– editor.
Title: Furthering fair housing : prospects for racial justice in America's
    neighborhoods / edited by Justin P. Steil, Nicholas F. Kelly, Lawrence J. Vale,
    and Maia S. Woluchem.
Description: Philadelphia : Temple University Press, 2021. | Includes
    bibliographical references and index. | Summary: "Examines the Department
    of Housing and Urban Development's 2015 Affirmatively Furthering Fair
    Housing (AFFH) Rule and its potential to reduce housing discrimination
    and promote integration in the United States"— Provided by publisher.
Identifiers: LCCN 2020022309 (print) | LCCN 2020022310 (ebook) |
    ISBN 9781439920725 (cloth) | ISBN 9781439920732 (paperback) |
    ISBN 9781439920749 (pdf)
Subjects: LCSH: Discrimination in housing—United States. | Housing policy—
    United States. | Race relations—United States.
Classification: LCC HD7288.76.U5 F79 2021 (print) | LCC HD7288.76.U5 (ebook)
    | DDC 363.5/9900973—dc23
LC record available at https://lccn.loc.gov/2020022309
LC ebook record available at https://lccn.loc.gov/2020022310

9 8 7 6 5 4 3 2 1

Contents

Acknowledgments

We would like to thank the many, many individuals who helped make this book possible over the course of four years. First, we thank all the authors in the volume, who worked with us through multiple drafts of their chapters. Second, we thank the dozens of city officials, public housing authority leaders, federal officials, and others who put together fair housing plans, spoke with us, and worked with us to make those documents public. Third, we thank the civil rights advocates who have tirelessly worked across generations to create more equal access to opportunities and to advance visions of a democratic, just, multiracial nation.

This volume began with a symposium in the fall of 2016, supported by the Massachusetts Institute of Technology (MIT) Department of Urban Studies and Planning. For helping guide the creation of that symposium and moderate many of the panels, we thank Ingrid Gould Ellen, who was at the time a visiting professor at MIT. For working closely with us to help plan the symposium and co-teach a class on the Affirmatively Furthering Fair Housing (AFFH) Rule at MIT, we are grateful to Ezra Haber Glenn. Harriette Crawford and Phil Sunde proved to be instrumental in helping put on the conference, and Takeo Kuwabara assisted us throughout, including advertising the symposium and helping us set up a website. Eran Ben-Joseph, as the head of MIT's Department of Urban Studies and Planning, offered financial and collegial support for the symposium from the beginning. We also thank Karmen Cheung, Jessie Lee Heneghan, and Will Monson for assistance with logistics and advertising, and Lee Fennell, William Fischel, Jeffrey Lubell, David Harris, Janine Anzalota, and Chrystal Kornegay for participating in the event. Additionally, we are grateful to all the participants in the symposium for their helpful questions and comments.

The process of transforming the discussions that began at the symposium into this book proved to be predictably lengthy. In addition to all the authors who patiently worked with us, we would like to thank many of the folks who helped us along the way. Reed Jordan was fundamental in helping track down Assessments of Fair Housing (AFHs) for the research in the chapter he coauthored as well as in conceiving the idea to launch a website collecting the work (available at furtheringfairhousing.mit.edu). Hayley Flores helped us take the website idea from concept to reality. For help with notes, we thank Valeria Alvarado and Francis Goyes. We appreciated the feedback received on our chapter and previous related research at several conferences, including the Association of Collegiate Schools of Planning conference and two gatherings at the University of Pennsylvania: The Fair Housing Act at 50 and US Housing Policy—The Future of What Works, with special thanks to Vincent Reina for his inclusion of this work there. We offer special gratitude to Aaron Javsicas and the entire team at Temple University Press for helping see this project through from inception to completion with enthusiasm, engagement, and patience.

Conflicts over spatial and racial justice have recurred throughout the history of the United States. We are indebted to the centuries of struggle for equal rights and anti-racist policies and hope this book can be a helpful tool as we consider how to translate desires for racial justice into plans and policies. The chapters in this volume suggest that, with the right policies at the federal level, many local officials are ready to play a needed role in addressing some of the long-standing inequalities in resources and in access to opportunity in our cities and regions.

Furthering Fair Housing

Introduction

Introduction

Fair Housing

Promises, Protests, and Prospects for
Racial Equity in Housing

JUSTIN P. STEIL, NICHOLAS F. KELLY,
LAWRENCE J. VALE, AND MAIA S. WOLUCHEM

Introduction: A New Round of Fair Housing Struggle

In the United States, the paired struggle for fairness in housing and for equality of access to opportunity is as old as the nation itself. It is a struggle with many battles, yielding both significant gains and lamentable reversals. This book centers on the most recent of these struggles: a regulation, little known outside housing policy circles, called the Affirmatively Furthering Fair Housing (AFFH) Rule, which was issued by the Department of Housing and Urban Development (HUD) in 2015. The AFFH Rule was immediately attacked by a variety of critics, suspended by the Donald Trump administration in 2018, and then rescinded in 2020. But the debate leading up to the implementation of the rule and the lessons learned from it have the potential to reshape national housing policy, local government actions to encourage more equal access to place-based opportunities, and the landscape of racial equity more broadly. At a time of renewed national reckoning about the role of structural racism in American society, debate over the AFFH Rule is a product of that struggle and its microcosm. As future administrations consider how to address intertwined concerns of housing affordability and racial disparities in access to resources, reflection upon the AFFH Rule will be a crucial starting point.

The Affirmatively Furthering Fair Housing Rule

On July 15, 2015, President Barack Obama's HUD secretary, Julián Castro, announced the finalization of the AFFH Rule, the most significant federal effort in a generation to address long-standing, pervasive residential segregation by race and to increase equality of access to place-based opportunities, such as high-performing schools or access to jobs. Pointedly, Castro made the announcement in Chicago, one of America's most racially segregated metropolitan areas.

Nearly fifty years earlier, the Fair Housing Act of 1968 had outlawed the denial of housing on the basis of race, color, religion, or sex. That landmark legislation had also instructed all executive departments and agencies to administer their programs "in a manner affirmatively to further" fair housing.[1] Although federal officials occasionally made efforts to address the separate and unequal neighborhoods that have characterized U.S. metropolitan areas for more than a century, the Fair Housing Act's mandate to take active steps to reduce disparities in access to place-based opportunities essentially withered on the vine. Indeed in the United States, the history of fair housing, and of racial equity more broadly, has been a famously long struggle, fraught with repeated cycles of promises, protests, backlash, and uncertain prospects for success.

Over the five decades since the passage of the Fair Housing Act, Republican and Democratic administrations have largely declined to require states or localities to take meaningful steps to reduce segregation or disparities in access to opportunity as the act's mandate to affirmatively further fair housing required. While levels of Black-white segregation have declined somewhat since the Fair Housing Act's passage, they remain high, and levels of Latinx-white segregation have remained largely unchanged over the past half-century.[2] Research has consistently found that higher levels of metropolitan-area segregation are associated with lower levels of socioeconomic mobility for all residents and with negative impacts on the life chances of African American and Latinx children and young adults,[3] including wider gaps in educational attainment, employment, and earnings;[4] negative health outcomes;[5] and reduced political power.[6] Deindustrialization, suburbanization, and widening income polarization have interacted with continuing racial residential segregation to contribute to the creation and intergenerational transference of neighborhood contexts characterized by concentrated, racialized poverty.[7]

With this mounting evidence of associations between segregated metropolitan areas, high-poverty neighborhoods, and negative outcomes for social mobility and socioeconomic opportunity, the Obama administration devoted substantial efforts to create the AFFH Rule to finally implement the 1968 act's mandate. As enacted, the AFFH Rule requires HUD to provide grant recipients with uniform data about residential segregation and disparities in access to place-based resources and opportunities, and HUD created a publicly accessible website that generates customized maps and tables for each jurisdiction and its surrounding region. The rule requires HUD grantees to engage with their residents to create local strategies to address disparities by race, national origin, family status, disability, and other protected characteristics in access to amenities or risks such as quality schools, proximity to employment, and exposure to environmental hazards. The rule then requires municipalities to submit plans to HUD, called Assessments of Fair Housing (AFHs). By mandating local creation of specific measurable goals and actions to reduce segregation and increase access to opportunity, the AFHs link these planning and assessment efforts to the availability of future HUD funding.[8]

To operationalize the AFFH Rule, HUD created the AFFH Assessment Tool, which contains questions that guide grantees through effective completion of their fair housing plans. The assessment tool has several key elements, including a community participation section that requires municipalities to gather public input on fair housing issues, make their draft plans public, solicit community feedback, and address those comments and concerns before submission. It also asks municipalities how they have addressed prior fair housing goals and how that progress or lack of progress has influenced the selection of current goals. Municipalities are required to analyze the HUD-provided data and additional local data, including data on segregation and integration along lines of race and ethnicity, national origin, English proficiency, and disability; racially or ethnically concentrated areas of poverty; disparities along protected class lines in access to high-performing schools, employment, transportation, low-poverty neighborhoods, environmentally healthy neighborhoods, and disproportionate housing needs; data on access to opportunity for the residents of publicly supported housing; data on access to opportunity for individuals with disabilities; and an analysis of fair housing enforcement, outreach capacity, and resources.

Based on this assessment of data and information gathered during public engagement activities, the assessment tool asks grant recipients to identify pressing local fair housing challenges and then to pinpoint and to prioritize the factors that contribute to those issues, particularly those that limit realistic opportunities to live in a variety of neighborhoods and drive disparities in access to opportunity. Finally, the tool asks grant recipients to set goals designed to overcome those contributing factors, to clarify how each goal addresses that contributing factor, and to set out metrics, milestones, time frames, and parties responsible for achieving the goals. Crucially, to ensure implementation, HUD requires that metrics, milestones, and strategies be included in subsequent Consolidated Plans, Annual Action Plans, and Public Housing Authority Plans.

HUD timed the due dates for the AFHs to precede the due dates for Community Development Block Grant (CDBG) Consolidated Plans and

Public Housing Authority Plans, which must include fair housing elements from the AFHs. The AFFH Rule obligates HUD to review fair housing plans within sixty days; any plan not reviewed within sixty days is deemed accepted. HUD reviews each AFH to evaluate whether the program participant has met the rule's requirements for analysis, assessment, and goal setting, and the rule mandates that HUD reject an AFH if it is found to be inconsistent with fair housing or civil rights requirements or is substantially incomplete. For any AFH that is not accepted, the rule requires HUD to provide in writing the reasons for nonacceptance and guidance as to how the AFH should be revised to be accepted.

In Fiscal Year 2019, HUD's Community Planning and Development department disbursed $7.7 billion in block grants and related funding to more than 1,200 state and municipal governments. The block grant programs all require state and local governments to conduct annual and long-term strategic planning for their use of these funds in what is known as the Consolidated Plan process. Withheld block grant funding for failure to complete the AFH process would represent a significant financial burden for some HUD program participants—and potentially an effective incentive to comply with the AFFH regulation. Similarly, HUD also requires public housing agencies to conduct annual and long-term planning and produce a Public Housing Authority Plan. To receive block grant funds, program participants must submit a Consolidated Plan to HUD every three to five years and certify that they will comply with all statutory and regulatory requirements, including the AFFH provision.

In the process of its development and after its release, the AFFH Rule was praised and criticized. From the Right, it was decried as social engineering and a federal takeover of the suburbs.[9] Conservative members of Congress tried repeatedly to repeal or undermine the rule after its passage.[10] From the Left, it was criticized as unlikely to be effective, given only blunt enforcement mechanisms.[11] Some took issue with its focus on racial segregation rather than racial equity.[12] Yet others heralded the rule as the most significant step forward for addressing place-based inequality in the United States since the passage of the Fair Housing Act itself in 1968.[13]

This book analyzes multiple dimensions of this new rule, including failures of past efforts to reduce segregation, how the AFFH Rule was crafted, what the effects of the rule have been so far, and how it interacts with other pressing contemporary housing issues, such as gentrification. Work on the book began with a series of public workshops in 2016 about the AFFH Rule as it was initially being implemented. We have worked to update the chapters as much as possible, as the landscape has changed dramatically over and over again in the intervening years. The book lays out criticisms of the AFFH Rule from the Left and the Right and then, given the efforts of the

Trump administration to curtail it, asks where we can go from here. By examining the near past and the distant past, we seek to identify promising new directions for future policies and practices.

The Role of Place in Socioeconomic Mobility and Racial Equity

Over the past half-century, socioeconomic mobility in the United States has declined dramatically. Ninety percent of children born in the 1940s grew up to earn more than their parents, compared to only 50 percent of children born in the 1980s.[14] These backward steps have not been experienced evenly. As socioeconomic mobility has declined broadly across America, the economic gains experienced by African American households immediately following the civil rights movement have largely reversed. The majority of African American households whose parents were in the middle class in the post–civil rights era have experienced downward mobility since, moving lower in the income distribution today than they were in their parents' generation.[15]

These trends are even more dramatic when considering how directly place shapes a child's chances of moving up the economic and social ladders. Neighborhood characteristics are strong predictors of upward socioeconomic mobility, especially for children starting out in the lower half of the income distribution.[16] In particular, the degree of racial and economic segregation in a metropolitan area dramatically influences children's upward economic advancement. The socioeconomic characteristics of neighborhoods are particularly powerful predictors of the educational and economic attainment of African American and Latinx young adults, whose neighborhoods are by and large physically separate and materially unequal from the neighborhoods in which white young adults grow up.[17] Today, residential segregation by race nationwide remains high, and income segregation is increasing, exacerbating gaps in intergenerational mobility by race.[18]

These trends are intertwined with a widening wealth gap that further reinforces economic inequality, particularly by race. For the majority of U.S. homeowners, their homes are their most valuable assets. Thus, one reason for the substantial racial and ethnic disparities in wealth is the disparity in rates of homeownership and in its financial returns. Homeownership rates in the United States reached record highs in 2004 and 2005, when more than three out of every four (76 percent) white non-Hispanic households were homeowners. But even at this peak, only half of Black households (49 percent) and Latinx households (50 percent) owned their own homes.[19] The economic growth in the first decade of the 2000s and the devastating recession beginning in 2008 were caused in part by the increased global investment in U.S.

homes, commodified through the packaging of home mortgage loans into securities. The precipitous decline in home values and the increased rate of foreclosures after 2008 contributed to a widening of the racial wealth gap between white and non-white households. In 2016, the median white household had a net worth of $171,000, nearly ten times the median Black household's net worth of $17,600 and roughly eight times the median Latinx household's net worth of $20,700.[20] By 2019, the white homeownership rate had fallen to 73 percent, while the Black homeownership rate had fallen to 41 percent and the Latinx rate to 47 percent—leaving a 26 to 32 percentage point gap in homeownership rates by race and ethnicity.[21] Even looking solely at those who do own their homes, white homeowners have substantially more net housing wealth, or home equity, than non-white homeowners.[22]

As homeownership rates have declined over the past decade, housing costs for renters have risen—in many cities, faster than renters' incomes. Increasing rent burdens for low- and moderate-income households have contributed to the rise of the most active local and national movements for affordable housing in recent memory. For instance, in 2018 and 2019, tenants' rights activists in Oregon and California won the passage of state laws enabling rent regulation, while tenants in New York strengthened existing rent regulations. Affordable housing organizers in Minneapolis worked with the mayor and city council to enact a "Minneapolis 2040" plan that changed zoning: across the roughly 75 percent of the city previously zoned for single-family homes, construction of three-family (or more) homes is now generally allowed.[23] Similarly, the Oregon state legislature enacted a law in 2019 requiring the creation of multifamily zoning in municipalities statewide. At the same time, conversations about racial equity, especially after the rise of the Black Lives Matter movement, continue to capture public attention and spur a focus on the wide and persistent racial wealth gap as well as racial disparities in measures of access to opportunity.

A home, of course, is also much more than just an asset. The level and quality of neighborhood-based resources are powerful predictors of individual life chances. The condition, security of tenure, and location of one's home, whether owned or rented, all have substantial impacts on one's health, well-being, and socioeconomic mobility. The structure of governance in the United States makes access to crucial public services and resources, such as schools or policing, dependent on the location of one's home.[24] In consequence, the level or quality of these services varies substantially based on jurisdiction or neighborhood. Indeed, differentiation by residential location in the United States is part of a spatial structure that organizes our social lives.[25]

Neighborhoods are not just separated by race, ethnicity, and income; they are also unequal.[26] The average Latinx or African American individual lives in a neighborhood with a substantially higher poverty rate (8 to 10 percentage points) and a lower-performing local school (16 to 22 percentage points) than the average white individual.[27] Neighborhoods shape families across generations, and the inequality of those neighborhoods must be conceptualized as a central dimension of social stratification and racial inequality in the United States.[28]

Because housing policy lies at the intersection of declining socioeconomic mobility and persistent racial and ethnic inequality in wealth and income, housing in recent years has become an issue of greater significance in national politics than has been seen in decades. From mortgage underwriting to foreclosures, rent regulation to evictions, housing cost burdens to exclusionary zoning, gentrification and Yes in My Backyard (YIMBY) organizations, housing policy issues have inspired an array of contemporary local and national social movements. The AFFH Rule connects these movements to the ongoing struggle for racial equality. It also creates leverage to make real changes in local and regional policy.

Nationally, the AFFH Rule has been referenced and expanded upon by a range of actors. Democratic presidential candidates in the 2020 cycle, including Bernie Sanders, Elizabeth Warren, Cory Booker, Kamala Harris, Pete Buttigieg, Amy Klobuchar, and former HUD secretary Julián Castro, all released housing plans that, at least in part, aimed to address disparities in access to place-based resources and opportunities. Sanders proposed national just-cause eviction requirements and rent regulation as well as investments in public housing and housing choice vouchers. He also proposed making federal housing and transportation funds contingent on remedying restrictive zoning ordinances and using HUD's authority to encourage state and local land-use policies that advance racial, economic, and disability integration. Warren proposed an expansive plan to reform land-use rules that restrict affordable housing construction and further racial segregation and recommended investments that would begin to close the racial wealth gap through targeted homeownership assistance. Warren's proposal also increased funding for public housing and strengthened protections for renters. Castro released a detailed plan to expand the housing choice voucher program, prohibit discrimination based on source of income, create a renters' tax credit, invest in subsidized housing, create federal land-use guidelines, and to use an expanded CDBG program to require zoning reforms that would advance fair housing and reduce racial disparities. Harris proposed a federal tax credit designed to ease the burden of rents for low- and moderate-income households. Booker proposed a federal tax credit for renters paying more than 30 percent of their income on rent and offered policies designed to restrain exclusionary zoning.

The eventual Democratic party candidate, Joe Biden, ultimately proposed a plan also aiming to directly address place-based racial disparities.

His plan included restoring and implementing the AFFH Rule, conditioning receipt of federal CDBG and transportation funding on the elimination of exclusionary zoning regulations, strengthening the Community Reinvestment Act, maintaining existing disparate impact liability under the Fair Housing Act, reinstating the power of the Consumer Financial Protection Bureau to investigate discriminatory lending, providing housing choice vouchers to all eligible households, creating a new first-time homebuyer tax credit, creating a new renter's tax credit, helping tenants facing eviction access legal assistance, and allocating increased funding and tax credits to affordable housing production. Perhaps just as important as the details of any of these plans is the fact that these presidential candidates generated new public dialogue about housing affordability and racialized wealth disparities that had been largely absent from previous campaigns.

This public dialogue is further strengthened by the immense power exercised through protest, particularly in the wake of the intertwined health, social, economic, and political crises of 2020. The unprecedented force of the 2020 resurgence of the Black Lives Matter movement has moved conversations about the pervasiveness of white supremacy in U.S. society to the forefront, contributing to significant changes in public perception about racial discrimination, particularly among white audiences. Importantly, the movement has sharpened this growing recognition of the nature of racial discrimination faced by Black Americans, providing a clearer lens through which to view the AFFH Rule.

In 2016, the Movement for Black Lives platform articulated a call to end the war on Black people and a call for reparations—including reparations to atone for long-standing housing discrimination. In addition, the movement demanded divestment from policing and prisons; investment in education and health care; community control over schools and public safety, together with participatory budgeting processes; and reforms to existing political processes that would support independent Black political power and Black self-determination. The platform also called for economic justice, including reforming the tax code, strengthening workers' rights, devoting resources to encourage cooperative or collective ownership, and delivering a right to land, clean air, clean water, and housing. Although the 2020 protests were sparked initially by police violence in a context of enduring white supremacy, the participation of millions of Americans nationwide helped underscore a growing understanding that racism must be understood not as individualized prejudice but as systematic white supremacist subordination—as ideologies, policies, and practices that normalize and perpetuate racialized inequalities. This movement pointedly underscores the deep historical roots undergirding the AFFH Rule, giving it renewed urgency. Seen this way, the racialized disparities in homeownership rates or neighborhood resources that the rule was designed in part to address must be seen as products of racism and a white supremacist social and economic order.

In response to the momentum of the Black Lives Matter movement, Donald Trump countered by continuing to stoke division, especially along racial lines. Among many elements of his response, he reasserted his widespread resentment of protestors and dissent, reaffirmed support for white supremacists, and continued to double down on his racist and divisive rhetoric. Reminiscent of his 2016 campaign, his calls for "law and order" were shouted over the calls for justice, even as protests continued through all fifty states throughout the summer of 2020. His actions illuminated a clear connection between racist ideologies and the policy decisions that uphold these divisions, especially urban and regional policies that continue to enable neighborhood-based socioeconomic and racial inequality. In July he tweeted:

> At the request of many great Americans who live in the Suburbs, and others, I am studying the AFFH housing regulation that is having a devastating impact on these once thriving Suburban areas. Corrupt Joe Biden wants to make them MUCH WORSE. Not fair to homeowners, I may END!

Critics and pundits widely viewed Trump's invocation of the AFFH Rule as an attempt to reverse declining suburban support by further inflaming racial divides. In the following weeks, Trump continued this rhetoric, evoking segregationist fearmongering from the 1960s. He claimed that because of the AFFH Rule, "Your home will go down in value and crime rates will rapidly rise" and that the rule "will totally destroy the beautiful suburbs. Suburbia will be no longer as we know it."[29] On July 23, 2020, the Trump administration issued a final rule titled "Preserving Community and Housing Choice" that repealed the 2015 AFFH Rule.

These statements that presaged the rule's repeal highlight the ways that the struggle for racial justice extends across every urban block and suburban front yard. In so doing, it clarified and amplified what is at stake in the fight to revive—or "END"—the AFFH Rule. Addressing racial disparities in housing produced by white exclusion and resource hoarding requires a complex reimagining of multiple dimensions of our collective ways of life. The work of the AFFH Rule is to root out the ways in which white supremacy has become physically embedded in the American landscape.

The Meaning of Fair Housing

Although much of the dialogue around housing centers on matters of affordability and only implicitly engages issues of fairness, the dialogue is not often explicitly framed in terms of "fair housing." It is worth stepping back, then, to ask what "fair housing" is and what acting "affirmatively to further" it should entail. The dual mandate of the Fair Housing Act, to end discrimination and "to provide . . . for fair housing throughout the United States," raises the question of what is—or should be—"fair" about housing.

As Alexander von Hoffman illustrates in Chapter 1 of this volume, civil rights activists created the "open housing" movement (as it was originally called) during World War II. The movement for open housing gained momentum in the 1950s and 1960s through challenges to government-sponsored or enforced housing segregation and to the widespread use of racially restrictive covenants that prohibited non-white or non-Christian individuals from purchasing housing. The term "open housing" captures fair housing's first meaning in its goal of opening housing opportunities that were denied on the basis of race or religion. The second, affirmative meaning of fair housing—to reduce segregation and increase access to opportunity—embodies a broader and arguably more controversial set of policy aspirations for a more inclusive, equal, and "fair" society. One of the Fair Housing Act's sponsors, Senator Walter Mondale, saw the goal of the act ultimately as the creation of "truly integrated neighborhoods."[30]

How exactly one interprets what it means to create fairness in housing, however, is complex. The AFFH Rule identifies a mandate to "overcome the legacy of segregation, unequal treatment, and historic lack of access to opportunity in housing," but what form that overcoming should take has been a crucial point of division in housing policy for decades. As Edward Goetz points out in Chapter 5, this mandate could be interpreted in at least three ways: first, as opening up exclusionary communities to new residents; second, as dismantling structural incentives that perpetuate racially segregated living patterns; or third, as working to actively integrate residential patterns, even if this integration has the consequence of significantly changing the composition of neighborhoods that have historically been predominantly populated by people of color. The chapters that follow explore the tensions among these different interpretations.

The History of Fair Housing:
From 1866, to 1968, to 2015

To fully understand the significance of housing policy in reproducing inequality and to effectively engage in the contemporary policy debates regarding housing, it is revealing to look back at two key historical moments: first, the Reconstruction period and subsequent rise of racial residential segregation; and second, the civil rights movement and the push for the Fair

Housing Act of 1968. The advances and the setbacks of these earlier rounds of struggle frame the challenges faced by the AFFH Rule.

The Reconstruction Amendments and the Civil Rights Act of 1866

In the midst of the Civil War, Congress passed the Thirteenth Amendment to the Constitution, and in 1865, the states ratified it, abolishing slavery and involuntary servitude throughout the nation and giving Congress the power to enact further legislation to enforce the amendment. Almost as soon as the Civil War had ended and the Thirteenth Amendment had been ratified, however, white officials in the South began to resist emancipation. States and municipalities enacted Black Codes (laws that applied only to African American individuals) to re-create the social and economic structure of slavery, criminalizing "vagrancy" to force freed individuals to sign labor contracts with white employers, allowing sheriffs to hire out Black "vagrants" to white employers to work off their sentences, and providing that Black employees who left before the end of a contract would forfeit all their wages for the year and could be arrested and returned to their "masters."[31] State and local officials generally refused to enforce whatever limited rights their newly enacted state constitutions actually granted to African American residents, white citizens used violent intimidation and terror to oppress Black neighbors, and white planters collaborated to compel freed slaves to work for their former masters or other planters on terms dictated by the employer. Carl Schurz, investigating the progress of Reconstruction, noted that the freed man was "not only not permitted to be idle" but "positively prohibited from working or carrying on a business for himself" and "[wa]s just as much bound to his employer 'for better and for worse' as he was when slavery existed in the old form."[32]

Despite this exploitation of Black labor, arguably the most pressing problem facing freed men and women was access to land.[33] During the Civil War, some freed slaves were able to access land abandoned by former plantation owners, but in 1865, President Andrew Johnson's Amnesty Proclamation stripped that property from the freed men and women and returned it to white plantation owners.[34] Land—"this absolutely fundamental and essential thing to any real emancipation of the slaves—was continually pushed by all emancipated Negroes and their representatives in every Southern state," W. E. B. Du Bois observed. Appeals to state and federal officials for land, however, were "met by ridicule, [and] by anger."[35]

Promise
In response to Southern efforts to effectively re-enslave the newly freed men and women, the Republican majority in Congress enacted the nation's first

civil rights law, the Civil Rights Bill of 1866. President Johnson vetoed the legislation, arguing that the bill "intervenes between capital and labor and attempts to settle questions of political economy through the agency of numerous officials," but Congress overrode the veto.[36] Reinforcing the Thirteenth Amendment, Congress intended for the legislation to make everyone born in the United States truly full citizens. The statute stated that all

> shall have the same right in every State and Territory in the United States to make and enforce contracts; to sue, be parties and give evidence; to inherit, purchase, lease sell hold, and convey real and personal property; and to full and equal benefit of all laws and proceedings for the security of person and property as is enjoyed by the white citizens, and shall be subject to like punishment, pains, and penalties and to none other, any law, statute, ordinance, regulation, or custom, to the contrary notwithstanding.[37]

In light of the Black Codes, Congress recognized the urgent need for federal protections against discrimination by the states. As important, Congress also recognized the danger of private discrimination by white individuals and white collectives, acting to deny African American men and women equal social and economic rights, especially equal rights in land. In his veto, President Johnson complained about the congressional recognition of the asymmetry of political, legal, and social power in a context of white supremacy, arguing that "the distinction of race and color is by the bill made to operate in favor of the colored and against the white race" and presaging contemporary arguments regarding "reverse discrimination."[38]

As the struggle between Republican legislators and President Johnson continued, congressional leaders sought to enshrine the civil rights protections in a constitutional amendment and thus protect them against a later congressional repeal. Congress proposed the Fourteenth Amendment in 1866, and the states ratified it in 1868, solidifying the citizenship of all those born within the United States; prohibiting states from depriving citizens of life, liberty, and property without due process of law; and prohibiting states from denying to any person within their jurisdiction the equal protection of the laws.

The Thirteenth, Fourteenth, and later Fifteenth (prohibiting discrimination on the basis of race in voting) Amendments held out the promise of a Reconstruction that could bring forth a true multiracial democracy. Together, these Reconstruction amendments transformed the Constitution from a document that was designed to protect the rights of individual white male property holders from interference by the state into a document that made it possible for the federal government to protect the rights of all those within the United States from discrimination by those states.[39] Electorates voted large numbers of African American officials into almost every level of public office, from city councils, to state legislatures, to Congress. For a brief moment, Black men (although not yet women) were part of the structure of governance, and "poor men were ruling and taxing rich men."[40]

Protest

White elites' opposition to Reconstruction, however, only intensified as African American elected officials revealed the falsity of white supremacist myths. Further, the economic situation of the South after the Civil War was dire. Industrialization was transforming not only the northern economy but also the southern one. White plantation owners still owned land but now found it much more difficult to extract labor at no or very low cost. White and Black workers without property struggled to survive. Nationally, the fledgling labor movements, in the words of Du Bois, "never had the intelligence or knowledge, as a whole, to see in Black slavery and Reconstruction, the kernel and meaning of the labor movement in the United States," and the hope for a "union of democratic forces never took place."[41] After the disputed 1876 presidential election, northern Republicans agreed to remove federal troops from the South, cede control back to the white planter elites, and essentially abandon the freed people in exchange for awarding the White House to Republican Rutherford B. Hayes. "Redeemer" governments quickly took power across the South, rewriting state constitutions to further disenfranchise and disempower Black citizens.

Still, farmers' alliances, including the National Farmers' Alliance and the Colored Farmers' Alliance, sprung up in the 1880s and 1890s and solidified into the Populist or People's Party, seeking to strengthen direct democracy through such changes as the direct election of U.S. senators and to enact policies equalizing the playing field between small farmers and industry, such as a graduated income tax. Georgia Populist Party leader Tom Watson addressed racially mixed crowds of farmers, saying that "the colored tenant is in the same boat as the white tenant, the colored laborer with the white laborer, and that the accident of color can make no difference in the interests of farmers, croppers, and laborers."[42] In North Carolina, the fusion of Republican and Populist voters won control of the North Carolina General Assembly, governorship, and most of the U.S. congressional seats in a powerful alliance of Black and white Republicans and small farmers. This Black-white political alliance precipitated the only coup d'état in U.S. history, in the Wilmington Massacre of 1898, when white Democratic party leaders led a mob of thousands of white supporters to terrorize the Black community, murder scores of Black residents, and overthrow the democratically elected, multiracial fusion government, chasing the elected leaders from the city.[43]

Prospects

The Civil Rights Bill of 1866 and the Reconstruction amendments held out the promise of a multiracial democracy, including crucial protections for basic rights and the ability to acquire and transfer property. But the Civil Rights Bill of 1866 failed to address the overwhelming inequity in land ownership by race that divided the South and the nation. In the words of Du Bois:

> To emancipate four million laborers whose labor had been owned, and separate them from the land upon which they had worked for nearly two and a half centuries, was an operation such as no modern country had for a moment attempted. The German and English and French serf, the Italian and Russian serf, were, on emancipation, given definite rights in the land. Only the American Negro slave was emancipated without such rights and in the end this spelled for him the continuation of slavery.[44]

Nevertheless, these first, contested steps taken by Fourteenth Amendment and the Civil Rights Bill of 1866 charted a direction for future civil rights organizations, such as the National Association for the Advancement of Colored People (NAACP), to chip away at the assumptions undergirding white supremacy and to assert Black citizenship and property rights. It would take until 1968 to pass the Fair Housing Act, but five decades of grassroots organizing and legal cases based on the Fourteenth Amendment and the Civil Rights Bill of 1866, such as *Buchanan v. Warley* (1917), *Shelley v. Kraemer* (1948), and *Jones v. Alfred H. Mayer Co.* (1968), prepared the legal and intellectual groundwork.

The Fair Housing Act of 1968

Following the end of Reconstruction, white collective violence against Black residents of integrated neighborhoods at the end of the eighteenth and beginning of the nineteenth centuries forced African American neighbors from their homes and neighborhoods, creating a more segregated metropolitan landscape. Following Baltimore's passage of a municipal segregation ordinance in 1910, cities across the South passed laws "requiring . . . the use of separate blocks for residences, places of abode and places of assembly by white and colored people respectively."[45] After the NAACP successfully challenged explicit municipal racial zoning provisions pursuant to the Fourteenth Amendment's Equal Protection Clause in *Buchanan v. Warley*

(1917), white strategies to solidify separate and unequal living patterns focused increasingly on the diffusion of private racially restrictive covenants in white communities.

Beginning in the early 1900s, real estate developers marketed middle-class suburban living in planned neighborhoods. These developers promoted deed restrictions governing the use of properties as a noteworthy amenity. Some covenants also included explicit prohibitions on residence by non-white people. These binding covenants ran with the property deed and generally prohibited all future purchasers from selling to non-white, and often non-Christian, buyers. The National Conference on City Planning provided a platform that helped these racially restrictive covenants spread countrywide, while the National Association of Real Estate Boards revised its code of ethics in 1924 to prohibit real estate agents from "introducing into a neighborhood a character of property or occupancy, members of any race or nationality, or any individual whose presence will clearly be detrimental to property values in that neighborhood."[46]

In the midst of the Great Depression, Congress created the Federal Housing Administration (FHA) to insure mortgages and to facilitate long-term loans with fixed monthly payments. To systematize appraisals and underwriting, the FHA also created an underwriting manual that urged the use of "proper zoning and deed restrictions" to protect against changes that diminished "desirable neighborhood character." It stated that the "more important among the adverse influential factors are the ingress of undesirable racial or nationality groups" and gave higher ratings to those properties and neighborhoods that had restrictive covenants in place.[47]

In 1935, the federal Home Owners' Loan Corporation (HOLC) created "Residential Security Maps" that color-coded neighborhoods of major cities according to appraisers' view of their profitability for mortgage lending, driven in part by racial or ethnic composition. Neighborhoods seen as higher lending risks were shaded red, leading to the term "redlining" to describe the denial of loans or financial services because of a neighborhood's racial or ethnic composition. The FHA provisions and the HOLC maps emboldened discrimination by real-estate agents, banks, sellers, and landlords.

As a result of the combination of these public and private policies, between 1880 and 1940, levels of segregation increased substantially nationwide. In 1880, an African American household had a one-in-two chance of having a non–African American neighbor. By 1940, that likelihood had declined to just over one in three.[48]

Civil rights organizations, such as the NAACP, developed political and legal campaigns to challenge public policies and private practices that excluded African American homeseekers from white neighborhoods—from municipal segregation ordinances, to racially restrictive covenants, to redlining—and from white schools. As discussed above, litigation by the NAACP led the Supreme Court to invalidate segregation ordinances in *Buchanan v. Warley* (1917). In another case brought by the NAACP concerning racially restrictive covenants, *Shelley v. Kraemer* (1948), the Court held that, even if the Constitution did not prohibit private racial discrimination, courts could not enforce private racially restrictive covenants because court enforcement would constitute state action in violation of the Fourteenth Amendment's Equal Protection Clause. Perhaps best known among these cases is Thurgood Marshall's victory in *Brown v. Board of Education* (1954), wherein the Supreme Court held that "separate educational facilities are inherently unequal" and that segregation in public education deprived Black students of their right to the equal protection of the laws guaranteed by the Fourteenth Amendment.[49] Even after *Brown*, however, racial discrimination in housing by lenders, brokers, landlords, and other private actors continued to be legally permissible and pervasive. The real estate development and financing practices that facilitated suburbanization after World War II essentially blocked Black households from the opportunity to move to these new suburban developments and continued to limit their ability to accumulate home equity.

As public and private investment in suburban land and infrastructure grew after World War II, property values in many inner-city neighborhoods began to fall. To confront this urban decline, Congress created national urban-renewal programs in the Housing Acts of 1949 and 1954. These acts provided federal funds to municipalities to acquire land, raze existing structures, and pave the way for private construction. Cities frequently used the program to demolish poor, and often predominantly non-white, neighborhoods that were categorized as "blighted," uprooting and displacing large numbers of Black, Latinx, and immigrant residents.

In 1966, Martin Luther King Jr. and the Southern Christian Leadership Conference (SCLC) announced a collaboration with the Coordinating Council of Community Organizations on the Chicago Freedom Movement, comparing residential segregation to colonization and seeking "to bring about the unconditional surrender of forces dedicated to the creation and maintenance of slums and ultimately make slums a moral and financial liability upon the whole community."[50]

King subsequently noted the parallels between spatial control through plantations under slavery and spatial control through metropolitan segregation: "The plantation and ghetto were created by those who had power, both to confine those who had no power and to perpetuate their powerlessness. The problem of transforming the ghetto, therefore, is a problem of power—confrontation of the forces of power demanding change and the forces of power dedicated to the preserving of the status quo."[51]

Focused on securing "open housing," the movement led marches through the summer of 1966 into all-white neighborhoods on Chicago's southwest and northwest sides to expose white opposition to residential integration and, in King's words, to "draw this hate into the open."[52] The marchers were consistently jeered, taunted, and met with violence from hostile white residents. King pointed out that "many whites who oppose open housing would deny that they are racists."[53] Against this hostility to neighborhood integration, however, King had little concrete progress to show, even after seven months of marches, protest, and meetings.

King and the movement struggled to effectively organize Chicago's culturally and economically diverse Black residents and faced mounting opposition from many white residents. That August, the movement's leaders announced plans to march through the all-white town of Cicero, where, fifteen years earlier, thousands of white residents had rioted for days after an African American World War II veteran, Harvey E. Clark, and his family had attempted to move into an apartment there. The Illinois governor ultimately had to call in the National Guard to stop the violence, and the Clark family left the state.

With local white leaders fearful of a new round of violence in Cicero and King struggling to gain traction among Black Chicagoans, he and other civil rights leaders met with Illinois governor Otto Kerner and Chicago mayor Richard Daley and agreed to call off the marches into white neighborhoods; in turn, city officials agreed to do more to promote fair housing. Civil rights leaders generally saw the agreement as a failure. Indeed, the city did little to fulfill its commitments, and the Chicago Real Estate Board would not even agree to drop its legal challenge to Chicago's largely ineffective fair housing ordinance. King that summer nevertheless highlighted the importance of tenant union organizing and pathways to homeownership as well as Black-owned banks. In his presidential address to the SCLC, King focused largely on access to housing and schools and on the spatial dimensions of inequality, urging members to continue the fight:

> Let us be dissatisfied until the tragic walls that separate the outer city of wealth and comfort from the inner city of poverty and despair shall be crushed by the battering rams of the forces of justice. Let us be dissatisfied until those who live on the outskirts of hope are brought into the metropolis of daily security. Let us be dissatisfied until slums are cast into the junk heaps of history, and every family will live in a decent, sanitary home. Let us be dissatisfied until the dark yesterdays of segregated schools will be transformed into bright tomorrows of quality integrated education. Let us be

dissatisfied until integration is not seen as a problem but as an opportunity to participate in the beauty of diversity.[54]

The limited success of the Chicago open housing campaign was one of King's relative failures in the civil rights movement. The struggles of the campaign highlight the vociferous opposition and violent resistance that efforts to promote racially integrated living patterns provoked in the past and still provoke today.

Promise

During the summer of 1967, more than 150 uprisings erupted in cities across the country, triggered by racially discriminatory housing policies and urban inequality generally. President Lyndon Johnson convened the National Advisory Commission on Civil Disorders, commonly known as the Kerner Commission after its chair, Otto Kerner. The Kerner Commission's report, released in February 1968, described the nation as "moving toward two societies, one black, one white—separate and unequal."[55] The report determined that housing discrimination, residential segregation, and economic inequality were causing increasing societal division, and it recommended that Congress "enact a comprehensive and enforceable open housing law."[56]

President Johnson and Senator Mondale had pushed for a federal fair housing bill in 1966 and 1967, without success. Mondale recalled, "A lot of civil rights was about making the South behave and taking the teeth from [southern segregationist] George Wallace," but the proposed fair housing law "came right to the neighborhoods across the country. This was civil rights getting personal."[57]

On April 4, 1968, King was assassinated, and the threat of widespread civil unrest loomed. Senator Jacob Javits, speaking in support of the Fair Housing Act, warned that "the crisis of the cities ... is equal to the crisis which we face in Vietnam."[58] Mondale, the primary drafter of the Fair Housing Act, cautioned that "our failure to abolish the ghetto will reinforce the growing alienation of white and black America. It will ensure two separate Americas constantly at war with one another."[59]

Congress recognized that discriminatory housing practices hurt not only individuals who were denied access to housing but the whole community. Mondale emphasized that citywide problems were "directly traceable to the existing patterns of racially segregated housing."[60] The sponsors of the Fair Housing Act pointed out that cities were overburdened and underfinanced specifically as a result of discrimination in housing. For instance, Mondale stated that the Fair Housing Act was necessary to address the "declining tax base, poor sanitation, loss of jobs, inadequate education opportunity, and urban squalor" that central cities faced.[61]

Congress repeatedly framed the Fair Housing Act as legislation intended to address the complex web of challenges that discrimination in housing had entrenched in segregated metropolitan areas. Senator Edward Brooke emphasized that the "tax base on which adequate public services, and especially adequate public education, subsists has fled the city," and he noted that the objective of the Fair Housing Act "must [be to] move toward [the] goal" of recreating "adequate services in the central city" by rooting out systemic discrimination.[62]

Within a week of King's assassination, Congress finally passed the Fair Housing Act, often referred to as the "last plank" of civil rights legislation. It set out the goal of providing for fair housing throughout the nation and fulfilling two promises. First, the Fair Housing Act prohibited discrimination in housing on the basis of race, color, religion, and national origin (and subsequently, after amendments in 1974 and 1988, sex, disability or handicap, and familial status).[63] Second, the Fair Housing Act required that "all executive departments and agencies shall administer their programs and activities relating to housing and urban development (including any Federal agency having regulatory or supervisory authority over financial institutions) in a manner affirmatively to further the purposes of this subchapter."[64] In short, the Fair Housing Act held out the promise of ending discrimination in housing and bringing about "fair housing" more broadly throughout the United States.

Protest

Following the 1968 presidential election of Republican Richard Nixon, George Romney became the HUD secretary and took steps to fulfill the act's promise to affirmatively further fair housing. As one strategy, Romney sought to deny HUD funding to wealthy municipalities that used a variety of exclusionary practices, such as overly restrictive land-use regulations or discriminatory provision of basic urban infrastructure. In his own words, Romney sought to break up the "high-income white noose" around Black communities.[65] President Nixon, however, actively sought to undermine Romney's open communities efforts, stating that "this country is not ready at this time for either forcibly integrated housing or forcibly integrated education."[66] Nixon's opposition ultimately contributed to Romney's resignation. In short, before efforts to realize the affirmatively furthering provision could truly begin, they were blocked from the top of the executive branch.

Nixon instead advanced his concept of "the New Federalism" through the Housing and Community Development Act of 1974, which consolidated multiple federal funding streams into the CDBG program, with the aim of "providing decent housing and a suitable living environment and expanding economic opportunities, principally for persons of low and moderate income."[67] The 1974 act was required to comply with Title VI of the Civil Rights Act of 1964 (prohibiting discrimination in programs receiving federal assistance) but conspicuously did not include any reference to the Fair Housing Act, implying that Nixon was happy to allow states and localities receiving HUD funding to avoid complying with the requirement to affirmatively further fair housing.[68]

In 1983, Congress amended the CDBG program to specify that HUD should award grants only if the grantees demonstrated that they would affirmatively further fair housing, clarifying again that state and local recipients of HUD's largest source of community development funds had a central role to play in opening access to housing.[69] In 1988 and again in 1995, HUD issued regulations stating that CDBG recipients would be considered in compliance with the obligation to further fair housing if recipients "conduct an analysis to identify impediments to fair housing choice within the jurisdiction, take appropriate actions to overcome the effects of any impediments identified through that analysis, and maintain records reflecting the analysis and actions."[70] HUD, however, rarely reviewed these Analyses of Impediments (AIs), and there were essentially no consequences for incomplete, inadequate, or nonexistent filings.

Eventually, in 2009, HUD conducted a study in which it asked a sample of participating jurisdictions to produce AIs for review and found that more than a third of jurisdictions failed to produce one at all.[71] The HUD study concluded that "only a minority of jurisdictions have an AI readily available to the public" and that "citizens seeking to obtain AIs would not consistently find them readily available."[72] Conducting a systematic review of completeness, the HUD study found that nearly half of the AIs that the department actually did receive and review needed improvement or were of poor quality. Specifically, HUD noted that "a sizable proportion of the AIs reviewed did not contain key aspects recommended for inclusion by the Fair Housing Planning Guide" and that many of the AIs "were completed in a cursory fashion only."[73] A Government Accountability Office (GAO) study of AIs conducted the following year similarly found that more than a third of them were out of date. The study also found that the analyses included few measurable objectives or time frames and were generally not signed by the grantees' highest-ranking local officials, effectively making it impossible to establish clear accountability.[74] The HUD study and the GAO study reinforced the findings of the bipartisan National Commission on Fair Housing and Equal Opportunity, cochaired by former HUD secretaries Jack Kemp and Henry Cisneros, which found that "the current federal system for ensuring fair housing compliance by state and local recipients of housing assistance has failed."[75] The commission determined that "HUD requires no evidence that anything is actually being done as a condition of funding and it does not take adverse action if jurisdictions are directly involved in discriminatory actions or fail to affirmatively further fair housing."[76]

These minimal requirements in the decades after Congress enacted the Fair Housing Act illustrate the struggle to realize the act's promise of reducing persistent racial disparities in access to opportunity. In what some have referred to as "our federalism," substantial power to exclude continues to rest with local governments.[77] And political will for the federal government to curb those exclusionary powers is generally lacking.

Prospects

The Fair Housing Act offered a crucial tool in the fight to realize its first promise: the fight against discrimination in housing. Enforcement has been limited, however, by a combination of lack of awareness by victims of discrimination, low levels of enforcement by the government agencies empowered to implement the act, and relatively weak penalties for lawbreakers.[78] Nevertheless, audit studies over the past three decades have suggested that explicit discrimination in housing has decreased and taken somewhat more subtle forms, such as non-white homeseekers' being shown fewer units or offered fewer financing options.[79] The Fair Housing Act has been less effective, however, in fulfilling its second promise: to reduce overall segregation. In this case, the structures that encourage and perpetuate segregation are entrenched in our local government boundaries, municipal financing structures, and homeownership policies. Continuing asymmetrical preferences for neighborhood racial composition combine with metropolitan fragmentation, exclusionary zoning, and regressive local tax policies to generate neighborhoods that remain separate and unequal.

To address the structural dimensions of continuing place-based disparities in access to resources requires giving life to the AFFH mandate of the Fair Housing Act. Unlike the direct anti-discrimination provisions of the Fair Housing Act, under which any "aggrieved person" can file suit, courts have generally been skeptical of a "private right of action" for individuals to sue directly to challenge failures by HUD and its grantees to affirmatively further fair housing.[80] Advocates have nevertheless sought creative ways to realize the potential power of the provision in such cases as *Resident Advisory Board v. Rizzo* (E.D. Pa. 1976), in which Philadelphia residents eligible for subsidized housing sued the mayor and city officials, alleging that they violated the AFFH provision by blocking construction of public housing in an all-white South Philadelphia neighborhood.[81] The appellate court upheld the district court's decision in favor of the residents but based liability on the provisions in Section 3604 of the Fair Housing Act, prohibiting the denial of housing on the basis of race, and sidestepped the question of private rights of action under Section 3608's AFFH provision.[82] In *NAACP, Boston Chapter v. HUD* (1st Cir. 1987), the NAACP challenged the city of Boston's and HUD's failure to use Urban Development Action Grant funds to create low-income housing in areas that would give households "a true choice of location."[83] Then-Judge (now Supreme Court Justice) Stephen Breyer wrote that although Section 3608 does not create a private right of action directly enforceable in court, it could be reviewed under an Administrative Procedure Act claim if the governmental actions were arbitrary and capricious in failing to affirmatively further fair housing. Another creative approach was seen in *United States* ex rel. *Anti-discrimination Center of Metro New York, Inc. v. Westchester County.*[84] The Anti-Discrimination Center of Metro New York sued Westchester County under the False Claims Act in 2006 for falsely certifying the county's compliance with fair housing regulations, when it had not, in fact, taken any steps to analyze or address impediments to fair housing. The United States joined the lawsuit, ultimately coming to a settlement in 2009. In 2011, HUD began withholding millions of dollars in funding from Westchester because the county had failed to comply with the settlement agreement; it finally accepted Westchester's eleventh submission of an AI in 2017 only after the change in presidential administrations.

These cases suggest that the AFFH provision has the potential to have a substantial impact on the construction and siting of affordable housing and on municipal and regional planning, but clear guidelines and federal enforcement are lacking. Such were the hopes of advocates when the Obama administration started working on the AFFH Rule. They engaged with HUD in imagining what form the rule could take.

As work on the AFFH Rule began, the legacy of the litigation discussed above revealed the difficulty of addressing local exclusion and regional inequality within a federal system that rests on strong protections for states and popularly entrenched localism. Given that there are limited avenues for either private or public enforcement through the courts for the Fair Housing Act's AFFH provision, the most viable path forward entailed having HUD use its administrative powers to set directives for state and local governments to advance racial equity.[85] As described by Raphael W. Bostic, Katherine O'Regan, Patrick Pontius, and Nicholas F. Kelly in Chapter 2, the AFFH Rule relies on localities' undertaking rigorous analysis and creating meaningful goals to meet the fair housing requirements and then honestly evaluating their progress toward those goals. The AFFH Rule thus arguably takes the form of an equality directive, albeit one without explicit federal goal setting. As with other equality directives, in which federal agencies set objectives for state and local governments to advance, responsibility falls to federal agencies to use their administrative powers strategically to ensure local compliance.[86] As the discussion below of comments submitted regarding the proposed rule reveals, concerns about effective enforcement were paramount for civil rights advocates as well as for localities and public housing authorities.

One of the tensions that shaped the drafting of the AFFH Rule was the long-standing strain between advocates of what have sometimes been called "place-based" and "people-based" investments. Some fair housing advocates have especially favored investments that support household geographic mobility—for instance, through housing choice vouchers combined with the calculation of small area fair market rents and the provision of robust housing counseling. An important early milestone in this approach came with the settlement of *Hills v. Gautreaux*, 425 U.S. 284 (1976), a case challenging racial discrimination by HUD and the Chicago Housing Authority; the resolution required the construction of new "scattered-site" public housing in Chicago and the creation of the Gautreaux Assisted Housing program, providing housing vouchers for Chicago Housing Authority tenants to use in racially integrated neighborhoods across the region. Research involving the participants in the assisted housing program found socioeconomic benefits for children and helped inspire the subsequent Moving to Opportunity for Fair Housing (MTO) program administered by HUD in the 1990s.[87] Recent research on the MTO program has found further support for the positive educational and income effects that mobility to neighborhoods with lower poverty rates can have on young children.[88] Similarly, research on some of the developments that followed the *Southern Burlington County NAACP v. Mt. Laurel*, 336 A.2d 713 (1975) decision by the New Jersey Supreme Court (requiring municipalities statewide to zone in such a way as to enable the construction of their fair share of affordable housing) also found substantial improvements in socioeconomic outcomes for children in more economically integrated neighborhoods.[89] Advocates of this people-based or mobility approach often emphasize that all households should have the freedom to live where they choose and argue that—given historical and continuing opposition to meaningful community investment—supporting household mobility is most likely to lead to substantial improvements in outcomes for young people and in reducing racial disparities in socioeconomic outcomes over the long term. In Chapter 7, Michael C. Lens reviews some of the research regarding the MTO program and the implications of that research for the AFFH Rule; in Chapter 8, Megan Haberle identifies obstacles and opportunities in the rule for advancing racial and economic integration.

An emphasis on place-based investments encourages the allocation of public and private capital to neighborhoods that have experienced historic disinvestment and that currently experience high poverty rates and economic isolation. Advocates of this approach often emphasize the importance of place-based social networks to household well-being and the cultural and psychological significance of connections to place as well as the costs of moving, the burdens of which are often unequally distributed. Chester Hartman noted decades ago that people should have a "right to stay put" if they choose and that the realization of that right requires investments that make neighborhood-based public services and amenities more equal.[90] In Chapter 5, Edward Goetz sets out several arguments from the Left in favor of place-based investments; in Chapter 4, Howard Husock presents a conservative argument against an undue emphasis on mobility.

Attempting to rigidly confine individuals or groups to either category, however, is not particularly productive, as organizations with leanings in both directions have largely come to appreciate the importance of simultaneous support for voluntary household mobility and for concerted investments in comprehensive community revitalization. Many now encourage a "place-conscious" approach to investing in people and neighborhoods.[91] Indeed, "comprehensive approaches that combine and coordinate sustained, long-term investments in multiple areas—such as affordable housing, early childhood education, quality schools, access to primary medical care, and a range of social supports—and track progress towards common goals over time, adjusting course when necessary" combined with "organizing efforts that build power and self-direction among residents" are critical.[92]

HUD's efforts to draft the proposed AFFH Rule had to navigate among these tensions and find what its officials came to call "a balanced approach" to furthering fair housing.[93] As discussed in Chapter 2, HUD expended significant effort on community engagement, working with civil rights advocates, affordable housing developers, public housing authorities, and other stakeholders. One of the basic innovations of the proposed rule was to actually define what "affirmatively furthering fair housing" should entail. HUD defined it as "taking meaningful actions that, taken together, address significant disparities in housing needs and in access to opportunity, replacing segregated living patterns with truly integrated and balanced living patterns, transforming racially and ethnically concentrated areas of poverty into areas of opportunity, and fostering and maintaining compliance with civil rights and fair housing laws."[94] The definition notably highlights that advancing racial and economic integration and investing in the transformation of economically isolated areas into ones rich with opportunity are central aspects of furthering fair housing. This articulation of a balanced approach was arguably central to gaining the strong support of civil rights organizations, community development groups, affordable housing developers, fair housing advocates, and others for the proposed rule. Although some anxiety remained on both sides about what its effects would be, the support for it was wide, as discussed below.

HUD officials were also careful to include attention to all protected classes in the proposed AFH process. HUD defined "fair housing choice" in the AFFH Rule as meaning "that individuals and families have the information, opportunity, and options to live where they choose without unlawful discrimination and other barriers related to race, color, religion, sex, familial status, national origin, or disability."[95] It further clarified that "for persons with disabilities, fair housing choice and access to opportunity include access to accessible housing and housing in the most integrated setting appropriate to an individual's needs as required under Federal civil rights law, including disability-related services that an individual needs to live in such housing."[96] As discussed in Chapter 3, several of the HUD grantees that completed early AFHs noted the role of the rule in catalyzing new attention to disability access in housing. Of the first AFHs that were submitted after the AFFH Rule's implementation, HUD rejected several for failing to address the integration of disabled households or failing to analyze and to set out goals to confront discrimination on the basis of national origin.[97]

The 2015 Affirmatively Furthering Fair Housing Rule, and Beyond

The history of fair housing from the nineteenth century until today forms the backdrop for this volume's central focus on more recent innovations. Ultimately, we look beyond the current stalemate over the AFFH Rule to envision new possibilities for next steps. Bringing together scholars from across the political spectrum and a wide range of disciplines, we examine the promises, protests, and prospects for fair housing in the next decade and beyond.

Promises

By structuring this volume to convey promises, protests, and prospects, we acknowledge the significance of a tortuous history of partial starts and setbacks but keep our focus on future possibilities. The AFFH Rule builds on the complex historical struggle for open housing that von Hoffman—a historian based at Harvard's Joint Center for Housing Studies—describes in Chapter 1. Von Hoffman explores the distinction—and sometimes even tension—between efforts to end discrimination in housing and efforts to affirmatively foster racial integration as well as debates over the meaning and significance of "the ghetto."

As Bostic, O'Regan, Pontius, and Kelly describe in Chapter 2, HUD worked carefully to overcome internal institutional divides and external opposition to issue the final AFFH Rule in July 2015. As key players in the process while working at HUD during the Obama administration, Bostic, O'Regan, and Pontius highlight some of the challenges to drafting the rule, including tensions between the department's planning and enforcement arms. This chapter shows how many of the key debates among fair housing and affordable housing advocates entered into internal contestation within HUD. The authors outline the process of crafting the rule, securing buy-in within HUD, compromising across departments, persevering in the face of delays, and ultimately succeeding in issuing the new rule—a process that took virtually the entire Obama administration to execute. One of the difficult debates they reveal revolved around whether the approach should be consensual and planning-based or focused more on punitive enforcement through legal action. The authors make a full-throated defense of the former, arguing that the rule was written with long-term planning processes in mind, designed to change conversations within municipalities around the country and, over time, to build a less segregated, more equal metropolitan America. Finally, the authors focus on some of the rule's key innovations, such as facilitating local determination of priorities, conceiving of the AFH as a meaningful planning tool for future action integrated with other planning requirements, and empowering communities with data so that they could effectively engage in a dialogue about unique local obstacles and strategies.

Civil rights organizations, including the NAACP, the NAACP Legal Defense Fund, the National Council of La Raza, the National Urban League, the Equal Rights Center, the Lawyers' Committee for Civil Rights Under Law, the Disability Rights Legal Center, the National Gay and Lesbian Task Force, and others, enthusiastically supported the AFFH Rule in public comments to HUD during the notice and comment period. For instance, the NAACP described the proposed regulations as "a very important step towards achieving Congress' vision about how the Fair Housing Act should be a tool for creating equal opportunity in our country."[98] Civil rights organizations generally offered vocal support for the proposed rule together with suggestions to strengthen it, largely by increasing community engagement requirements, offering incentives for regional collaboration in AFHs, setting higher expectations for performance by grantees, requiring grantees to make timely and concrete progress toward achieving their fair housing goals, creating a process for residents and advocates to challenge AFHs, and ensuring that HUD allocated effective resources to review AFHs. A joint letter from a diverse coalition of forty-one civil rights organizations, including the American-Arab Anti-Discrimination Committee, Asian Americans Advancing Justice, the Human Rights Campaign, the Leadership Conference on Civil and Human Rights, The National Coalition for Asian Pacific American Community Development, The National Consumer Law Center, the National Women's Law Center, the Opportunity Agenda, and PolicyLink, noted that by "establishing a framework that holds recipients of federal funding accountable, this rule will promote thriving, diverse communities that can meet the challenges of the 21st century."[99] The National Council of La Raza emphasized its belief that the proposed rule "w[ould] offer better protections for a family's right to obtain adequate and safe housing of one's choosing" than existing regulations, but, like many other civil rights organizations, it also noted that "the success of these changes is highly dependent on accountability through rigorous outreach and enforcement," encouraging HUD to require more robust community outreach, set higher standards of performance for grantees, and make enforcement of the AFFH Rule a priority.[100] The National Community Reinvestment Coalition similarly endorsed the proposed rule, encouraging HUD to require grantees to maximize citizen participation throughout the assessment process, to require grantees to consider more information beyond the data provided by HUD, to require grantees to identify quantifiable performance benchmarks, and to allocate resources for enforcement.[101]

Several civil rights organizations enthusiastically supported the AFFH Rule and called for a stronger emphasis on integration and mobility. For instance, the NAACP Legal Defense Fund described the rule as a "tremendous first step" toward further advancing the Fair Housing Act but asked HUD to clarify that the "the central purpose of the Fair Housing Act's affirmatively furthering fair housing mandate is to promote integration" and encouraged HUD to adopt more robust enforcement mechanisms, to require measurable performance standards of grantees, and to more expressly weave the fair housing requirements into the Consolidated Plan and Public Housing Authority Annual Plans.[102] The Lawyers' Committee for Civil Rights Under Law noted that "there is a serious imbalance between housing opportunities available to low income people—with a dearth of opportunities in low poverty areas with quality schools, good employment opportunities, and proximity to transportation assets compared to opportunities existing in high poverty, segregated areas" and called for the AFFH Rule to "promote a better balance of housing choices for people who are members of protected classes than currently exists."[103] The Poverty and Race Research Action Council, writing on behalf of itself and more than two dozen other civil rights and fair housing groups, expressed concern that the proposed rule did not go far enough to ensure compliance, arguing that "[a]s civil rights advocates, we do not object to HUD's basic premise—that part of the fair housing mandate must include the radical improvement of segregated, higher poverty neighborhoods where many low-income families will continue to reside even after strong voluntary desegregation efforts," but expressing concern that the proposed rule did not forcefully enough put forth the "primary integrative purpose" of the provision.[104] The letter encouraged HUD to "make it clear that the primary purpose of the 'community revitalization' prong of the AFFH rule is to direct non-housing economic and community assets into these neighborhoods: assets like enhanced school resources, economic development, job training, improved parks, full service grocery stores, and community policing."[105] The letter also expressed concern about HUD's capacity to review the AFHs and encouraged the department to avoid its routine review altogether, instead substituting an audit-based and complaint-triggered review process, providing more guidance in the rule on what constitutes an acceptable AFH, and creating a procedure through which local advocates could object to HUD's approval of an AFH.[106]

Community organizing groups and affordable housing advocates generally expressed support for the proposed AFFH Rule as well, while also raising concerns about potential effects on community reinvestment efforts. National People's Action, a federation of twenty-nine grassroots organizations in eighteen states working together for racial and economic justice, endorsed the rule while cautioning that "too much emphasis on promoting integration and overcoming segregation (as important as these goals are and even in the name of eliminating concentrations of poverty in minority areas)[. . .] can be used to undermine the legitimate needs of existing minority communities where, in fact, most minority families will live out their lives."[107] The National Low Income Housing Coalition "commend[ed] HUD for undertaking a multi-year effort to obtain the views of a wide range of stakeholders" and "enthusiastically support[ed] the proposed improvements," while also requesting that HUD "recognize that affirmatively furthering fair housing may entail devoting resources to improve areas of concentrated racial and ethnic poverty by preserving and improving affordable housing, and by implementing investment policies that augment access to essential community assets for protected class residents who wish to remain in their communities—while protecting them from the forces of displacement."[108]

Although they indicated support for the goals of the proposed AFFH Rule, many public housing authorities, by contrast, expressed skepticism and concern about the regulations. The Council of Large Public Housing Authorities warned "that the proposed rule sends mixed messages about how PHAs' [Public Housing Authorities'] current operations comply with their obligation to affirmatively further fair housing; offers inadequate protections to PHAs that strive to meet their obligations; and imposes an unfunded mandate on PHAs that are already suffering from severe budget cuts to their current operations."[109] The National Association of Housing and Redevelopment Officials similarly voiced apprehension "that this highly procedural proposed rule will add significant administrative burden for PHAs and other HUD grantees while doing very little to actually promote fair housing outcomes," leading to "small communities opting out of federal programs and resources being diverted away from actually serving the populations intended to benefit from the regulations."[110]

Few conservative public policy research institutions submitted comments. While on the campaign trail, Ben Carson wrote an article in the *Washington Times* describing the AFFH Rule as a "mandated social-engineering scheme," much like, he said, the desegregation efforts after *Brown v. Board of Education* (1954).[111] He criticized these "government-engineered attempts to legislate racial equality" as examples of "failed socialist experiments."[112] Many individuals also submitted comments in opposition to the rule, articulating similar concerns about "social engineering,"[113] expressing disapproval of the regulation on the grounds that it would "subvert private property laws and limit if not eliminate any or all future suburban development,"[114] and urging HUD to "return land use control to the local governments."[115]

HUD responded to hundreds of such comments, revised the rule, and issued the final regulation in 2015. One of the most surprising things about its initial rollout was HUD's engagement and enforcement. In Chapter 3, Nicholas F. Kelly, Maia S. Woluchem, Reed Jordan, and Justin P. Steil analyze fair housing plans from the first forty-nine municipalities that submitted AFHs before the tool was suspended in 2018. The authors code every goal in every AFH, finding that the rule led to more goals with measurable objectives or new policies than did the prior AI process. Many of the municipalities engaged in meaningful community dialogues that produced innovative, rigorous goals to reduce segregation and increase access to opportunity. These authors also code the goals according to a variety of other measures, finding that the AFHs included goals focused on place-based and mobility policies, zoning changes, efforts at combating displacement, and regional collaborations, among other things. This diversity of goal types represents the broad array of policies that municipalities proposed to fulfill the AFFH mandate. The authors also find a statistically significant relationship between the level of segregation in a community and whether the fair housing plan set out measurable objectives or proposed new policies, suggesting that some of the most segregated communities were taking the most meaningful steps to further fair housing.

Protests

Even after its passage, the AFFH Rule continued to be contested. Once it was promulgated, civil rights advocates expressed concerns about its enforceability. Others criticized its focus on segregation and on racially and ethnically concentrated areas of poverty, as compared to the need for community investment and affordable housing. For instance, planning and policy scholar Goetz argues in Chapter 4 that the existence of spatial inequality does not necessarily mean that spatial integration is the right solution. He argues that criticism by some fair housing advocates of the construction of more affordable housing in neighborhoods with high poverty rates draws on and reinforces negative views toward affordable housing more generally. Attempts to dismantle public housing to further integration, he suggests, benefit developers, who profit from the construction, and harm communities of color, who bear the burden of relocation.

In Chapter 5, the Manhattan Institute's Husock similarly critiques the AFFH Rule, this time from a conservative perspective, as an ineffective way of improving the prospects of low-income people of color. Instead of integration, Husock, like Goetz, advocates for greater investment in low-income neighborhoods. He does not question the research demonstrating the importance of neighborhoods for the long-term economic outcomes of children. Instead, he questions the practicality of scaling up the AFFH Rule and challenges the general skepticism among mobility advocates about place-based approaches. He situates these critiques in the recognition that past government efforts have often undermined the same low-income neighborhoods that the current AFFH Rule aims to support. Husock points out that many neighborhoods cleared by urban renewal were not as impoverished as commonly thought and held high levels of social and political capital. In short, he argues against environmental determinism and in favor of the idea that low-income areas can be "good neighborhoods."

Promises

In this book's final section, we turn to three chapters that look beyond the AFFH Rule to address a select number of issues that show how we might grapple with fair housing challenges in the years to come.

In housing policy today, perhaps no issue provokes as vocal a response as that of gentrification. The interaction of gentrification with fair housing concerns raises a set of particularly vexing policy questions. In Chapter 6, Been, a former commissioner of the New York City Department of Housing Preservation and Development and subsequently a deputy mayor of Housing and Economic Development for New York City, examines how policymakers, advocates, and scholars should think about how to affirmatively further fair housing in the context of gentrification. New York is a particularly compelling case through which to examine the intersection of fair housing and gentrification, as it is simultaneously one of the most segregated metropolitan areas in the country with some of the most intense gentrification pressures, as well as the city with the nation's largest public housing authority and most powerful municipal housing preservation and development agency. In recent years, New York has also been home to a growing tenant movement focused on strengthening and expanding rent regulation, which it accomplished in 2019, and fighting against displacement, often by seeking to intervene in the city's proposed neighborhood based re-zonings. Been examines these issues in relation to the affordable housing crisis in New York City and the city's efforts to address it. She confronts difficult policy tradeoffs evident in such policies as efforts to allow for more density in many neighborhoods in New York—many of them low-income—which have stoked fears of increased displacement. From a fair housing context, she engages the concern that increased investment in such neighborhoods may remedy years of disinvestment while also contributing to racial and economic integration—but through the mechanism of gentrification. Conversely, efforts to prevent displacement can, at times, further concentrate poverty and exacerbate segregation. Finally, she confronts the ways that zoning interacts with efforts to promote integration, examining how a variety of zoning changes affect residential segregation and integration. Been explores these questions through her practical experience shaping housing policy in New York City, moving us forward in understanding this intersection of crucial issues facing America's cities.

In Chapter 7, University of California, Los Angeles planning professor Lens offers a way to improve the AFFH process through paying greater attention to a crucial measure of opportunity: the relative presence or absence of crime. He reviews the literature on neighborhood effects, finding that poverty, crime, and school quality are three primary indicators associated with changes in outcomes for low-income children. Lens also evaluates the literature on neighborhood preferences of low-income families who participated in the MTO program, arguing that crime and violence are primary concerns for those participants wanting to move. Lens then notes that the AFFH tool currently lacks a key metric of neighborhood quality: crime data. He shows how tract-level crime data, while difficult to collect, have become more common. This availability means that is now possible to add in the most significant missing variable in the current AFFH tool.

Finally, in Chapter 8, Haberle, who directs housing policy at the Poverty & Race Research Action Council, analyzes how the AFFH Rule created a policy context for rigorous efforts to reduce segregation while also facing a number of hurdles to achieve that reality. These barriers include discrimination, local zoning decisions, federal funding, and bureaucratic structures within public housing authorities that tend to reinforce jurisdictional fragmentation. Haberle also discusses past problems with enforcing the Fair Housing Act, which may continue in future AFFH enforcement. These problems range from HUD's lack of commitment to fair housing to an unwillingness to leverage its funding over states and localities to incentivize compliance. She discusses the double-edged sword of local control over fair housing in the AFFH Rule—it allows for experimentation but may also be a way to avoid accountability. Haberle points to the lack of prior performance metrics as key to HUD's previous inability to hold grant recipients accountable. She argues that participation in the AFFH process could spark a cooperative federalism, creating new coalitions and public understandings. Haberle also notes that the AFFH's focus on regional issues could be an innovative way to confront our fragmented metropolitan regions that reinforce segregation. Given federal efforts to undermine the AFFH Rule, she points to the possibility of overlaying the AFFH onto the housing choice voucher and low-income housing tax credit programs as a way to achieve many of the same goals.

Conclusion

The post-Obama attacks on civil rights protections have extended to a set of crucial policies created over the prior decade to begin to address powerful place-based inequalities in resources and access to opportunity. The AFFH Rule became a key target of these attacks. As discussed above, HUD in 2018 initially suspended and then subsequently proposed revising the AFFH Rule.[116] In 2019, HUD released its proposal for an alternative AFFH Rule.[117] The proposed rule eliminated any focus on disparities between protected classes in access to opportunities and made no mention of segregation.

To say the least, this reorientation marked a dramatic pullback. The 2015 rule had defined AFFH to mean addressing "significant disparities in housing needs and in access to opportunity, replacing segregated living patterns with truly integrated and balanced living patterns, transforming racially and ethnically concentrated areas of poverty into areas of opportunity, and fostering and maintaining compliance with civil rights and fair housing laws."[118] The 2019 proposed revisions, by contrast, redefined AFFH as "reducing obstacles within the participant's sphere of influence to providing fair housing choice."[119] It went on to define fair housing choice as merely ensuring that "within a HUD program participant's sphere of influence, that individuals and families have the opportunity and options to live where they choose, within their means, without unlawful discrimination related to race, color, religion, sex, familial status, national origin, or disability."[120]

In short, the proposed revisions eliminated the effort to address centuries of discrimination in housing policy on the basis of race, national origin, religion, sex, familial status, and disability that had been the core of the 2015 rule and jettisoned the focus on disparities in access to place-based opportunities and their relationship to socioeconomic mobility. Instead, the 2019 proposed revisions introduced narrow language focusing on eliminating intentional discrimination and presented an effort to facilitate the construction of market rate housing by eliminating state and local regulations. To evaluate progress toward fair housing, the proposal suggested that HUD would use measures of housing costs, the availability of "complete plumbing or kitchen facilities," vacancy rates, and "rates of subpar Public Housing conditions" as well as measures of lead poisoning, disability access, and voucher use.[121] Instead of looking holistically at the interaction between land use, housing policy, environmental quality, economic development, educational access, transportation, and social mobility as the 2015 rule had done, the 2019 proposal returned to a siloed focus on housing alone and to rudimentary measures of housing quality that would be easy for jurisdictions to meet (for example, more than 99 percent of occupied housing units in 2017 had complete plumbing and kitchen facilities).

This proposed evisceration of the 2015 AFFH Rule is part of a broad assault on civil rights protections in housing. For instance, HUD in 2019 also issued a proposed rule revising the 2013 rule implementing the Fair Housing Act's disparate impact standard. In *Texas Department of Housing and Community Affairs v. The Inclusive Communities Project* (2015), the Supreme Court confirmed that claims of discrimination under the Fair Housing Act could be brought on the basis of a policy's disparate impact, without direct evidence of an intent to discriminate. Yet under the Trump administration, HUD sought to undermine the essential ability to look at not just the intent of policies but also their effects.

In 2020, HUD abruptly issued a new final rule that repealed the AFFH Rule altogether. The 2020 rule essentially rewrote two crucial terms. First, it redefined "fair housing" to mean "housing that, among other attributes, is affordable, safe, decent, free of unlawful discrimination, and accessible as required under civil rights laws." Second, it redefined "affirmatively further" to mean "to take any action rationally related to promoting any attribute or attributes of fair housing." With these new definitions in place, the 2020 rule required HUD grantees to certify only that they had taken "*any*" action linked to fair housing. The earlier revisions proposed in 2019 gutted the 2015 effort to address place-based disparities associated with race, disability, family status, or other protected characteristics in access to resources. The 2020 final rule went even further by completely eliminating any affirmative responsibility to advance fair housing, allowing whatever step a locality proposed related to "affordable," "safe," or "decent" housing to suffice.

To Trump and his supporters, the problem with the 2019 proposed changes was that "the HUD approach did not go far enough." What they wanted, though, was not further enforcement of fair housing but, instead, a rule that would enable HUD to "do more . . . to empower local communities and to reduce the regulatory burden of providing unnecessary data to HUD." In his tweets accompanying the repeal, Secretary Ben Carson described the AFFH Rule as a "ruse for social engineering under the guise of desegregation" that essentially turned HUD "into a national zoning board." The repeal followed Trump's claims via Twitter and virtual town halls that the AFFH Rule was "not fair to homeowners" and that it would be "bringing who knows who into your suburbs, so your communities will be unsafe and your housing values will go down." Evoking racialized claims of neighborhood decline and white grievance, Trump further tweeted that "people have worked all their lives to get into a community, and now they're going to watch it go to hell. Not going to happen, not while I'm here." Trump tweeted after the repeal, "I am happy to inform all the people living their Suburban Lifestyle Dream that you will no longer be bothered or financially hurt by having low income housing built in your neighborhood. . . . Your housing prices will go up based on the market, and crime will go down. I have rescinded the Obama-Biden AFFH Rule. Enjoy!"

Fair housing advocates have already had substantial victories in their efforts to protect important civil rights regulations, however. In 2017, HUD tried to undermine the Small Area Fair Market Rents Final Rule—something that the agency had finalized just one year earlier. The Small Area Fair Market Rents Rule provides that instead of determining housing choice voucher payment standards by using a metropolitan areawide fair market rent estimate, PHAs can use fair market rents calculated for each zip code within the metropolitan area, thus enabling housing choice voucher tenants to access areas with lower poverty rates and with greater resources by deploying a housing subsidy adequate to cover higher rents in those areas. After HUD sought to withdraw the Small Area Fair Market Rents Rule in 2017, fair housing advocates successfully sued under the Administrative Procedures Act to reinstate it, enabling the Small Area Fair Market Rents Rule's implementation in a growing number of metropolitan areas across the country.

The 2020 repeal of the AFFH Rule, along with the proposed revisions to the disparate effects rule, represents another cycle of retreat from the promises of fair housing, just like the ones that had occurred in the nineteenth and twentieth centuries. In the run-up to the 2020 presidential election, as the struggle for suburban voters intensified and the Black Lives Matter movement directed attention to racial inequality, the AFFH Rule suddenly emerged into the limelight: Democratic presidential candidate Joe Biden expressed his intention to reinstate it, while Trump highlighted his repeal. As the conclusion to this book affirms, our intention here is to find ways to regain momentum in the simultaneous fight for fair and affordable housing. Many of the chapters that follow draw insights from the process through which the AFFH Rule was passed to help identify how a future policy can be made. Other chapters illuminate what the AFFH Rule accomplished during the brief time when it was actually in effect. Collectively, critically, and constructively, we have tried to evaluate the 2015 AFFH Rule. Ultimately, having identified several of its strengths and weaknesses, we envision some ways in which fair housing policies can be revised, improved, and given new life.

ENDNOTES

1. 42 U.S.C. § 3608.
2. Jorge De la Roca, Ingrid Gould Ellen, and Katherine M. O'Regan, "Race and Neighborhoods in the 21st Century: What Does Segregation Mean Today?" *Regional Science and Urban Economics* 47 (July 2014): 138–151.
3. Raj Chetty, Nathaniel Hendren, Patrick Kline, and Emmanuel Saez, *Where Is the Land of Opportunity? The Geography of Intergenerational Mobility in the United States* (Cambridge, MA: National Bureau of Economic Research, January 2014).
4. David M. Cutler and Edward L. Glaeser, "Are Ghettos Good or Bad?" *Quarterly Journal of Economics* 112, no. 3 (August 1, 1997): 827–872; Jorge De la Roca, Ingrid Gould Ellen, and Justin Steil, "Does Segregation Matter for Latinos?" *Journal of Housing Economics* 40 (June 2018): 129–141.
5. Ingrid Gould Ellen, "Is Segregation Bad for Your Health? The Case of Low Birth Weight," *Brookings-Wharton Papers on Urban Affairs* (2000): 203–229.
6. Elizabeth Oltmans Ananat and Ebonya Washington, "Segregation and Black Political Efficacy," *Journal of Public Economics* 93, no. 5–6 (2009): 807–822.
7. Douglas S. Massey and Nancy A. Denton, *American Apartheid: Segregation and the Making of the Underclass* (Cambridge, MA: Harvard University Press, 1993), 10; Lincoln Quillian, "Segregation and Poverty Concentration: The Role of Three Segregations," *American Sociological Review* 77, no. 3 (June 1, 2012): 354–379; Patrick Sharkey, *Stuck in Place: Urban Neighborhoods and the End of Progress toward Racial Equality* (Chicago: University of Chicago Press, 2013); Paul Jargowsky, "The Architecture of Segregation" (Century Foundation, August 7, 2015), available at https://tcf.org/content/report/architecture-of-segregation/.
8. 24 CFR §§ 5.150 et seq. The provisions of the AFFH Rule are discussed in greater detail in Chapter 2.
9. For example, Ben Carson, "Experimenting with Failed Socialism Again: Obama's New Housing Rules Try to Accomplish What Busing Could Not," *Washington Times*, July 23, 2015, available at https://www.washingtontimes.com/news/2015/jul/23/ben-carson-obamas-housing-rules-try-to-accomplish-/.
10. H.R.482 - Local Zoning Decisions Protection Act of 2017, 115th Congress (2017–2018).
11. For example, Poverty and Race Research Action Council, Comment re: Proposed Rule Affirmatively Furthering Fair Housing, Docket No. FR-5173-P-01, September 17, 2013.
12. For example, National People's Action, Comment re: Proposed Rule Affirmatively Furthering Fair Housing, Docket No. FR-5173-P-01, September 17, 2013.
13. For example, National Association for the Advancement of Colored People, Washington Bureau, Comment re: Proposed Rule Affirmatively Furthering Fair Housing, Docket No. FR-5173-P-01, September 16, 2013.
14. Raj Chetty, Nathaniel Hendren, Patrick Kline, Emmanuel Saez, and Nicholas Turner, "Is the United States Still a Land of Opportunity? Recent Trends in Intergenerational Mobility," *American Economic Review* 104, no. 5 (2014): 141–147.

15. Sharkey, *Stuck in Place*, 4.

16. Chetty et al., "Where Is the Land of Opportunity?"

17. De la Roca, Ellen, and O'Regan, "Race and Neighborhoods in the 21st Century"; De la Roca, Ellen, and Steil, "Does Segregation Matter for Latinos?"; Sharkey, *Stuck in Place*; Ingrid Gould Ellen, Justin P. Steil, and Jorge De la Roca, "The Significance of Segregation in the 21st Century," *City and Community* 15, no. 1 (2016): 8–13.

18. De la Roca, Ellen, and O'Regan, "Race and Neighborhoods in the 21st Century"; Sean F. Reardon and Kendra Bischoff, "Income Inequality and Income Segregation," *American Journal of Sociology* 116 (2011): 1092–1153.

19. U.S. Department of Commerce, Bureau of the Census, "Housing Vacancies and Homeownership. Table 16: Quarterly Homeownership Rates by Race and Ethnicity of Householder: 1994 to Present," 2019, available at https://www.census.gov/housing/hvs/data/histtabs.html.

20. Jesse Bricker et al., "Changes in U.S. Family Finances from 2013 to 2016: Evidence from the Survey of Consumer Finances," *Federal Reserve Bulletin* 103, no. 3 (2017), available at https://www.federalreserve.gov/publications/2017-September-changes-in-us-family-finances-from-2013-to-2016.htm.

21. U.S. Department of Commerce, Bureau of the Census, "Housing Vacancies and Homeownership."

22. Bricker et al., "Changes in U.S. Family Finances from 2013 to 2016."

23. "Minneapolis 2040," accessed May 12, 2019, available at https://minneapolis2040.com/.

24. Yonah Freemark, Justin P. Steil, and Kathleen Thelen, "Varieties of Urbanism: A Comparative View of Inequality and the Dual Dimensions of Metropolitan Fragmentation," *Politics and Society* (2020), available at https://doi-org.libproxy.mit.edu/10.1177/0032329220908966.

25. Robert J. Sampson, *Great American City: Chicago and the Enduring Neighborhood Effect* (repr., Chicago: University of Chicago Press, 2012), 21.

26. Justin P. Steil, Jorge De la Roca, and Ingrid Gould Ellen, "Desvinculado y desigual: Is segregation harmful to Latinos?" *Annals of the American Academy of Political and Social Science* 660, no. 1 (2015): 57–76; Justin P. Steil and Laura Humm Delgado, "Limits of Diversity: Jane Jacobs, the Just City, and Anti-subordination," *Cities* 91 (2019): 39–48.

27. De la Roca, Ellen, and O'Regan, "Race and Neighborhoods in the 21st Century."

28. Sharkey, *Stuck in Place*, 6.

29. Kevin Liptak, "Trump Pitches White Suburban Voters in Blatantly Political White House Event," *CNN*, July 16, 2020, available at https://www.cnn.com/2020/07/16/politics/donald-trump-white-suburbs/index.html.

30. 114 Cong. Rec. 3422 (1968).

31. Theodore Brantner Wilson, *The Black Codes of the South* (Tuscaloosa: University of Alabama Press, 1965).

32. Carl Schurz, "Report on the Condition of the South," S. Exec. Doc. No. 39-2 (1865), reprinted in Carl Schurz, *Speeches, Correspondence and Political Papers of Carl Schurz*, ed. (New York: G. P. Putnam's Sons, 1913), 325.

33. W. E. B. Du Bois, *Black Reconstruction in America, 1860–1880* (New York: Harcourt, Brace and Company, 1935), 601.

34. Ibid., 602–603.

35. Ibid., 601.

36. Andrew Johnson, *The Papers of Andrew Johnson, Volume 10* (Knoxville: University of Tennessee Press, 1967), 319.

37. 42 U.S.C. § 1981.

38. Johnson, *The Papers of Andrew Johnson*, 319.

39. Eric Foner, *Reconstruction: America's Unfinished Revolution* (New York: Harper-Collins, 1989).

40. Du Bois, *Black Reconstruction in America*, 419.

41. Ibid., 353, 239.

42. C. Vann Woodward, "Tom Watson and the Negro in Agrarian Politics," *Journal of Southern History* 4, no. 1 (1938): 14–33.

43. Elizabeth A. Herbin-Triant, *Threatening Property: Race, Class, and Campaigns to Legislate Jim Crow Neighborhoods* (New York: Columbia University Press, 2019).

44. Du Bois, *Black Reconstruction in America*, 661.

45. Baltimore, Maryland, Ordinances and Resolutions of the Mayor and City Council of Baltimore Passed the Annual Session 1910–11, 379 (1911). See generally Justin P. Steil and Laura Delgado, "Contested Values: How Jim Crow Segregation Ordinances Redefined Property Rights," in Global Perspectives on Urban Law, ed. Nestor Davidson and Geeta Tewari (London: Routledge, 2018), 7–26; Justin P. Steil and Camille Z. Charles, "The Sociology of Segregation and Fair Housing," in *Perspectives on Fair Housing*, ed. Wendell Pritchett, Susan Wachter, and Vincent Reina (Philadelphia: University of Pennsylvania Press, forthcoming).

46. National Association of Real Estate Boards, "1924 Code of Ethics," June 6, 1924, available at http://archive.realtor.org/sites/default/files/1924Ethics.pdf.

47. Daniel Aaronson, Daniel Hartley, and Bhashkar Mazumder, "The Effects of the 1930s HOLC 'Redlining' Maps" (Federal Reserve Bank of Chicago, August 3, 2017), available at http://eh.net/eha/wp-content/uploads/2017/08/Aaronson.pdf.

48. Trevon D. Logan and John M. Parman, "The National Rise in Residential Segregation," *Journal of Economic History* 77, no. 1 (2017): 127–170.

49. *Brown v. Board of Education of Topeka*, 347 U.S. 483 (1954).

50. Martin Luther King, "King Encyclopedia," speech given on March 18, 1966, available at http://mlk-kpp01.stanford.edu/index.php/encyclopedia/encyclopedia/enc_chicago_campaign.

51. Martin Luther King, "Where Do We Go from Here?" address delivered at the eleventh annual SCLC Convention, August 16, 1967, available at https://kinginstitute.stanford.edu/king-papers/documents/where-do-we-go-here-address-delivered-eleventh-annual-sclc-convention.

52. Stephen B. Oates, *Let the Trumpet Sound: The Life of Martin Luther King, Jr.* (New York: Mentor, 1985), 388.

53. Ibid., 413.

54. King, "Where Do We Go from Here?"

55. The National Advisory Commission on Civil Disorders, *Report of the National Advisory Commission on Civil Disorders* (Washington, DC: National Institute of Justice, 1968).

56. Ibid.

57. Nikole Hannah-Jones, "Living Apart: How the Government Betrayed a Landmark Civil Rights Law," *ProPublica*, June 25, 2015, available at https://www.propublica.org/article/living-apart-how-the-government-betrayed-a-landmark-civil-rights-law.

58. 114 Cong. Rec. 2703 (1968).

59. 114 Cong. Rec. 2274 (1968).

60. 114 Cong. Rec. 2276 (1968).

61. 114 Cong. Rec. 2274 (1968).

62. 114 Cong. Rec. 2280 (1968).

63. See Section 804(a), which makes it unlawful "to refuse to sell or rent after the making of a bona fide offer, or to refuse to negotiate for the sale or rental of, or otherwise make unavailable or deny, a dwelling to any person because of race, color, religion, sex, familial status, or national origin" (42 U.S.C. § 3608(d)); and Section 804(b), which provides that "it shall be unlawful for any person or other entity whose business includes engaging in real estate-related transactions to discriminate against any person in making available such a transaction, or in the terms or conditions of such a transaction, because of race, color, religion, sex, handicap, familial status, or national origin" (42 U.S.C. § 3608(e)).

64. Sec. 808(d), codified as 42 U.S.C. 3608(d).

65. Hannah-Jones, "Living Apart."

66. Robert Mason, *Richard Nixon and the Quest for a New Majority* (Chapel Hill: University of North Carolina Press, 2014), 149; Christopher Bonastia, *Knocking on the Door: The Federal Government's Attempt to Desegregate the Suburbs* (Princeton, NJ: Princeton University Press, 2008).

67. Pub. L. 93–383, title I, § 101, Aug. 22, 1974, 88 Stat. 633.

68. Pub. L. 93–383, title I, § 109, Aug. 22, 1974, 88 Stat. 649.

69. Pub. L. 98–181; 42 U.S.C. § 5304(b)(2), 5306(7)(B).

70. 53 Fed. Reg. 34,416 (Sept. 6, 1988); 60 Fed. Reg. 1,878 (Jan. 5, 1995); see 24 C.F.R. §§ 91.225(a)(1) and 91.325(a)(1).

71. U.S. Department of Housing and Urban Development, Policy Development Division, Office of Policy Development and Research, *Analysis of Impediments Study* (Washington, DC: U.S. Department of Housing and Urban Development, 2009).

72. Ibid.

73. Ibid., 15.

74. Government Accountability Office, *Report: HUD Needs to Enhance Its Requirements and Oversight of Jurisdictions' Fair Housing Plans* (Government Accountability Office, September 2010).

75. National Commission on Fair Housing and Equal Opportunity, *The Future of Fair Housing: Report of the National Commission on Fair Housing and Equal Opportunity* (National Commission on Fair Housing and Equal Opportunity, 2008), 44.

76. Ibid.

77. Richard Briffault, "Our Localism: Part I—The Structure of Local Government Law," *Columbia Law Review* 90, no. 1 (1990): 1–115.

78. Michael Schill, "Implementing the Federal Fair Housing Act: The Adjudication of Complaints," in *Fragile Rights within Cities: Government, Housing, and Fairness*, ed. John M. Goering (Lanham, MD: Rowman and Littlefield, 2007), 143–176.

79. Margery Austin Turner, Rob Santos, Diane Levy, Doug Wissoker, Claudia Aranda, and Rob Pitingolo, "Housing and Discrimination against Racial and Ethnic Minorities 2012" (Urban Institute, 2013); Devah Pager and Hana Shepherd, "The Sociology of Discrimination: Racial Discrimination in Employment, Housing, Credit, and Consumer Markets," *Annual Review of Sociology* 34, no. 1 (2008): 181–209.

80. Robert G. Schwemm, "Overcoming Structural Barriers to Integrated Housing: A Back-to-the-Future Reflection on the Fair Housing Act's Affirmatively Further Mandate," *Kentucky Law Journal* 100 (2011): 125.

81. 425 F. Supp. 987, 1013–21 (E.D. Pa. 1976), aff'd in part, rev'd in part, 564 F.2d 126 (3d Cir. 1977).

82. *Resident Advisory Board v. Rizzo*, 564 F.2d 126 (3d Cir. 1977).

83. 817 F.2d 149, 161 (1st Cir. 1987).

84. *United States* ex rel. *Anti-Discrimination Center of Metro New York v. Westchester County*, No. 668 F. Supp. 2d 548, 563, 570–71 (S.D.N.Y. 2009).

85. Olatunde C. A. Johnson, "Beyond the Private Attorney General: Equality Directives in American Law," *NYU Law Review* 87 (2012): 1339; Olatunde C. A. Johnson, "Overreach and Innovation in Equality Regulation," *Duke Law Journal* 66 (2016): 1771; Justin P. Steil, "Antisubordination Planning," *Journal of Planning Education and Research* (forthcoming), available at https://doi.org/10.1177/0739456X18815739.

86. Justin P. Steil and Nicholas F. Kelly, "The Fairest of Them All: Analyzing Affirmatively Furthering Fair Housing Compliance," *Housing Policy Debate* 29, no. 1 (2019): 85–105.

87. Xavier de Souza Briggs, ed., *The Geography of Opportunity: Race and Housing Choice in Metropolitan America* (Washington, DC: Brookings Institution Press, 2005).

88. Raj Chetty, Nathaniel Hendren, and Lawrence F. Katz, "The Effects of Exposure to Better Neighborhoods on Children: New Evidence from the Moving to Opportunity Experiment," *American Economic Review* 106, no. 4 (2016): 855–902.

89. Douglas S. Massey, Len Albright, Rebecca Casciano, Elizabeth Derickson, and David N. Kinsey, *Climbing Mount Laurel: The Struggle for Affordable Housing and Social Mobility in an American Suburb* (Princeton, NJ; Princeton University Press, 2013).

90. Chester Hartman, "The Right to Stay Put," in *Land Reform, American Style*, ed. Charles. C. Geisler and Frank. J. Popper (Totowa, NJ: Rowman and Allanheld, 1984), 302–318; see also Kathe Newman and Elvin K. Wyly, "The Right to Stay Put, Revisited: Gentrification and Resistance to Displacement in New York City," *Urban Studies* 43, no. 1 (2006): 23–57.

91. Margery Austin Turner, "Beyond People versus Place: A Place-Conscious Framework for Investing in Housing and Neighborhoods," *Housing Policy Debate* 27, no. 2 (2017): 306–314.

92. Nancy Andrews and Dan Rinzler, "Holistic Place-Based Investments," in *The Dream Revisited: Contemporary Debates about Housing, Segregation, and Opportunity*, ed. Ingrid Ellen and Justin P. Steil (New York: Columbia University Press, 2019), 233–234.

93. There have often been fierce debates between these two perspectives, as Bostic, O'Regan, Pontius, and Kelly describe in Chapter 2; see also David Imbroscio, "'United and Actuated by Some Common Impulse of Passion': Challenging the Dispersal Consensus in American Housing Policy Research," *Journal of Urban Affairs* 30, no. 2 (2008): 111–130; Xavier de Souza Briggs, "Maximum Feasible Misdirection: A Reply to Imbroscio," *Journal of Urban Affairs* 30, no. 2 (2008): 131–137. Mary Pattillo has written about a conundrum intertwined with mobility approaches: that the promotion of integration by race or by class "as the means to improve the lives of Blacks stigmatizes Black people and Black spaces and valorizes Whiteness as both the symbol of opportunity and the measuring stick for equality. In turn, such stigmatization of Blacks and Black spaces is precisely what foils efforts toward integration" (in *The Dream Revisited: Contemporary Debates about Housing, Segregation, and Opportunity*, ed. Ingrid Ellen and Justin P. Steil [New York: Columbia University Press, 2019], 30). Others, such as Goetz in this volume, suggest that a focus on mobility can in some contexts pave the way for gentrification, developer profit, and the dispersal of Black communities. Critic of an emphasis on place-based investments have argued that these policies, despite decades of efforts, have not meaningfully changed the racially and economically unequal geographies of the United States and have instead continued to perpetuate segregated and unequal living patterns.

94. 24 C.F.R. § 5.152.

95. Ibid.

96. Ibid.

97. Justin P. Steil and Nicholas F. Kelly, "Survival of the Fairest: Examining HUD Reviews of Assessments of Fair Housing," *Housing Policy Debate* 29, no. 5 (2019): 736–751.

98. National Association for the Advancement of Colored People, Washington Bureau, Comment re: Proposed Rule Affirmatively Furthering Fair Housing, Docket No. FR-5173-P-01, September 16, 2013.

99. Letter from forty-one national civil rights, fair housing, women's, disability, LBGT [Lesbian, Bisexual, Gay, Transgender], and consumer organizations, and labor unions, Comment re: Proposed Rule Affirmatively Furthering Fair Housing, Docket No. FR-5173-P-01, September 17, 2013.

100. National Council of La Raza, Comment re: Proposed Rule Affirmatively Furthering Fair Housing, Docket No. FR-5173-P-01, September 17, 2013.

101. National Community Reinvestment Coalition, Comment re: Proposed Rule Affirmatively Furthering Fair Housing, Docket No. FR-5173-P-01, September 17, 2013.

102. NAACP Legal Defense Fund, Comment re: Proposed Rule Affirmatively Furthering Fair Housing, Docket No. FR-5173-P-01, September 17, 2013.

103. The Lawyers' Committee for Civil Rights Under Law, Comment re: Proposed Rule Affirmatively Furthering Fair Housing, Docket No. FR-5173-P-01, September 17, 2013.

104. Poverty and Race Research Action Council, Comment re: Proposed Rule Affirmatively Furthering Fair Housing, Docket No. FR-5173-P-01, September 17, 2013.

105. Ibid.

106. Ibid.

107. National People's Action, Comment re: Proposed Rule Affirmatively Furthering Fair Housing.

108. National Low Income Housing Coalition, Comment re: Proposed Rule Affirmatively Furthering Fair Housing, Docket No. FR-5173-P-01, September 17, 2013.

109. Coalition of Large Public Housing Authorities, Comment re: Proposed Rule Affirmatively Furthering Fair Housing, Docket No. FR-5173-P-01, September 17, 2013.

110. National Association of Housing and Redevelopment Officials, Comment re: Proposed Rule Affirmatively Furthering Fair Housing, Docket No. FR-5173-P-01, September 17, 2013.

111. Carson, "Experimenting with Failed Socialism Again."

112. Ibid.

113. Sharon Howard, Comment re: Proposed Rule Affirmatively Furthering Fair Housing, Docket No. FR-5173-P-01, August 12, 2013.

114. Chris Brown, Comment re: Proposed Rule Affirmatively Furthering Fair Housing, Docket No. FR-5173-P-01, August 14, 2013.

115. Ibid.

116. 83 Fed. Reg. 683, January 5, 2018; 83 Fed. Reg. 23927, May 23, 2018.

117. 85 Fed. Reg. 2041, January 14, 2020.

118. 24 C.F.R. § 5.152.

119. 85 Fed. Reg. 2041, 2053, January 14, 2020. It further delineated three dimensions of this choice: "protected choice," "which means access to housing without discrimination"; "actual choice," "which means not only that affordable housing options exist, but that information and resources are available to enable informed choice"; and "quality choice," "which means access to affordable housing options that are decent, safe, and sanitary."

120. 85 Fed. Reg. 2041, 2053, January 14, 2020.
121. Ibid.

NOTE REGARDING CAPITALIZATION:

Throughout this volume, we have capitalized "Black" but not "white." As a social construction, race is also a construction of language. Some style guides recommend writing "white" and "black" in all lowercase letters. Lori L. Tharps has made a case for why she "refuse[s] to remain in the lower case" and have her "culture . . . reduced to a color." As Tharps and others have highlighted, Du Bois fought to have the "n" in Negro capitalized nearly a century ago, and when the *New York Times* ultimately agreed, in 1930, the editorial board wrote, "In our 'style book' 'Negro' is now added to the list of words to be capitalized. It is not merely a typographical change; it is an act of recognition of racial self-respect for those who have been for generations in 'the lower case.'" If "Black" is capitalized, should "white" then also be capitalized? Some style guides accept the capitalization of both for consistency. Touré explains that he chooses to capitalize "Black" and write "white" in lowercase because he believes that "'Black' constitutes a group, an ethnicity equivalent to African-American, Negro, or, in terms of a sense of ethnic cohesion, Irish, Polish, or Chinese" but that whiteness does not merit the same treatment. Touré notes that "most American whites think of themselves as Italian-American or Jewish or otherwise relating to other past connections that Blacks cannot make because of the familial and national disruptions of slavery." Because "Black speaks to an unknown familial/national past it deserves capitalization," but white does not. We agree.

Promises

1

The Origins of the Fair Housing Act of 1968

ALEXANDER VON HOFFMAN

With the passage of Title VIII of the Civil Rights Act of 1968, better known as the Fair Housing Act, a decades-long struggle to end racial injustice in American housing came to a triumphant climax. In the first part of the twentieth century, civil rights activists successfully fought to ban racial zoning and eliminate racially restrictive covenants. Advocates for fair housing then took on the federal government's policies that fostered racial segregation, especially those of the Federal Housing Administration (FHA). They built a movement, starting in New York City, with the five-year long campaign to desegregate Stuyvesant Town, a large publicly subsidized privately developed urban redevelopment project. Out of that effort came the National Committee Against Discrimination in Housing (NCDH), which in turn encouraged fair housing campaigns and legislation in dozens of states and towns across the country.

In the 1960s, fair housing advocates set their sights on a national prohibition on discrimination in all housing, public and private, on the basis of race, creed, or national origin. They successfully pressured President John Kennedy to issue an executive order to that end in late 1962, but it was far more limited than they had hoped. Then, in the midst of civil rights ferment and urban uprisings of the late 1960s, many reformers began to see predominantly African American urban neighborhoods as pathological places that fostered poverty and violence. In arguing for the passage of the Fair Housing Act, liberals in Congress explained that the law was necessary to rescue African Americans from such "racial ghettos."

Activists expanded their goals from simply banning discriminatory practices to breaking up these "racial ghettos" and integrating neighborhoods throughout metropolitan areas. Although its proponents insisted that the Fair Housing Act was necessary to eliminate the ghetto, the majority of its provisions targeted discrimination in real estate transactions. The complex factors, from exclusionary zoning to socioeconomic inequality to household preferences for particular neighborhood characteristics, that shape settlement patterns and that reproduce racial segregation make the prospects for widely integrated neighborhoods unclear, even with the newer Affirmatively Furthering Fair Housing (AFFH) Rule. Although the introduction to this volume has already noted some of the key historical themes and precedents, some additional aspects of this history are worth recounting to explain the struggle and potential of the quest to further fair housing.

Public and Private Segregation and Its Early Opponents

During the early decades of the twentieth century, more than a million African Americans moved from the rural South to America's urban centers in what has come to be known as "the Great Migration." In the great cities of the nation, many of the new arrivals clustered in central locations, helping create neighborhoods with high concentrations of Black residents—greater than the proportion of foreign-born groups in their respective immigrant quarters, and longer lasting. The most important cause of highly concentrated Black settlement patterns was white people's hostility to their presence. Whites' antagonism toward Blacks was frequently organized and at times violent. Dozens of African Americans died at the hands of whites in ugly mob actions, the most notorious of which occurred in Chicago and East St. Louis in 1919 and Detroit in 1925 but which persisted into the mid-twentieth century.[1]

Whites took many other measures short of violence to prevent African Americans from living among them. White real estate brokers and lenders frequently would not serve Black customers, property managers of white-occupied apartment buildings refused to rent to Blacks, homebuilders rarely built houses for African Americans, and white homeowners often would not sell their homes to African Americans. Several city governments passed racial zoning ordinances. After the Supreme Court ruled racial zoning unconstitutional in 1917, white real estate developers and homeowners who wanted to prevent African Americans from moving to their neighborhoods shifted strategies. They drew up private agreements requiring that all neighborhood residents would not sell or rent their property to Negroes. These racially restrictive covenants, which were also used against Jews and other unwanted population groups, took the form of either attachments to property deeds or agreements between fellow property owners.[2]

Formed in 1909 to end racial discrimination in America, the National Association for the Advancement of Colored People (NAACP) first campaigned against racial zoning and then during the 1940s spearheaded the fight against racial covenants. Under its founder Thurgood Marshall, the NAACP Legal Defense and Educational Fund pursued two basic lines of legal attack. First, its attorneys recognized the validity of racial covenants as voluntary private agreements but opposed their enforcement by the courts as unconstitutionally discriminatory "state action" similar to racial zoning laws.[3] Second, they argued that the covenants were inimical to a sound public policy by presenting sociological evidence that covenants forced African Americans to live in substandard racial ghettos—a term that several authors used to evoke the Jewish ghettos in Europe organized and enforced by the Nazis.[4]

In May 1948, the Supreme Court heard two racial covenant cases grouped together, *McGhee v. Sipes* and *Shelley v. Kraemer*, and ruled against enforcement of racially restrictive covenants. The court affirmed the state action theory that the NAACP had argued and held that the state courts' upholding of these restrictive covenants deprived the Black plaintiffs of their property rights in violation of the Fourteenth Amendment's prohibition against a state's denying any person within its territory equal protection under the laws.[5]

At the same time as opponents of housing discrimination challenged court enforcement of private restrictive covenants, they also knew that government housing agencies were themselves directly engaged in forms of discriminatory state action. The nation's public housing program, created in the 1930s, blatantly enforced segregation of the races in the great majority of public housing projects. The United States Housing Authority (USHA) had established a Racial Relations Service, but despite being staffed by such integrationists as Frank S. Horne, it had done little to integrate public housing.[6]

Several factors inhibited officials from integrating government-sponsored public housing projects. In the segregated South, public housing was politically popular, but to local officials, integration of housing projects was unthinkable.[7] In the North, the situation was not much better. In Chicago, Elizabeth Wood, the liberal executive secretary of the Chicago Housing Authority, tried to place small numbers of Blacks in new, predominantly white public housing in the central city and on the city's outskirts, but even this limited policy provoked massive white violence in 1946 and 1947. Wood then lost a struggle with the city council over the location of a host of new public housing projects, after which Blacks were largely constrained to public housing projects in Black neighborhoods.[8]

The public housing movement bequeathed several leaders to the effort to prohibit housing discrimination, the most prominent of whom were Robert C. Weaver and Charles Abrams. As a member of the "Black Cabinet" in Franklin D. Roosevelt's administration, Weaver had held several federal government positions, including special assistant in the public housing division of the Works Progress Administration (WPA). In 1948, he published *The Negro Ghetto*, a seminal work on the problem of discrimination, and in 1965, President Lyndon Johnson appointed him to be the first secretary of the Department of Housing and Urban Development (HUD). A lawyer by profession, Abrams in 1933 helped draft legislation to establish the New York City Housing Authority and then served as that public housing body's counsel. In the 1950s, he became the first chairman of the New York State Commission against Discrimination. During his long career, Abrams not only applied his legal expertise to solving housing and civil rights issues but also wrote prolifically to sway public opinion on these matters.[9]

As veterans of the public housing movement, such opponents of housing discrimination usually did not dwell on the sins of the public housing program, which was a key component of liberals' postwar policy agenda. Instead, they saved their wrath for the FHA, the federal government agency established in 1935 to insure mortgage loans and promote single-family homeownership. Supporters of public housing reviled the FHA as a rival to their own program and a tool of the private housing industry, which they blamed for creating the nation's slums and then doing nothing to provide homes to low-income people.[10]

For their part, civil rights advocates denounced the FHA for aggressively pursuing a policy of containment of African Americans in the ghetto. For years, FHA regulators encouraged the use of racially restrictive covenants. Even after the Supreme Court's decision, agency officials believed that *Shelley* did not prevent them from honoring mortgages on covenanted properties. Moreover, the FHA's underwriting manual specifically warned against insuring loans to Blacks or to owners in racially mixed neighborhoods. In the view of Abrams, the FHA's "racial policy . . . could well have been culled from the [Nazi] Nuremburg laws."[11]

After the *Shelley* decision, the NAACP applied intensive pressure on the FHA to modify its policies. Walter White, the chief executive of the NAACP, protested personally to President Harry Truman. Marshall met repeatedly with the solicitor general to submit drafts of revised FHA regulations and sternly lectured FHA officials against following local segregation customs. In 1947, the agency finally agreed to delete offending references to race in its underwriting manual, but not until late 1949 did it agree to deny insurance to mortgages with racial covenants. Even so, the FHA continued to encourage development of suburbs, such as Westlake in Daly City, California, and Levittown, Pennsylvania, that were closed to African Americans. Under presidents Kennedy and Johnson, the FHA gradually improved, but in the late 1960s, the agency was still approving segregated developments and working with developers and owners who discriminated against Blacks.[12]

The Legacy of Stuyvesant Town

In New York City, a long campaign to desegregate the pioneer urban redevelopment project Stuyvesant Town led to the founding of the first organizations dedicated specifically to eliminating discrimination in housing. With support from Robert Moses, New York's controversial urban-planning power broker, the Metropolitan Life Insurance Company initiated the Stuyvesant Town project in 1943. The project enraged liberal public housing supporters because it forcibly removed low-income families without rehousing them and used public money (in the form of tax exemptions) to support a private real-estate venture. Worst of all, the rental policy for the new project blatantly banned minorities.[13] Outraged civil rights and public housing advocates enlisted many liberal organizations, including the American Civil Liberties Union (ACLU), the NAACP, and the American Jewish Congress, to fight to integrate Stuyvesant Town. Eventually, in January 1952, Metropolitan Life succumbed to the pressure and adopted a nondiscriminatory rental policy.[14]

Although the anti-discrimination forces had won a great moral victory, the new rental policy had little effect. Relatively few African Americans moved to Stuyvesant Town, mainly because few applied for admittance: low incomes and long waiting lists for apartments deterred many, and a reluctance to endure expected white hostility no doubt kept others away. However, the battle to integrate Stuyvesant Town had profound effects beyond the boundaries of the housing project. In 1948, the representatives of sixteen groups involved in the campaign organized the New York State Committee on Discrimination in Housing to agitate for fair housing. The new organization sponsored path-breaking legislation in the city and the state that made it illegal to discriminate in publicly aided and private housing developments.[15]

After the passage of the Housing Act of 1949, the members of the New York State Committee on Discrimination in Housing saw the potential for action on a national scale and, in 1950, founded a new organization, the National Committee Against Discrimination in Housing (NCDH) to coordinate activities in the cause of what was originally called "democratic housing" but soon became known as either open or fair housing. Until its demise in 1987, the NCDH was the only national organization dedicated to wiping out racial discrimination in the housing field. Fittingly enough, Weaver and Abrams, two old friends and leaders in the struggles against restrictive covenants and Stuyvesant Town, served as the first president and vice president of the NCDH.[16]

First Steps toward Fair Housing

The NCDH focused on fighting discrimination rather than the patterns of racial change in neighborhoods, a far more complex phenomenon. As the author of a 1960 report funded by the Ford Foundation explained, eliminating discriminatory conduct would be easier and more effective than trying to change prejudiced attitudes, and changing laws was the most effective way to change conduct and the factors that encouraged prejudiced attitudes. Hence, the NCDH drafted model anti-discrimination laws for cities and states and lobbied the federal Housing and Home Finance Agency (HHFA) to encourage open or nondiscriminatory occupancy policies in new FHA-supported private housing and all public housing. In the private sphere, it worked with local interracial housing committees in Norfolk and Minneapolis and campaigned to get developers to sell homes to African Americans. After a decade of work, advocates of "open housing," a term that evoked unrestricted real estate markets, could point to thirty-two cities and ten states that had prohibited discrimination in government-supported developments.[17]

By 1960, the anti-housing discrimination advocates had begun to make headway in reforming private real-estate activity. The growing civil rights movement raised the consciousness of many white Americans and spurred ordinary citizens to form fair housing committees in hundreds of communities across the United States. Some committees encouraged local governments to bar discrimination and invited African Americans to move to their communities, although as a practical matter in affluent suburbs, such as Boston's Natick and Wellesley, Blacks were unlikely to come in significant numbers. An increasing number of states and cities passed anti-discrimination laws. In one of those states, New Jersey, representatives of local organizations formed a New Jersey Committee against Discrimination and, with the aid and advice of the NCDH, mounted a publicity and legal campaign against developer William Levitt, who notoriously had refused to sell to Blacks, that forced him to reverse policy and sell to non-whites. Such decentralized local efforts multiplied during the civil rights era, so that on the eve of the passage of the Fair Housing Act of 1968, the NCDH counted twenty-one states, the District of Columbia, five counties, and seventy-five cities and villages that had enacted open housing statutes.[18]

Beyond its encouragement of local endeavors, the NCDH relentlessly pursued federal policies that would end discrimination. During the 1960 U.S. presidential campaign, the NCDH persuaded both parties to adopt open housing planks. Candidate Kennedy raised the hopes of public housing and civil rights advocates when he promised that if elected, he would outlaw housing discrimination by federal agencies with a "stroke of a pen." After the election, however, frustration set in when it became clear that the new president was in no hurry to issue an executive order. Abrams, recently installed as the president of the NCDH, helpfully sent Kennedy a sweeping draft order that would have banned discrimination in all forms of federally assisted housing and all federally regulated and assisted lending institutions, but to no avail.

The hopes of the advocates were raised again when, at year's end, Kennedy nominated Weaver, the NCDH's former president, to head the federal HHFA. Yet the president, wary of political repercussions, refused to act on the executive order to prohibit housing discrimination by federal agencies. Abrams initiated a national lobbying effort to force the president's hand. Finally, in the fall of 1962, Kennedy issued a limited order that directed all federal departments, but particularly the HHFA, "to take all action necessary and appropriate to prevent discrimination because of race, color, creed, or national origin" in any housing the government owned, financed, or supported through loan insurance, *in the future*. Needless to say, open housing advocates were highly disappointed.[19]

Changing Perceptions of the Ghetto

By the mid-1960s, the social and political context of the movement to end housing discrimination had begun to change. The northern and urban migrations of African Americans had slowed to a virtual halt. Large numbers of whites continued to move from city neighborhoods into the suburbs, opening large new territories in which Black people could settle.

The transition process, however, created dual real estate markets in which demand for homes in old neighborhoods was low among whites and high among African Americans. Unscrupulous real estate agents and investors, known as "blockbusters," exploited this situation by scaring whites into selling homes at discount prices in "changing neighborhoods" and then charging high prices to Blacks to purchase such houses, a practice sometimes made worse by requiring the onerous contract method of sale. Although widely condemned for causing wholesale racial change, blockbusters were a symptom, not a cause, of the discriminatory real estate market. Hence, the NCDH's leaders believed that such exploitation constituted not civil rights violations but fraud and worried that trying to suppress it might prevent Blacks from purchasing homes in previously white neighborhoods.[20]

As African Americans spread across the cities and into the inner suburbs, their accommodations improved. Density levels and the number of substandard dwellings dropped; gone were the desperately tight housing market, overcrowding, and kitchenette apartments of the early postwar years. In many cities, the degree of urban segregation actually declined.[21]

As middle-class African Americans departed for middle-class districts, the proportion of low-income, unemployed, and single-parent households living in predominantly African American central-city areas increased. Crime rates, which rose throughout the country during the 1960s, escalated dramatically in the core areas of large cities. Just as the southern civil rights movement triumphed with the passage of the Civil Rights Act of 1964, violent disorders broke out in the Hough neighborhood of Cleveland and New York City's Harlem, followed by four years of similar upheavals in African American neighborhoods throughout the nation. The urban unrest, poverty, and rising crime rates convinced many observers that the nation's cities were in crisis. In response, scholars, civil rights advocates, and journalists launched a harsh attack on what they called "the racial ghetto" and redefined the goals of the fair housing movement. Since the 1940s, urban sociologists and civil rights activists had invoked the term "ghetto" to emphasize the injustice of housing discrimination, noting the correlation of overcrowded slums with social problems.[22]

Now, influenced by theories of a self-perpetuating "culture of poverty," scholars and reformers conceived of the ghetto as an oppressive place that inflicted poverty, dangerous housing, inferior schools, chiseling storekeepers, and brutal police upon its inhabitants. People who lived in such neighborhoods, according to studies of urban social pathology, faced almost insurmountable barriers to finding jobs or experiencing stable social lives. To such observers, the color gap in wealth seemed to be widening instead of narrowing as America's inner cities dissolved into a tangle of poverty, drugs, violence, and defeatism.[23]

In 1965, Kenneth Clark published *Dark Ghetto: Dilemmas of Social Power*, perhaps the most eloquent and influential expression of this concept of the ghetto as a source of social ills. Based on his experience with the government-funded Harlem Youth Opportunities Unlimited program, *Dark Ghetto* was not so much a report as an "anguished cry."[24] In it, Clark spells out the social problems he saw facing African Americans: "low aspiration, poor education, family instability, illegitimacy, unemployment, crime, drug addiction and alcoholism, frequent illness and early death." An internalized sense of inferior racial status with its attendant despair and hatred, he adds, aggravated the problems of urban poverty.[25]

A primary source of these social problems, Clark strongly believes, was the physical environment that hemmed in its inhabitants behind an "invisible wall." "The pathologies of the ghetto community," he writes, "perpetuate themselves through cumulative ugliness, deterioration, and isolation." Echoing anti-slum reformers of the early twentieth century, Clark charges that unsafe, deteriorating, and overcrowded housing was killing off the residents of Harlem.[26] During the mid-1960s, many politically liberal Americans, including the president of the United States, adopted the view that the isolation of the ghetto interlocked with past injustice and present prejudice to harm African Americans in complex and profound ways. As Congress debated the Voting Rights Act of 1965, President Johnson echoed Clark in a speech at Howard University in which he described African Americans as "a separated people" in "a world of decay ringed by an invisible wall."[27]

To Break Up the Racial Ghetto

In the ferment over civil rights and the inner city, the open housing reformers widened the scope of their agenda beyond simply ending discriminatory practices; they wished to eliminate that invisible wall altogether. In 1965, the NCDH launched a nationwide campaign for open occupancy that deliberately moved "beyond the issue of discrimination *per se* to those broad social, economic, and political factors which support and extend the ghetto walls." That October, the NCDH organized a national conference, attended by participants from 132 cities and 32 states, on the theme of "How to Break Up the Racial Ghetto."[28] The following year, the NCDH participated in the White House Conference on Civil Rights and helped draft and then promoted housing goals, such as building low-cost housing in suburbs and developing racially inclusive new towns, that went further than merely removing barriers to free selection of housing.[29]

Yet for all their dislike of the ghetto, open housing leaders overestimated the value that many African American residents of inner-city neighborhoods placed on racial integration. The NCDH's own newsletter in 1963 summarized a Philadelphia study that found that when choosing a home, most African Americans unsurprisingly looked first for good-quality housing and neighborhood amenities. "Integration as such," the study concluded, "was a secondary consideration."[30] In 1964, a study of middle-class Black families dislocated by urban renewal projects in Boston found that almost all had moved to other predominantly Black neighborhoods, most often because they liked the inexpensive housing there and wanted to be near friends and relatives. "Negroes do not move [out of Black neighborhoods]," one African American woman displaced by urban renewal explained, "because they feel more comfortable with other Negroes." Whether this sentiment was widespread or not, it indicated that some Blacks did not consider living in integrated neighborhoods to be their highest priority.[31]

In New York City, where almost all homes were covered by extensive fair housing laws, open housing advocates ran a massive educational program from 1964 to 1965 to "convince Negroes that good housing is also integrated

housing." After fifteen months of trying to help minority households obtain
housing in predominantly white neighborhoods, however, "Operation Open
City" could only point to eighty families who had found "mainstream"
homes. African Americans were reluctant to move to predominantly white
neighborhoods for many reasons—including costs of housing, desire to be
near family and friends, and/or the expectation of white hostility—which
complicated the task of integrating urban neighborhoods beyond what reformers usually thought was necessary.[32]

Chicago 1966

The Chicago Freedom Movement, a coalition led by Dr. Martin Luther
King, also discovered the difficulties of trying to transform urban dwelling
patterns. In 1966, as the sense of "urban crisis" deepened, King and other
leaders of the Southern Christian Leadership Conference (SCLC) came to
Chicago to begin the northern drive of the civil rights movement and chose
to make housing their central issue. The Chicago Freedom Movement ab-
sorbed the anti-ghetto principles of the open housing movement. "To wipe
out slums, ghettos, and racism," the leaders declared, "we must create an
open city with equal opportunities and equal results."[33]

Following the precepts of open housing advocates, the Chicago Freedom
Movement's leaders declared that particular agents—slumlords, real estate
brokers, savings and loan associations, the Chicago Housing Authority—
were orchestrating the city's segregated residential patterns. By staging
anti-discrimination demonstrations, the leaders hoped to pressure Chicago's mayor, Richard J. Daley, and the city's other powerbrokers to order the
agents of segregation to cease and desist.[34]

The housing campaign, however, did not turn out as planned. The Chicago Freedom Movement held prayer vigils and marches in the city's all-
white communities. In working-class white neighborhoods, such as Gage
Park, they were confronted not by real estate agents and lenders but by
mobs of stone-throwing whites whose hostility surpassed anything that
the veterans of the civil rights movement had ever encountered in response
to their demonstrations. The marches generated little support. The city's
newspapers, which had originally greeted King warmly, soured on the campaign, and few residents of Chicago's Black neighborhoods responded. That
August, at a summit meeting with the mayor, city officials, and real estate
executives, the civil rights leaders won only token concessions to their demands for open housing.[35]

One of the agreements the Chicago Freedom Movement's leaders ob-
tained was the establishment of an open housing service, which would
aim to place a thousand racial minority families in white communities

throughout the Chicago area. As with New York's "Open City" campaign, however, the program did not reach its ambitious goals. The service encountered many obstacles, including not only the difficulty of finding white landlords willing to rent or sell to Blacks but also low levels of interest among Chicago's African Americans in moving to white neighborhoods. The housing service's African American staff members encountered resistance from Black Chicagoans to the idea of moving out of their neighborhoods, including residents who believed that the program was a scheme to dilute Blacks' political strength. Moreover, a majority of the applicants to the housing service, according to social scientist Brian J. L. Berry, were more interested in finding decent housing than in moving to integrated neighborhoods— and more than a third of them were content to live in predominantly Black neighborhoods. After a year of operation in a city with three hundred thousand Black households, the service had placed only 46 of 537 applicants, and of these only about 15 had moved to all-white communities. In the end, embattled working-class communities, such as Gage Park and Cicero—not to mention wealthy North Shore suburbs, such as Winnetka—remained lily white.[36] Although the Chicago campaign had more lasting success on the legal front with the *Gautreaux* cases filed in 1966, it would take thirty years of struggle to carry out these court orders. Meanwhile, Chicago remained one of the nation's most highly segregated cities.[37]

The Black Power Challenge to Housing Integration

In the late 1960s, the open housing movement began to face a formidable challenge from an array of civil rights leaders, policy makers, and intellectuals who disavowed the anti-ghetto policies of the open housing crusade and expressed instead a strong sense of racial solidarity among African Americans and an emphasis on empowering predominantly Black neighborhoods. Within the civil rights movement, the rising popularity of the idea of Black Power challenged the fundamentally integrationist principles of open housing. Inspired in part by Malcolm X and frustrated by the failure of Democratic Party to seat the Mississippi Freedom Democratic Party at the 1964 National Convention, Stokely Carmichael, a freedom rider and leader of the Student Nonviolent Coordinating Committee (SNCC), began to rally support for a Black Power philosophy that helped precipitate a split between the increasingly militant and Black nationalist groups, such as SNCC and the Congress of Racial Equality (CORE), and the more moderate and integrationist organizations, such as SCLC and the NAACP.

Black Power advocates rejected the notion that Blacks had to live in white neighborhoods to improve their lives. As Carmichael said, "We were never fighting for the right to integrate, we were fighting against white supremacy."

In Chicago, supporters of Black Power opposed King's leadership of the Chicago Freedom Movement and the goal of an open city by appealing to the reluctance of Blacks to move to white neighborhoods. "Is token integration the solution to our problem?" SNCC leaders asked the city's Black residents. "Would you move your family into Gage Park? Who is kidding who?"[38]

At the same time, the idea of curing poverty and hopelessness from within afflicted communities presented another alternative to the goal of open housing. The grassroots community organizing projects of Saul Alinsky's Industrial Areas Foundation in such cities as Chicago and Rochester, New York, and the programs of Black Panther Party chapters in Oakland and San Francisco, California, and other cities popularized the empowering of inner-city residents where they lived. Influenced by the push for community organization and Black empowerment, federal government programs began to reflect the goal of strengthening rather than abandoning troubled neighborhoods. The Community Action Program, a part of Johnson's War on Poverty legislation, called for the "maximum feasible participation" of the residents of areas receiving federal funds to shape federal programs to remedy their social problems. The Model Cities program, another Johnson initiative passed in 1966, aimed at producing a coordinated attack by government and nonprofit agencies at the local level on housing, employment, and other social problems within the slums and blighted areas of particular communities.[39]

In 1966, Frances Fox Piven and Richard A. Cloward, activists and scholars of these community action programs, articulated their own case against integrationist urban policies. In a direct slap at the open housing movement, they pointed out that the multitude of legal reforms and education campaigns had failed to alter patterns of residential segregation. Citing the historical precedents for ethnic self-help efforts, Piven and Cloward embraced the concept of racial separatism and urged reformers to abandon the goal of desegregation because it was delaying urgently needed improvements in the inner city.[40]

The challenges posed by rival policies, however, only stiffened the resolve of the integrationist leaders of the open housing movement. Horne, the chair of the NCDH executive committee, blasted critics of open housing for wishing to "polish up" the ghetto, which he had learned long ago that "traditional racist-oriented forces" had created. The ghetto must be destroyed, Horne declared, because it "is the bar sinister; it is the Pandora's box out of which fly segregated schools, segregated lives and violence in the streets." Federal slum rehabilitation and Model Cities programs, he charged, compromised with an evil akin to "Attila or Hitler or Beelzebub."[41]

In 1967, the NCDH took aim at the community-based Model Cities program in a widely publicized broadside titled *How the Federal Government*

Builds Ghettos. The NCDH manifesto recited the history of discriminatory policies of the FHA and the federal public housing administration and the current government practices that upheld segregated living patterns. Although the authors called for withholding all federal funding that benefited all-white communities, their chief goal was to persuade the federal government to force the FHA to implement aggressive anti-discriminatory measures and compel local governments to adopt affirmative open housing policies in Model Cities, urban renewal, public housing, and federal programs.[42]

Ironically, Weaver, now secretary of HUD, was forced to respond to charges similar to those he himself had made. In response to the NCDH manifesto, he issued a memo that ordered HUD undersecretaries to meet nondiscrimination requirements or answer to him. Then, in an effort to satisfy both sides in the ghetto debate, Weaver announced that HUD was pursuing policies to break down segregation and to build up the inner city, foreshadowing the "balanced approach" that the fair housing rule would take four decades later.[43]

A First Try for a National Fair Housing Law

In the midst of the debates about Black Power and the explosions of violence that marked the urban crisis era, advocates for fair housing pressed the federal government to expand Kennedy's limited executive order against housing discrimination. They sought an executive order, rather than a new law, for the practical reason that issuing an executive order would avoid a risky battle over what the liberal lobbying organization Americans for Democratic Action termed "a sensitive political issue." The Johnson administration rejected that approach because of concerns about its constitutionality and instead in April 1966 included the fair housing measure as part of its proposed civil rights legislation. Title IV of the proposed Civil Rights Act of 1966 contained much of the language, some of it verbatim, that would be enacted two years later as the Fair Housing Act. The bill banned any refusal to sell or rent a home, offer real estate services, make a housing loan, or show a dwelling available for sale or rent because of race, color, religion, and national origin.[44]

Unlike the later Fair Housing Act, the 1966 Civil Rights Act gave HUD a subsidiary role: it placed primary responsibility for enforcement of its fair housing provisions with the attorney general and relegated the secretary of HUD to investigating and referring complaints of housing discrimination. Under a section titled "Assistance by the Secretary of Housing and Urban Development," the act also ordered HUD to study and issue reports on housing discrimination. The last provision of this section reiterated and strengthened the gist of Kennedy's 1962 executive order by instructing

HUD to administer its programs "in a manner affirmatively to further the policies of this title." The language of the provision, including the word "affirmatively," echoes a bill of particulars that the NCDH submitted to the White House in April 1966 while the legislation was being drafted. Castigating HUD officials at all levels who refused to follow nondiscriminatory practices, the NCDH cataloged numerous HUD subagencies and programs that tolerated or actively discriminated against African Americans.[45]

The long history of efforts by the NCDH and civil rights groups to reform government practices, internal HUD documents, and the language of the provision itself indicate that the authors of the legislation inserted the "affirmatively further" phrase to galvanize department officials to implement federal programs—especially the FHA, public housing, and Model Cities—in ways that neither discriminated against Blacks nor encouraged racial segregation.[46]

But the time was not yet ripe for a federal open housing law. In Chicago, working-class whites revolted against the Democrats for allowing the fair housing marches and voted to defeat the liberal Illinois senator, Paul Douglas. In California, a two-year battle over fair housing legislation resulted in voters passing a constitutional amendment that protected property owners' rights and throwing out the liberal governor Pat Brown in favor of Ronald Reagan. In Washington, the Civil Rights Act of 1966 passed in the House but failed in the Senate. The Senate minority leader, Illinois Republican Everett Dirksen, blamed the bill's open housing provisions, which he had adamantly opposed.[47]

President Johnson and the liberals in Congress nonetheless continued to press for legislation that would ban discrimination in housing. In August 1967, Walter Mondale, the Democratic senator from Minnesota, introduced a fair housing bill that would empower HUD to prevent anyone from engaging in racial discrimination with regard to housing transactions. Under this bill, HUD could investigate incidents of discrimination, initiate complaints, and, if negotiation failed, issue cease-and-desist orders. Nonetheless, the Fair Housing Act of 1967 seemed unlikely to pass. The House of Representatives Subcommittee on Housing and Urban Affairs held hearings, but, believing that the time was not right, the members chose not to submit the bill to the House.

The Legislative Arguments for Fair Housing

Debates over the nature of the ghetto permeated the hearings on fair housing legislation, which took place in 1966 and 1967. Congressional representatives and committee hearing witnesses alike portrayed African Americans as helpless victims who were imprisoned in ghettos, exaggerating the plight of Black city dwellers for dramatic effect. Supporting the 1966 bill, for example, Republican representative Charles Mathias of Maryland asserted that fair housing would free African Americans from the "physical shackles of the ghetto." HUD secretary Weaver declared that discrimination in housing "chain[ed] almost all nonwhites" to ghettos and a life of deprivation.[48]

The ghettos, the fair housing proponents explained, took a heavy toll on their inhabitants. In his testimony to the House Subcommittee on Housing and Urban Affairs, NCDH cofounder Algernon Black, speaking for the ACLU, echoed Clark's *Dark Ghetto* when he explained that the cost of the forced existence in the racial ghetto could be measured "in the health, the life expectancy, juvenile delinquency, mental illness, family disorganization, a tremendous cost in suffering, in waste of talent, in destruction of motivation to learn and work, in the victims who live in the ghetto." Making a legal argument to the subcommittee, Attorney General Ramsey Clark argued that discrimination in housing deprived Blacks of the "equal protection" guaranteed by the Fourteenth Amendment by forcing them to live in underserved and inadequate ghetto living environments.[49]

The fair housing law, Senator Mondale repeatedly argued, was necessary to eliminate America's racial ghettos. Without it, he asserted, "black racists" who advocated for separatism could demonstrate that white Americans were forcing African Americans to live in rotting ghettos. The matter was urgent, Mondale and several witnesses argued, because the ghetto was a primary cause of the violence rocking American cities. Putting an exclamation point on this argument, the authors of the highly influential Kerner Commission report, which was published in March while the bill was under consideration, presented the ghettos as a prima facie example of an unequal racially divided society and pinned much of the blame for urban riots on them.[50]

Mondale, however, often explained that the fair housing law would not by itself eliminate the ghettos. He and other witnesses, including administration officials, insisted that fair housing was essential but acknowledged that other efforts—new housing outside the ghettos as well as education, jobs, health care, recreation, and social services—would also be necessary to help the low-income residents of America's inner-city neighborhoods.

In fact, Mondale and some witnesses argued that under the act's prohibition of housing discrimination, only middle-class Blacks would escape impoverished central-city neighborhoods. The law would put the American Dream within reach of respectable hard-working citizens, such as Navy officer Carlos Campbell and college professor Gerard Ferere, who both testified at the hearings that their attempts to find homes had been repeatedly rejected because of their race.

Some of the law's supporters even reassured fearful whites that low-income African Americans could not afford to buy houses in the suburbs.

Fair housing, Senator Edward Brooke of Massachusetts explained, "will scarcely lead to a mass dispersal of the ghetto population to the suburbs; but it will make it possible for those who have the resources to escape." Ironically, some fair housing supporters seemed willing to consign the poor to the dreadful ghettos they described to allay the fears of white suburbanites and their representatives of an invasion by low-income city dwellers.[51]

Other supporters of the Fair Housing Act agreed that eliminating discrimination in housing transactions would not be sufficient and pushed for a broader attack on the problem of the ghetto. Senator William Proxmire, a Democrat from Wisconsin, accused suburban governments of excluding members of racial minorities and poor people through zoning ordinances, building codes, and other forms of seemingly neutral land-use restrictions. Real estate professionals in favor of fair housing heartily agreed, testifying that large-lot zoning, community facility requirements, and local opposition to density of land use made it next to impossible to develop row houses or garden apartments, let alone multifamily buildings. NCDH executive director Edward Rutledge concurred, noting that suburban officials concerned about the cost of providing public services used a range of such legal and administrative devices to keep out low- and moderate-income families with children.[52]

To broaden the scope of the fair housing legislation, Proxmire suggested adopting what he called carrot and stick provisions. He proposed withholding HUD funding from places that used regulatory devices that inhibited the development of housing for people of low and moderate incomes and rewarding those jurisdictions that had made a clear effort to provide such housing. Several witnesses agreed with Proxmire, but Congress had little appetite for a sweeping approach that imposed penalties on communities.[53]

In January 1968, Johnson called on Congress to pass the Civil Rights Act, including the open housing provision. Soon thereafter, Mondale, working with liberal allies in the Senate, managed to attach his bill to legislation for protecting civil rights workers. Having held hearings and debated the bill extensively in previous sessions, Congress now chiefly struggled over procedural issues. In February and March, the Democratic leadership maneuvered to obtain additional votes to cut off a filibuster by Southern conservatives. The cloture effort gained almost enough votes when Senate minority leader Dirksen threw his support in return for weakening the bill's enforcement provision and reducing its coverage. In March, the release of the dramatic Kerner Commission report shook loose the remaining needed votes.[54]

After passing the Senate, the bill went to the House, where it appeared it might expire in the Rules Committee. But the assassination of King on April 4, and the ensuing violence in the streets of Washington, galvanized the House, which passed the Senate's version of the bill by a wide margin. On April 11, Johnson signed the Civil Rights Act of 1968 into law, including Title VIII.

The Provision That Inspired the Affirmatively Furthering Fair Housing Rule

Consistent with its history, the Fair Housing Act aimed to stop discrimination, first in the selling and renting of residences and second in the corollary activities of real estate brokering and lending. It covered anyone involved in private housing transactions, with the exceptions of owner-occupants who owned buildings with four or fewer dwellings or who sold their single-family houses without professional help. As in earlier proposed legislation, the Fair Housing Act prohibited discrimination in any form of real estate financing. Beside prohibiting real estate steering and redlining by lenders, the law included a new provision to ban the practice of blockbusting. The 1968 law placed HUD in charge of enforcement, but the agency could only act in response to individuals' complaints and use persuasion to change discriminatory behaviors or, as a last resort, refer the cases to the Justice Department.

Section 808 of the Fair Housing Act, which detailed its administration, twice replicated this phrase from the proposed 1966 legislation: "in a manner affirmatively to further the policies of this title." The first use of the phrase broadened the scope of responsibility to require all federal agencies to take action to prevent discrimination in any housing and urban development programs they carried out and cooperate with HUD in their efforts. The law's second invocation of the phrase, somewhat redundantly, ordered HUD also to administer its programs in accord with the Fair Housing Act. In both cases, as in the 1966 legislation, this language, as Mara Sidney points out, aimed at ensuring that federal officials incorporated fair housing principles into the FHA, public housing, urban renewal, and Model Cities.[55]

The directive to HUD, however, did not indicate what manner the agency should employ to affirmatively further the principles of fair housing. Perhaps the authors used vague language because they wished to avoid political controversy or to accommodate future circumstances. In any case, it was not until twenty years after the passage of the law that the federal government first began to codify methods for implementing fair housing policies.[56]

Another part of the same section set a precedent for the data sharing of the 2015 AFFH Rule. The Kennedy executive order created the President's Committee on Equal Opportunity in Housing to confer with and encourage government agencies and fair housing citizen groups to eliminate discrimination in government-assisted housing and facilities. The fair housing bills of the late 1960s shifted the authority for similar activities to the newly created HUD. The provision that became Section 808 of the Fair Housing Act specified ways that HUD, through its secretary, must assist the anti-discrimination cause: through studying and reporting housing discrimination practices and giving technical assistance to public or private agencies and institutions "which are formulating or carrying on programs to prevent or eliminate discriminatory housing practices." Then, as now, it made sense for HUD to coordinate with and support the fair housing efforts of state and municipal governments and local citizen organizations.[57]

The Conundrum of Housing Discrimination and Racial Segregation

In the first part of the twentieth century, pervasive racist attitudes among white Americans underpinned a wide range of individual and institutional conduct, laws, and policies intended to oppress African Americans. To begin to overthrow this system of racial bias, civil rights activists and reformers in the housing field chose to challenge the government's role in upholding racial inequity. The initial approach of the fair housing movement, thus, was to fight to end discriminatory policies, such as racial zoning, enforcement of racial covenants, and government-supported discrimination in real estate lending, brokering, and urban redevelopment projects, such as Stuyvesant Town. Ultimately, civil rights advocates strove to achieve fair housing legislation that would outlaw private acts of discrimination in housing transactions.

In their battles for equity in housing, fair housing advocates deployed the idea of the racial ghetto to symbolize the unjust consequences of racial prejudice in the housing sector. In the 1940s, advocates insisted that racial covenants and clauses in the FHA's underwriting manual helped segregate Blacks into compulsory ghettos, emphasizing the injustice of confining African Americans to certain places. Twenty years after the covenants had been banned and the FHA's manual had been revised, the supporters of a fair housing law governing private transactions asserted the evils of these racial ghettos, depicting them as miserable places of entrenched poverty that caused a wide range of social ills. Fair housing advocates accordingly stressed not only the need for anti-discrimination provisions but also the importance of breaking up the ghettos and integrating neighborhoods throughout metropolitan areas.

The authors of the Fair Housing Act, however, wrote a law aimed at preventing acts of discrimination by those involved in real estate transactions and the government agencies that supported them. Amendments passed in 1988 strengthened the law significantly, giving HUD the power to initiate complaints, issue subpoenas, and, if needed, order the Justice Department to commence litigation. In the following years, enforcement of the Fair Housing Act has waxed and waned from one presidential administration to another, but through complaints, field tests, and lawsuits, the law has helped curtail many instances of discrimination. In the 1990s, HUD attempted to encourage local officials to identify and counteract the practices that prevented members of racial minority groups and other protected classes from residing in their own jurisdictions. Applying the fair housing review criteria to all its programs in 1995, HUD required recipients of community planning and development funds to provide fair housing plans, called Analyses of Impediments (AIs), but problems with HUD's implementation led the agency in 2015 to propose the AFFH Rule.[58]

Meanwhile, advocates have supplemented the Fair Housing Act by filing lawsuits, many of them successful, against public housing authorities, suburban towns, developers, and landlords for racially discriminatory practices. They have also implemented programs to give low-income and minority families the option to move out of inner-city neighborhoods into affluent suburban communities. Like the programs initiated by fair housing advocates in the 1960s, these mobility programs have been painfully slow and moved relatively small numbers of people, but in many instances, they have benefited their participants.[59]

Although levels of Black-white segregation have declined somewhat nationally since the passage of the Fair Housing Act, they remain high. One important reason, as several scholars have pointed out, is the discrepancy between the goals of eliminating discrimination in housing and fostering integrated neighborhoods. "Housing discrimination and racial segregation," historian Wendell Pritchett writes, "are intimately related . . . [but] not the result of the same set of factors." Vigorous enforcement of anti-discrimination measures, then, will reduce injustice but not necessarily integrate neighborhoods.[60]

Residential patterns of population groups at any given time are the product of numerous factors. Racial discrimination in all its ugly forms continues to be an important factor. Racial disparities in wealth combined with the availability and cost of homes are also factors. As such, the web of land-use regulations—zoning, environmental protection of land, and restrictions on multifamily and other relatively dense residential structures—continues to inhibit the construction of multifamily and low-cost dwellings in high-income communities, limiting the availability of housing in those locations largely to the affluent.

Racial attitudes also influence the characteristics of neighborhoods, in particular the different perceptions of many whites and Blacks as to what proportion of the other's race constitutes a comfortably integrated neigh-borhood.[61] In addition, household incomes, the price of housing, and the personal priorities of individuals and households shape myriad decisions of where to live.

Indeed, fifty years after the passage of the Fair Housing Act, research-ers seeking to explain the persistence of residential racial segregation have come to similar conclusions as those of researchers in the 1960s: when choosing a home, people rely on personal relationships for information, de-sire proximity to family members and friends, and look for familiar types of neighborhoods. Ironically, perhaps, increasing numbers of communities have become integrated in just this way, as racial tolerance has spread and the number of places with amenities attractive to members of multiple races and ethnicities has grown.[62]

Although designed primarily to root out acts of explicit housing dis-crimination in the sale or rental of properties, the Fair Housing Act included a provision to ensure that the federal government would affirmatively fur-ther fair housing in its own programs. The AFFH Rule of 2015 clarified that this provision also required the active cooperation of local officials in removing discriminatory obstacles and encouraging racial minorities and other protected groups to live in their towns.

As such, the rule echoes the ideas expressed in the midst of the debate about the original fair housing legislation by anti-discrimination activists and Senator Proxmire, who called in vain for a broad effort that included local governments receiving federal housing and community development funding. Proxmire and others realized that many factors influence the ra-cial composition of communities. The complexity of causation in the past limited the effectiveness of anti-discrimination programs in reducing residential segregation. The question remains, then, whether the AFFH Rule, if properly implemented, could alter enough of the factors that shape America's racial settlement patterns to bring about a thorough integration of America's metropolitan areas.

ENDNOTES
1. During the 1940s and 1950s, whites attacked African Americans as they at-tempted to move to previously white or contested neighborhoods. Douglas S. Massey and Nancy A. Denton, *American Apartheid: Segregation and the Making of the Under-class* (Cambridge, MA: Harvard University Press, 1993), 26–35; Charles Abrams, *For-bidden Neighbors: A Study of Prejudice in Housing* (New York: Harper, 1955); Robert Weaver, *The Negro Ghetto* (New York: Harcourt Brace, 1948), 90–96; Dominic Capeci Jr., *Race Relations in Wartime Detroit: The Sojourner Truth Housing Controversy of 1942* (Philadelphia: Temple University Press, 1984); Arnold R. Hirsch, *Making the Second Ghetto: Race and Housing in Chicago 1940–1960* (Cambridge; Cambridge University Press, 1983).

2. Wendy Plotkin, "'Hemmed In': The Struggle against Racial Restrictive Covenants and Deed Restrictions in Post-WWII Chicago," *Journal of the Illinois State Historical Society* 94, no. 1 (April 1, 2001): 39–69; Michael Jones-Correa, "The Origins and Diffusion of Racial Restrictive Covenants," *Political Science Quarterly* 115, no. 4 (2000): 541–568.

3. Clement E. Vose, *Caucasians Only: The Supreme Court, the NAACP, and the Restrictive Covenant Cases* (Berkeley and Los Angeles, University of California Press, 1967), 57–64; Mark V. Tushnet, *Making Civil Rights Law: Thurgood Marshall and the Supreme Court, 1936–1961* (New York: Oxford University Press, 1994), 87–91. For a recent account of the legal campaign against restrictive covenants, see Jeffrey D. Gonda, *Unjust Deeds: The Restrictive Covenant Cases and the Making of the Civil Rights Movement* (Chapel Hill: University of North Carolina Press, 2015).

4. The anti-covenant writers, many encouraged by Marshall, included public housing expert Charles Abrams, editor Charles S. Johnson, and lawyer Loren Miller. Vose, *Caucasians Only*, 22–23, 57, 64–65, 160–161, 275n45; Stephen L. Wabsy, Anthony A. D'Amato, and Rosemary Metrailer, *Desegregation from Brown to Alexander: An Exploration of Supreme Court Strategies* (Carbondale: Southern Illinois University Press, 1977), 39; Mitchell Duneier, *Ghetto: The Invention of a Place, the History of an Idea* (New York: Farrar, Straus and Giroux, 2017), 24–32.

5. *Shelley v. Kraemer*, 334 U.S. 1 (U.S. 1948).

6. Weaver worked in the service as well. Philip G. Sadler, "The Dream and the Substance," manuscript, 1954, Records of the Intergroup Relations Branch, Records of the Public Housing Administration, RG 196, National Archives (hereafter NA), College Park, Maryland. For the history of the federal government's role in segregation, see Richard Rothstein, *The Color of Law: A Forgotten History of How Our Government Segregated America* (New York: Liveright, 2017).

7. Weaver, *The Negro Ghetto*, 165.

8. D. Bradford Hunt, *Blueprint for Disaster: The Unraveling of Chicago Public Housing* (Chicago: University of Chicago Press, 2010), 79–98; Martin Meyerson, *Politics, Planning, and the Public Interest: The Case of Public Housing in Chicago* (Glencoe, IL: Free Press, 1955); Hirsch, *Making the Second Ghetto*, 218–232.

9. Wendell E. Pritchett, *Robert Clifton Weaver and the American City: The Life and Times of an Urban Reformer* (Chicago: University of Chicago Press, 2008); A. Scott Henderson, *Housing and the Democratic Ideal* (New York: Columbia University Press, 2000).

10. Abrams, *Forbidden Neighbors*, 153–154; Arnold R. Hirsch, "Containment on the Home Front: Race and Federal Housing Policy from the New Deal to the Cold War," *Journal of Urban History* 26, no. 2 (January 2000): 171, 179. For examples of public housing advocates' censure of the FHA, see Eugenie Ladner Birch, "Edith Elmer Wood and the Genesis of Liberal Housing Thought, 1910–1942," (Ph.D. diss., Columbia University, 1976), 186; Catherine Bauer, "National Labor Organizations Want Public Housing; Attack F.H.A.," press release, American Federation of Labor Housing Committee, Building Trades Committee and Labor Housing Conference, February 18, 1936, cited in Mary Susan Cole, "Catherine Bauer and the Public Housing Movement, 1926–1937" (Ph.D. diss., George Washington University, 1975), 498; Charles Abrams, *The Future of Housing* (New York: Harper and Brothers, 1946), passim; Nathan Straus, *The Seven Myths of Housing* (New York: Knopf, 1944), 176.

11. David Freund, *Colored Property: State Policy and White Racial Politics in Suburban American.* (Chicago: University of Chicago Press, 2007), 155–162, 206–210; Rothstein, *The Color of Law*, 83–88; Kenneth T. Jackson, *Crabgrass Frontier: The Suburbanization of the United States* (New York: Oxford University Press, 1985), 207–210;

Weaver, *The Negro Ghetto*, 71–73, 143–148, 217–222; Charles Abrams, "The Segregation Threat in Housing," *Commentary* 7, no. 2 (February 1949): 123–131; Abrams, *Forbidden Neighbors*, 233–234.

12. Tushnet, *Making Civil Rights Law*, 97; Abrams, *Forbidden Neighbors*, 101–102, 233–234; Weaver, *The Negro Ghetto*, 149–154; National Committee Against Discrimination in Housing (NCDH), *How the Federal Government Builds Ghettos* (New York, 1967), available at https://catalog.hathitrust.org/Record/007131276; Wendell Pritchett, "Where Shall We Live? Class and the Limitations of Fair Housing Law," *Urban Lawyer* 35, no. 3 (Summer 2003): 426–427; Rothstein, *The Color of Law*, 76–79, 88–90.

13. Abrams, "The Segregation Threat in Housing," 125; Abrams, *Forbidden Neighbors*, 251–259.

14. Arthur R. Simon, *Stuyvesant Town, U.S.A.: Pattern for Two Americas* (New York: New York University Press, 1970); Pritchett, "Where Shall We Live?" 408–413.

15. The NCDH promoted a series of laws by New York City and New York State, starting with New York City's Brown-Isaacs Law of 1951 through the Sharkey-Brown-Isaacs Bill of 1957 and New York State Wicks-Austin Law of 1950 through the Metcalf-Baker Act of 1969. "Toward Democracy in Housing: The NCDH Story," *Trends in Housing* 4, no. 4 (August 1960): 4; Pritchett, "Where Shall We Live?" 431–439.

16. "Toward Democracy in Housing," 4–5.

17. Interestingly, the report urged that proponents of racially integrated housing not attempt to integrate socioeconomic groups, which would encounter much more resistance. Davis McEntire, *Residence and Race* (Berkeley: University of California Press, 1960), 352–355; Juliet Saltman, *Open Housing: Dynamics of a Social Movement* (New York: Praeger, 1978), 45–47; McEntire, *Residence and Race*, 5; "Toward Democracy in Housing," 4–5.

18. In 1965, NCDH reported twenty-seven active fair housing committees in the five boroughs of New York City alone. "Toward Democracy in Housing," 5; "Our Correspondents Report: Boston Suburbia," *Trends in Housing* 2, no. 6 (November 1958): 5; "US Supreme Court Lets NJ Law Stand," *Trends in Housing* 9, no. 3 (June 1965): 1, 6; "Capahosic Housing Conference," *Trends in Housing* 9, no. 3 (June 1965): 3; "Local FH Law Surge," *Trends in Housing* 12, no. 1 (January 1968): 1, 7. In his tabulation, Collins counted twenty-two states, one more than the NCDH, with open housing legislation. William J. Collins, "The Political Economy of State Fair Housing Laws before 1968," *Social Science History* 30, no. 1 (2006): 15–49. For the growth of local open housing activity, see Saltman, *Open Housing*.

19. "NCDH to Propose Executive Order—Kennedy Committed," *Trends in Housing* 4, no. 5 (September/October 1960): 1; "Weaver Confirmed as Housing Chief," *Trends in Housing* 5, no. 1 (January/February 1961): 1, 8; "Nationwide Drive on for Executive Order," *Trends in Housing* 5, no. 5 (September/October 1961): 1, 6; Henderson, *Housing and the Democratic Ideal*, 167–171; Carl M. Brauer, *John F. Kennedy and the Second Reconstruction*, Contemporary American History Series (New York: Columbia University Press, 1977), 210–211; John F. Kennedy, Executive Order 11063—Equal Opportunity in Housing, November 20, 1962.

20. Jack Rothman, "The Ghetto Makers," *The Nation*, October 7, 1961, 222–225; W. E. Orser, *Blockbusting in Baltimore: The Edmondson Village Story* (Lexington: University Press of Kentucky, 2003); Beryl Satter, *Family Properties: Race, Real Estate, and the Exploitation of Black Urban America* (New York: Metropolitan Books, 2009), 277; Rose Helper, *Racial Policies and Practices of Real Estate Brokers* (Minneapolis: University of Minnesota Press, 1969); "US Focus: Blockbusting," *Trends in Housing* 13, no. 4 (May 1969): 2.

21. Richard F. Muth, *Cities and Housing: The Spatial Pattern of Urban Residential Land Use* (Chicago: University of Chicago Press, 1969); Historic Census of Housing Tables—Crowding, available at https://www.census.gov/hhes/www/housing/census/historic/crowding.html; Historic Census of Housing Tables—Plumbing https://www.census.gov/hhes/www/housing/census/historic/plumbing.html; Peter G. Rowe, *Modernity and Housing* (Cambridge: Massachusetts Institute of Technology Press, 1993), 184; Massey and Denton, *American Apartheid*, 47.

22. St. Clair Drake and Horace R. Cayton, *Black Metropolis: A Study of Negro Life in a Northern City* (Chicago: University of Chicago Press, 1970), 174–213, 383; Loren Miller, "Covenants for Exclusion," *Survey Graphic* 36, no. 10 (n.d.): 543, 558; Weaver, *The Negro Ghetto*, 7, 257–259, 269–271; Abrams, *Forbidden Neighbors*, 73–78.

23. The anthropologist Oscar Lewis introduced the phrase "culture of poverty" in Oscar Lewis, Margaret Mead, and O. LaFarge, *Five Families: Mexican Case Studies in the Culture of Poverty* (New York: Basic Books, 1975). For the influence of Lewis's ideas and the concept of pathological ghetto culture, see Alice O'Connor, *Poverty Knowledge: Social Science, Social Policy, and the Poor in Twentieth-Century U.S. History* (Princeton, NJ: Princeton University Press, 2002), 113–123, 197–210; Duneier, *Ghetto*, 107–111; Joe T. Darden, "The Ghetto: A Bibliography," Exchange Bibliography (Council of Planning Librarians, July 1977), 4–5; Harlem Youth Opportunities Unlimited, *Youth in the Ghetto—A Study of the Consequences of Powerlessness and a Blueprint for Change* (New York: HARYOU, 1964); Michael Harrington, *The Other America: Poverty in the United States* (New York: Scribner, 1997); U.S. Department of Labor, Office of Policy Planning and Research, and Daniel Patrick Moynihan, *The Negro Family: The Case for National Action* (Washington, DC: U.S. GPO, 1965); Pierre DeVise, "Chicago's Widening Color Gap" (Chicago: Community and Family Study Center, University of Chicago, 1967); Elliot Liebow, *Tally's Corner: A Study of Negro Streetcorner Men* (Lanham, MD: Rowman and Littlefield, 2003); Lee Rainwater, *Behind Ghetto Walls: Black Families in a Federal Slum* (New Brunswick, NJ: Aldine Transaction, 2006).

24. Kenneth B. Clark, *Dark Ghetto: Dilemmas of Social Power* (New York: Harper and Row, 1965); Duneier, *Ghetto*, 85–138.

25. Clark and Myrdal, *Dark Ghetto*, 27; For an extensive assessment of Clark's views on Black poverty and the ghetto, see Duneier, *Ghetto*, 85–138.

26. Clark and Myrdal, *Dark Ghetto*, 12, 30–31, 106.

27. Lyndon B. Johnson, "To Fulfill These Rights" (June 4, 1965).

28. Saltman, *Open Housing*, 52–59; "Broad Course Charted to Break Up Ghettos," *Trends in Housing* 9, no. 5 (September/October 1965): 1 (quotation), 2, 4, 8–10.

29. "News Briefs," *Trends in Housing* 10, no. 2 (April 1966): 8; *The Report of the White House Conference to Fulfill These Rights, June 1–2, 1966, Washington, D.C.* (Washington, DC: Government Printing Office, 1966), 103–113; "Total Effort Urged to End Ghetto System," *Trends in Housing* 10, no. 9 (December 1966): 1–4.

30. "Study Cities Influences Which Deter Integration," *Trends in Housing* 7, no. 3 (June 1963): 2; Edward C. Banfield, *The Unheavenly City: The Nature and the Future of Our Urban Crisis* (Boston: Little, Brown, 1970), 92–95; Oscar Handlin, *The Newcomers: Negroes and Puerto Ricans in a Changing Metropolis* (New York: Doubleday, 1962), 93.

31. Lewis Watts, Howard E. Freeman, Helen M. Hughes, Robert Morris, and Thomas F. Pettigrew. *The Middle-Income Negro Family Faces Urban Renewal* (Boston: Department of Commerce and Development, Commonwealth of Massachusetts, 1964).

32. "Capahosic Housing Conference."

33. Alan B. Anderson and George W. Pikering, *Confronting the Color Line: The Broken Promise of the Civil Rights Movement in Chicago* (Athens: University of Georgia Press, 1986), 188–192; James R. Ralph Jr., *Northern Protest: Martin Luther King, Jr., Chicago, and the Civil Rights Movement* (Cambridge, MA: Harvard University Press, 1993), 88–90; Mary Lou Finley, "The Open Housing Marches: Chicago, Summer '66," in *Chicago 1966: Open Housing Marches, Summit Negotiations, and Operation Breadbasket*, ed. David J. Garrow (Brooklyn: Carlson Publishing, 1989), 7, 102.

34. Finley, "The Open Housing Marches," 8–9; Ralph, *Northern Protest*, 99–104; Anderson and Pikering, *Confronting the Color Line*, 197–199.

35. After his experience in Chicago, King downplayed housing issues and instead concentrated his efforts on helping low-income Americans obtain jobs and higher incomes. Ralph, *Northern Protest*, 56–57, 149–219; Anderson and Pikering, *Confronting the Color Line*, 191, 216–228, 237–271.

36. The figure for those who moved to white neighborhoods is extrapolated from Berry's calculation of the percentage of those applicants with neighborhood data regarding the number of people moving to different neighborhoods. Almost two-thirds of the placements moved to "transitional" neighborhoods, and more than half were placed in the polyglot Uptown neighborhood, home to white Appalachian migrants, Native Americans, and immigrants. Berry concluded that the housing service program was "a dismal failure." Anderson and Pikering, *Confronting the Color Line*, 260–261, 281; Brian J. L. Berry, *The Open Housing Question: Race and Housing in Chicago, 1966–1976* (Cambridge, MA: Ballinger Publishing, 1979), 27, 29, 46–62 ("dismal failure").

37. Flynn McRoberts, "Gautreaux Housing Program Nears End," *Chicago Tribune*, January 12, 1996; Fran Spielman, "Scattered-Site Could Spark Flight from City, Daley Says," *Chicago Sun-Times*, April 27, 1996; Fran Spielman and Art Golab, "Scattered-Site Housing Foes Fume," *Chicago Sun-Times*, May 2, 1996. For a review of the limitations and difficulties of relocation efforts, including Gautreaux, see Edward G. Goetz, "Housing Dispersal Programs," *Journal of Planning Literature* 18, no. 1 (August 2003): 3–16. For the legal saga, see Alexander Polikoff, *Waiting for Gautreaux: A Story of Segregation, Housing, and the Black Ghetto* (Evanston, IL: Northwestern University Press, 2005).

38. Catherine Ellis and Stephen Drury Smith, eds., *Say It Plain: A Century of Great African-American Speeches* (New York: New Press, 2005), 58; Anderson and Pikering, *Confronting the Color Line*, 275–276.

39. Economic Opportunity Act of 1964, P.L. 88–452, Title II, Section 202(a)(3); Demonstration Cities and Metropolitan Development Act of 1966 (Public Law 89–754).

40. "The Case against Urban Desegregation," *Social Work*, January 1967, 12–21; Frances Fox Piven and Richard A. Cloward, "Desegregated Housing—Who Pays for the Reformers' Ideal?" *New Republic*, December 17, 1966.

41. Frank Horne, "What Price, Rebuilding Ghettos as Ghettos?" Letter to the Editor in response to "Desegregated Housing," Piven and Cloward, *New Republic,* December 17, 1966, reprinted in *Trends in Housing* 11, no. 1 (January 1967): 4.

42. NCDH, *How the Federal Government Builds Ghettos.*

43. Robert Weaver to President Lyndon Johnson, memorandum, February 9, 1967; Robert Weaver to Harry C. McPherson Jr., memorandum, March 22, 1967, NCDH file, Subject Correspondence Files of Secretary Robert C. Weaver, Box 305, RG 207, NA; "US Is Labeled Ghetto Builder," *Trends in Housing* 11, no. 2 (February 1967): 1, 2-3.

44. Unlike its successor, however, the 1966 law applied only to real estate professionals and not to homeowners. "Executive Order on Housing," *Trends in Housing* 9, no. 4 (August 1965): 4; "NAACP Adopts Broad Plan to Accelerate Open Occupancy,"

ibid., 10; "1966 Civil Rights Act Dies in Senate," in *CQ Almanac 1966*, 22nd ed. (Washington, DC: Congressional Quarterly, 1967), 5; Civil Rights Act of 1966, H.R. 14765.

45. NCDH, "Bill of Particulars Submitted to the White House," April 22, 1966, reprinted in *How the Federal Government Builds Ghettos*, 5–13, uses "affirmatively," "affirmative action," and "affirmative programs" throughout the document.

46. An internal HUD committee chaired by Leonard Duhl argued that the phrase promoted a policy that was "both affirmative and aggressive" and recommended that Secretary Weaver write a memo to HUD program administrators that forcefully urged them to realize equal opportunity in housing, full participation by racial minorities in department affairs, and the "elimination of enforced ghettos and achievement of racially inclusive patterns and trends in housing." Although vague about actual steps, this latter demand echoed the concerns of many activists. The proposed memo went far beyond the language of the bill, however, and the HUD secretary rejected the recommendation to issue it. Civil Rights Act of 1966, H.R. 14765, Section 407(d), Section 409—quotation in subsection (e); "Report of the Work Group on Social Concerns," August 23, 1966; draft memorandum, disapproved by the secretary, August 24, 1966, Subject Correspondence Files of Secretary Robert C. Weaver, Box 305, RG 207, NA.

47. Darren Miles, "The Art of the Possible: Everett Dirksen's Role in Civil Rights Legislation of the 1950s and 1960s," *Western Illinois Historical Review* I (Spring 2009): 108–115; "1966 Civil Rights Act Dies in Senate."

48. Opponents also acknowledged the evils of the ghetto but denied that fair housing would remedy them. Mara S. Sidney, "Images of Race, Class, and Markets: Rethinking the Origin of U.S. Fair Housing Policy," *Journal of Policy History* 13, no. 2 (2001): 181–214; Fair Housing Act of 1967, Hearings, 9, 36; Minority views of Hon. Basil L. Whitener on HR 14765, Title IV, House Committee on the Judiciary, Civil Rights Act of 1966, a report to accompany H.R. 14765, 59.

49. Other witnesses, such as Roy Wilkins, the executive director of the NAACP, made the same point. Fair Housing Act of 1967, Hearings, 8–10, 105, 174.

50. At hearings on the 1967 bill held on August 21 that year, Mondale repeated the argument about "black racists" in his opening statement and twice more in colloquy with Attorney General Clark, at one point stating, "It seems to me that one of the biggest arguments that we give to the black racists is the existence of ghetto living." The chairman of the National Advisory Commission on Civil Disorders was Illinois governor Otto Kerner. Fair Housing Act of 1967, Hearings, 2, 22, 28 (above quote); for examples of Mondale and witnesses blaming the ghetto for recent violence, see testimony of Frankie M. Freeman, member of U.S. Civil Rights Commission, Fair Housing Act of 1967, Hearings, 76, 80, 83, 86; testimony of Roy Wilkins, 98; testimony of Rev. Robert F. Drinan, S.J., Dean, Boston College Law School, 127; testimony of Algernon Black, speaking for American Civil Liberties Union, 179; Sidney, "Images of Race, Class, and Markets," 195–196; U.S. Kerner Commission, *Report of the National Advisory Commission on Civil Disorders* (New York: Bantam Books, 1968).

51. A few open housing advocates opposed this approach. As early as 1965, George B. Nesbitt, the director of the federal housing agency's Low-Income Demonstration program, told an NCDH conference to abandon "upper-class-ism" that led to working only with middle-class people to integrate neighborhoods. Fair Housing Act of 1967, Hearings, 2, 27, 47–48; Sidney, "Images of Race, Class, and Markets," 196–198; "Broad Course Charted to Break Up Ghettos," 2–3.

52. Local fair housing organizations had long fought such restrictions. Fair Housing Act of 1967, Hearings, 73, 363–364, 217, 416–417; Sidney, "Images of Race, Class,

and Markets"; "'Feudal Caste System' in Greenwich, Conn.," *Trends in Housing* 10, no. 2 (April 1966): 8.

53. Fair Housing Act of 1967, Hearings, testimony of Proxmire, 73, 177–178, 417; Sidney, "Images of Race, Class, and Markets," 208.

54. The revised bill reduced HUD's ability to initiate actions against discriminating parties and exempted sales of single-family dwellings by owner-occupants who did not use real estate brokers. Jean E. Dubofsky, "Fair Housing: A Legislative History and a Perspective," *Washburn Law Journal* 8 (1969): 149–158; Fair Housing Act of 1967, Hearings before the Subcommittee on Housing and Urban Affairs of the Committee on Banking and Currency of the United States, Ninetieth Congress, First Session on S.1358, S. 2114, and S.2280, August 22 and 23, 1967.

55. Other agencies included, for example, the Department of Defense, which, in response to criticism for tolerating racial segregation, was attempting to ensure that all service members had equal access to housing close to military installations. Civil Rights Act of 1966, Title IV, Section 409(e); Civil Rights Act of 1968 (P.L. 90–284), Title VIII, Section 808(d); Fair Housing Act of 1967, Hearings, 80, 89–96, 106–107; Sidney, "Images of Race, Class, and Markets," 205.

56. In 1988, HUD, under pressure from the courts and at the request of the Department of Justice, introduced criteria for communities receiving Community Development Block Grant funds that required them to conduct AIs regarding fair housing choice and address any identified impediments. Sidney, "Images of Race, Class, and Markets," 205; HUD, Office of Fair Housing and Equal Opportunity, *Fair Housing Planning Guide* 1, 2–3; *Federal Register* 53, no. 172 (Tuesday, September 6, 1988), Rules and Regulations, 34430, 34434–34435, 33450, 34457, 34468–34469 (§ 570.904 Equal Opportunity and Fair Housing Criteria).

57. Executive Order 11063, Parts II, IV, and V; Civil Rights Act of 1966, Title IV, Section 409(a–c).

58. HUD, *Fair Housing Planning Guide*, 3–5; Raphael Bostic and Arthur Acolin, "The Potential for HUD's Affirmatively Furthering Fair Housing Rule to Meaningfully Increase Inclusion," 2018, 4–5, available at http://www.jchs.harvard.edu/sites/default/files/a_shared _future_potential_for_hud_affh_increase_inclusion.pdf; "Consolidated Submission for Community Planning and Development Programs," Federal Register, January 5, 1995, available at https://www.federalregister.gov/documents/1995/01/05/94-32150/consolidated -submission-for-community-planning-and-development-programs.

59. Goetz, "Housing Dispersal Programs"; Charles M. Haar, *Suburbs Under Siege* (Princeton: Princeton University Press, 1996); David Kirp, *Our Town: Race, Housing, and the Soul of Suburbia*, 1st ed. (New Brunswick, NJ: Rutgers University Press, 1996); John Goering and Judith D. Feins, *Choosing a Better Life? Evaluating the Moving to Opportunity Social Experiment* (Washington, DC: Rowman and Littlefield, 2003).

60. James A. Kushner, "Fair Housing Amendments Act of 1988: The Second Generation of Fair Housing," *Vanderbilt Law Review* 42 (1989): 1049–1120; Richard Sander, "Individual Rights and Demographic Realities: The Problem of Fair Housing," *Northwestern University Law Review* 82 (n.d.): 888–902; Sidney, "Images of Race, Class, and Markets," 206–207; Brian Patrick Larkin, "The Forty-Year 'First Step': The Fair Housing Act as an Incomplete Tool for Suburban Integration," *Columbia Law Review* 107, no. 7 (November 2007): 1617–1654; Pritchett, "Where Shall We Live?" 469–470.

61. Reynolds Farley, Elaine Fielding, and Maria Krysan, "The Residential Preferences of Blacks and Whites: A Four-Metropolis Analysis," *Housing Policy Debate* 8 (January 1, 1997): 763–800; Reynolds Farley, Charlotte Steeh, Tara Jackson, Maria

Krysan, Keith Reeves, "Continued Racial Residential Segregation in Detroit: 'Chocolate City, Vanilla Suburbs' Revisited," *Journal of Housing Research* 4, no. 1 (1993): 1–38; William A. V. Clark, "Residential Segregation in American Cities," in *Issues in Housing Discrimination 1*, A Consultation/Hearing of the United States Commission on Civil Rights, Washington, D.C. (November 12, 1985), 39.

62. Maria Krysan and Kyle Crowder, *Cycle of Segregation: Social Processes and Residential Stratification* (New York: Russell Sage Foundation, 2017); Laura Carrillo, Mary Pattillo, Erin Hardy, and Dolores Acevedo-Garcia, "Housing Decisions among Low-Income Hispanic Households in Chicago," *Cityscape* 18, no. 2 (May 1, 2016): 109–149; Kimberly Kobba and Edward G. Goetz, "Mobility Decisions of Very Low-Income Households," *Cityscape* 15, no. 2 (2013): 155–172; Ingrid Gould Ellen, *Sharing America's Neighborhoods: The Prospects for Stable Racial Integration* (Cambridge, MA: Harvard University Press, 2001); Michael Maly, *Beyond Segregation: Multiracial and Multiethnic Neighborhoods* (Philadelphia: Temple University Press, 2005). William Frey has found—despite the persistence of relatively high levels of Black segregation, especially in the old industrial North—an overall decline in segregation. William H. Frey, "Census Shows Modest Declines in Black-White Segregation," *Brookings*, December 8, 2015, available at https://www.brookings.edu/blog/the-avenue/2015/12/08/census-shows-modest-declines-in-black-white-segregation/.

2

Fair Housing from the Inside Out

A Behind-the-Scenes Look at the Creation of the Affirmatively Furthering Fair Housing Rule

RAPHAEL W. BOSTIC, KATHERINE O'REGAN, AND
PATRICK PONTIUS, WITH NICHOLAS F. KELLY

After nearly fifty years of federal inaction to meaningfully implement the "affirmatively furthering" fair housing mandate of the Fair Housing Act, how did the Department of Housing and Urban Development (HUD) and the Barack Obama administration successfully promulgate the Affirmatively Furthering Fair Housing (AFFH) Rule? As former leaders in HUD's Office of Policy Development and Research and the Office of the Secretary, we were part of the HUD-wide AFFH rule-making team that included dedicated, hard-working career staff who helped shepherd the rule from its internal HUD beginnings in 2009 through its final 2015 publication and implementation in 2016. This chapter describes our three perspectives regarding working at HUD, with Nicholas Kelly's help to bring our thoughts together. It provides an inside view of how the most significant federal effort in a half century to address segregation through the Fair Housing Act came to be. We hope that this story illustrates some of the struggles that persist in defining and implementing the Fair Housing Act's affirmatively furthering obligation as well as how we might overcome them by not permitting the dismantling of the AFFH Rule.

In this chapter, we describe how reforming the previous process landed on HUD's regulatory agenda and then delve into the long journey of consensus building within HUD, looking at the key phases of rule making and the mechanisms we used to succeed in promulgating a highly contentious regulation in a very challenging environment. We then provide an overview of several key policy innovations that came out of that process and are critical components of the final AFFH Rule. We demonstrate the value of an approach to affirmatively furthering fair housing that centers more on using the AFFH process as a practical *planning tool* rather than one that relies solely on *legal enforcement*.

After decades of insufficient progress in the capacity to affirmatively deliver fair housing at the national level, HUD was able to develop a framework that has great potential. Although the Donald Trump administration effectively suspended implementation of the final AFFH Rule, we hope that this chapter—and book—will help a future administration and the public better understand why this rule is important for our nation. In spite of its suspension and subsequent rescisssion, many communities around the country continued to use some of or all the pieces of the rule in their HUD planning. We see great potential to learn from those efforts so that it will be easier to pick up the ball in the future and continue to learn about, refine, and make improvements to the AFFH framework—all so that we can actually fulfill the goals set out in the Fair Housing Act more than fifty years ago.

A Brief Overview of Why the Department of Housing and Urban Development Decided to Undertake the Affirmatively Furthering Fair Housing Rule

Four key factors led Secretary Shaun Donovan and the HUD team to put the AFFH Rule on the policy agenda: the general understanding from fair housing advocates and community development practitioners of the inadequacies of the existing Analysis of Impediments (AI) process; an internal review by HUD corroborating these presumed deficiencies; most crucially, a report from the Government Accountability Office (GAO) that reiterated these points; and the damaging role of racial segregation and concentrated poverty given a new urgency by the foreclosure crisis and the differential impacts of hurricanes.

Prior to the AFFH Rule, a regulatory requirement and process were in place for communities receiving HUD formula grants (such as the Community Development Block Grant [CDBG]) as part of meeting their obligation to affirmatively further fair housing.[1] This process relied on a relatively broad, loosely defined AI (this regulatory requirement was part of the broader AFFH requirement listed in the Consolidated Plan regulations at 24 CFR Part 91), which all jurisdictions were required to complete as part of their HUD planning process. An AI was supposed to lay out all the impediments to fair housing choice in that particular locality so that the locality could undertake appropriate action to overcome the effects of those impediments.

Unfortunately, the AI process appeared to have many flaws in practice. First, many communities hired consultants to create the AIs rather than conduct the analyses themselves, and it was suspected that some local of-ficials may not have even read them. If true, it is hard to see how an AI could then inform any strategies to address the impediments. Second, HUD did not generally review AIs, so little was known about their quality or whether municipalities were conducting them regularly. Finally, there was no ex-plicit connection between any impediments identified in the AI and strate-gies to address them via a community's consolidated plan, which lays out the community's investment priorities for its major HUD funding stream. At base, the AI lacked any formal way to couple planning to meaningful action.

Aware of the suspected deficiencies in the AI process, Secretary Dono-van tasked HUD with conducting an internal review of some set of the AIs in 2009. Importantly, the GAO decided to conduct a similar assessment as well.[2] Both studies provided remarkably strong critiques of the AI process, finding it highly flawed and ineffective. The GAO report detailed a lack of clarity for the grantees and revealed that HUD had employed inconsistent compliance requirements over the last couple of decades.[3] Only 40 percent of jurisdictions could produce current AIs, and many of them were quite out of date. The GAO report called for Secretary Donovan to address the highly flawed AI process.

The failures of the AI process and HUD's limited AFFH efforts were made more salient by the ongoing foreclosure crisis and how it was par-ticularly debilitating in urban communities of color. Advancing fair hous-ing entered the Obama administration agenda in large part because of the continued realization that racial segregation and areas of concentrated dis-advantage had become the source for so much other damage and that our country had not done enough to address these issues. Sometimes things happen in waves. The 1968 Fair Housing Act was passed fewer than two months after release of the Kerner Commission's report, which attributed the spate of urban riots to racial segregation and the disparities in opportu-nity this creates.[4] Forty years later, President Obama and Secretary Dono-van were looking at segregated urban communities and feared that those same characteristics were continuing to drive persistent disadvantage and laying the groundwork for another round of negative impacts. We finally had a leadership environment that wanted to get it done.

Political scientists have theorized about what conditions are necessary for major policy changes like the AFFH Rule. John Kingdon's policy streams approach argues that policy windows like the one that opened during the AFFH process occur when (1) policy issues come to be seen as a problem, (2) political conditions change to enable the consideration of new policy ideas, and (3) policy communities have developed solutions to address the problem at hand. At least the first two streams were present in 2009: while advocates had known about the deficiency of the AI process for many years, the GAO report served as a "focusing event" that provided the extra initiative for change, and the election of President Obama and corresponding changes in staff at HUD were essential for putting the possibility of an AFFH process on the agenda.[5] But as the next section illustrates, there was far from a consensus on the appropriate policy solution.

The Long Process to Promulgate a Final Affirmatively Furthering Fair Housing Rule

So, how did the AFFH Rule become a reality? The story we tell here is one of consensus building of the highest order. A number of debates within the fair housing community as well as between fair housing and community development advocates made the process much more difficult. Indeed, our nickname for the AFFH process within HUD was "the Civil War Project" because even within the agency, this issue brought out that kind of passion and opposition. At times, these were angry meetings. It is worth emphasizing that this level of conflict was occurring fully *within* HUD, well before the initiative became public and we encountered some external opposition.

One source of that conflict was limited resources. We live in an environment and a society where resources are scarce and where federal agencies—especially HUD—do not have enough money to do all the things they might want to do. This situation fosters a zero-sum view, wherein every dollar spent in one area is simply seen as a dollar not spent in another. Staff from different program offices within HUD, and advocates for those programs outside HUD, often opposed any increased programmatic effort not in their own areas, even when they did not oppose the effort itself.

That was the backdrop for this entire discussion. In broad strokes, we aspired to have a collectively owned and meaningful AFFH process for all involved, one that would be useful for the grantees on the ground and in the actual community, not just useful for HUD. We wanted this process to be easy to understand—easy enough for one's parents to understand why AFFH matters; easy enough for regular people to be able to use public-facing data and tools to comprehend the current state of affairs in their community; and easy enough to create eureka moments of awareness, such as why are all of our communities of poor Black residents *here* and why are all the high-performing schools *there*? This process would give communities an avenue to discuss the complex issues of segregation and access to opportunity, which in turn would help citizens better understand their communities and what perpetuates disparities and make it easier to figure out what might be done to improve the situation.

A major challenge, though, was that we knew that the problems we were trying to address went back generations and that the amount of money we controlled in this process was small and dwindling. But we (and many others) believed that reforming the process for AFFH and making the assessment and planning tools actually useful and doable was important, and so we had high hopes, tempered with cautious optimism.

Phase 1—False Starts: Initial Failed Attempts (Late 2009 through End of 2010)

Despite many good intentions, the new AFFH rule-making process began in late 2009 with a series of failures. The first effort was launched in the Office of Fair Housing and Equal Opportunity (FHEO)—the office with the primary responsibility of managing AFFH and the AI process—but it was unable to gain support from other parts of HUD. Consequently, Secretary Donovan moved the rule-making process to the General Counsel's office. Staffers tried there but, again, failed.

After these initial two failures, Secretary Donovan was frustrated. He brought senior leadership together in the fall of 2010 to announce a "fair housing retreat" to force everyone to talk about what a new AFFH Rule could look like. At the meeting, he asked for the creation of a mission statement.

In trying to draft a mission statement, senior leadership faced a critical existential question about what AFFH means—is it a compliance or a planning process? Seen most broadly, HUD already had a substantial infrastructure established to eliminate discrimination, largely through enforcement by the FHEO office. That office funds nonprofits and legal aid organizations and offers technical assistance to tenants as well. Those programs focus primarily on enforcement and compliance.

Enforcement and compliance are vital, but a new AFFH Rule promised to be something different. The history of discrimination and segregation in this country has had lasting impacts that needed to be addressed proactively. The rationale behind the rule was that if we were going to move forward, we needed to do so affirmatively, with proactive purpose. We needed to actively use resources to try to redress those disparities and dismantle them. And so, in addition to stopping discrimination and its effects, the Fair Housing Act called on HUD to encourage communities to affirmatively create policies and use resources to make a difference.

HUD has an established infrastructure to support enforcement and compliance, but on the "affirmative" side, such infrastructure is far less robust. At the most basic level, HUD has a carrot and a stick. The enforcement and compliance are the stick; the AFFH Rule is the carrot. HUD has devoted substantial resources to the stick side, so communities have been largely reluctant to engage in these conversations. From their experience, when they have this conversation, they get pushback. Ultimately, we decided it was important to lift up the carrot to convey the agency's recognition that positive things could happen if we pursued strategies to advance fair housing and to signal that HUD wanted to help communities do that. So, that was the goal. The HUD leadership needed to carry out a process of rule setting that would garner this broader buy-in and get people to see AFFH as a planning tool—the first step in a longer series of events culminating in investments and actions.

For the AFFH process to be meaningful, we argued that it would have to have some teeth and that HUD would also have to have some "skin in the game" as a partner working with the grantees. This accountability had two important parts. The first was committing HUD to providing a clear, base-level set of data with a standard framework for analysis (what became the Assessment of Fair Housing [AFH] tool) and requiring grantees to submit their completed AFHs to HUD for review. The second was connecting this analysis to existing planning requirements for funding recipients—the Consolidated Plan for jurisdictions and the Public Housing Authority (PHA) plans required of PHAs. Rather than a jurisdiction's assessment potentially just sitting on a shelf, HUD would actually verify whether a grantee was then making investment decisions in its Consolidated Plan and PHA plan that related to issues raised in the AFH. This approach was how we thought we could best effect change.

It was hoped that the AFFH Rule and the AFH tool at the core of the rule would start a conversation within municipalities about addressing long-standing fair housing issues. We expected that this process would be incremental, a first step in a much longer game. Most grantees have three- to five-year planning cycles, and we were not going to address deeply rooted, systemic problems in five or even ten years. But the fact that communities would actually have to have this conversation was one of the most important pieces—it is one thing to know that fair housing barriers and disparities exist, but actually sitting down in a room with people in the community and facing them—you can't brush it off or laugh it off. The AFFH process was meant to force the conversation and also equip the public to discuss those issues.

The ideal outcome would be for communities to have a first conversation, use the AFH tool to complete and submit a first AFH with their goals, connect these goals to actions in their Consolidated and PHA Plans, and then repeat the process in five years. Then this process would become an incremental layer, an opportunity to discuss what was and wasn't working; this knowledge could then be used to modify their goals and strategies. It might not be until the third or fourth planning cycle—perhaps as far as twenty years down the road—when some communities would start seeing the needle really move. Ideally, a series of interrelated players would be working together. Then, through this process, communities would gain a very clear, transparent entry into what had been a hidden process bogged down by the baffling language of consultants during the AI era.

Resolving that the rule was meant to be a planning tool with some teeth for enforcement helped us land on a mission statement that we could use to start anew and kick off the second phase of the rule-making process.

Phase 2—Pivot to Success: Launch of the Affirmatively Furthering Fair Housing Council and Development of a Proposed Rule (January 2011 through July 2012)

We started the new process in February 2011 by launching a departmental AFFH Council with representation from all the core offices (e.g., Fair Housing and Equal Opportunity [FHEO], Community Planning and Development [CPD], Public and Indian Housing [PIH], Office of the General Counsel [OGC], Policy Development and Research [PD&R], and so forth) that would be integral to the process. In recognition of the inherent tensions between the offices charged with administering AFFH (FHEO and, to some degree, the OGC) and those that worked directly with the grantees that were subject to the AFFH obligation (CPD and PIH primarily), Secretary Donovan made PD&R the neutral lead convener for the rule-making group. We also began an external listening tour with a variety of urban and rural jurisdictions and PHAs from coast to coast to get initial thoughts on the AI process and what might improve it.

We set an ambitious timeline to have the draft rule ready by the summer of 2011, but in doing so, we were extremely naïve. Efforts had failed for two years previously, and dealing with race, integration, and other complex issues requires making major, complex policy decisions. It took much longer than expected. We met twice a week with the full rule-making council, where we would tee up and strive to resolve significant policy decisions: How should we define a racially concentrated area of poverty? What opportunity measures should we use (if we used them at all)? What kinds of maps should we provide?

Members of the council had widely different opinions, and the tension between planning and enforcement resurfaced. Many wanted to focus on making the AFFH Rule's language and implementation tools practical. But others argued that the AFH tool must pass a legal threshold of sufficiency to be useful for enforcement. When working on some element of the assessment tool or a key definition, we tried to make it practical (e.g., "If I worked for a city, I could do this, and if I'm a layperson in the community, I'll understand what we're trying to do."). But this kind of thinking quickly got very specific in terms of requirements for communities, and a strong faction insisted that this level of practical analysis was not sufficient, given the Fair Housing Act. This tension between planning practicality and legally sufficient compliance proved to be incredibly challenging despite the core foundation established by the secretary: that this process would be first and foremost for planning.

The whole process of getting all the different program offices within HUD on board took a full year-and-a-half. One group wrote draft language for a particular section of the rule, for example, while another wrote language for another section. When we could not resolve disagreements, we would take them to the secretary for resolution. Then we would go back to working. It was basically slowly moving the ball down the field. We were trying to be as transparent as possible across offices. Since everybody in the department owned a piece of it, this process could not be done behind the scenes. It was a game changer for the way HUD hoped (and hopes) to operate, but it made the process a lot longer.

Rather than just "write it up and publish it," we undertook an arduous, iterative process with key staff involved from each office as well as senior leadership. We constantly reiterated the importance of this rule's being departmental, something that everyone owns. Eventually, we reached agreement on the elements that we thought communities needed to analyze and had the proposed AFFH Rule and a starting outline for the AFH tool ready by mid-2012. Reaching this milestone included an extensive back-and-forth review process with the White House's Office of Management and Budget (OMB) and its Office of Information and Regulatory Affairs.

Phase 3—Unexpected Turbulence: Political Uncertainty and Delayed Publication of the Proposed Rule (July 2012 through July 19, 2013)

With our approval from OMB and positive meetings with the White House, we planned to publish the proposed AFFH Rule in the *Federal Register* and have President Obama announce it in a speech at the National Urban League Conference in New Orleans on July 25, 2012. But we quickly learned that major policies, such as AFFH, are not only extremely complex to develop inside one federal agency; they are also just as hard to roll out given the especially difficult and unpredictable politics that come with a presidential election year. Due to an unfortunate and completely unforeseen event not at all related to HUD and AFFH, the release of the proposed rule was delayed. We hoped this delay would be temporary, but this initial hiccup and the uncertainty of the upcoming election soon affected not only the AFFH Rule but all major regulations in the queue across the federal government.

Secretary Donovan tried valiantly to regain the "green light" for publication without the formal announcement by the president, but the entire regulatory engine had shut down by late August. We immediately went into a Plan B contingency mode, adapting much of the proposed rule as new guidance for the existing AI regulatory requirement should the administration change following the election. Fortunately, we did not need the contingency, but we naïvely thought we could pick up where we had left off and publish the new rule soon after the election.

The election delay necessitated a tremendous amount of work just to get back to where we had been in July. We ended up having to completely rebrief key offices in the White House and at OMB, which took up the entire first half of 2013. On July 19, 2013, we finally published the proposed AFFH Rule in the *Federal Register* after a very long journey, but this announcement was just the beginning of an even larger amount of work to come. We had basically lost an entire year.

Phase 4—The Final Push: Publishing and Implementing the Final AFFH Rule and AFH Tool (January 2014 through 2016)

Every proposed rule in the *Federal Register* goes through an extensive period of public review and comment. When the comment period on the proposed rule closed in late 2013, HUD had received well over one thousand comments to address in its final rule making. The long years of proposed rule making had exhausted almost all involved, but everyone knew that we had to dive back in and get this done. To set ourselves up for success, incorporate lessons learned from the proposed rule making, and adapt to leadership and personnel changes, we invested a significant amount of time in the winter of 2014 in establishing working norms and operating protocols. The primary neutral stewardship role had moved from PD&R to the Office of the Secretary, run by a senior adviser to the secretary. This person met with each key office career staff member to solicit feedback and then convened all the assistant secretaries and deputy secretaries to codify a full set of guidelines, expectations, and resource allocations for final rule making, something we had not had in place for the proposed rule making. These norms and protocols became the gold standard that everyone could use to anchor our shared ownership and accountability while trying to maintain civility during complex policy making. Although we had worked through many critical issues in proposed rule making, we had also punted many concerns, and many public comments homed in on critical issues that we still needed to resolve.

With a firm commitment for regular involvement from the secretary and the deputy secretary to each assistant secretary, a dedicated full-time career staff member from each core office, and the aforementioned set of norms and protocols in place, we officially launched final rule making in February 2014. This endeavor focused on two primary components: (1) addressing the thousand-plus comments and drafting the final rule's language; and (2) finalizing the first draft of the AFH tool, including the data, which would need to go through its own period of public review and comment.

We were working fervently to develop two sets of complex, interdependent language for the rule and the AFH tool. Most critically, we had to move these two pieces together at an urgent "lock-step" pace, as we knew that even if we published a final rule, we could not implement it without a fully vetted and approved AFH tool since that was how the public and our grantees would actually fulfill the AFFH obligation. And the clock was ticking to 2016, uncertainty around another major election, and whether the next administration would carry forward the AFFH torch. Additionally, HUD underwent a leadership change with the transition from Secretary Shaun Donovan to Secretary Julián Castro in the summer of 2014. Folks worked hard to get the incoming secretary up to speed and fully invested, as there was no guarantee he would have the same commitment to AFFH as his predecessor. Fortunately, Secretary Castro dove in and fully committed to releasing the new AFFH Rule.

The departmental HUD team worked around the clock in two overlapping work groups on the rule and the AFH tool. The process of reaching consensus on the AFH tool was incredibly difficult, because it often involved relitigating policy issues ostensibly agreed upon months earlier during the proposed rule making. Compromises on vague language resurfaced once we needed to get specific and concrete, issues reopened that some believed had already been resolved, and the turnover in players at senior appointee levels did not help. But we persevered due to the hard work and determination of everyone involved, especially the dedicated career staff from each office.

On September 26, 2014, HUD published a proposed AFH tool, which went through significant public review and comment and then further revision by HUD staff for most of 2015. Simultaneously, the same core group of HUD staff worked diligently on the final rule. After a *very long* journey, HUD published the final AFFH Rule in the *Federal Register* on July 16, 2015. But the fun did not end for the AFFH team: we continued to refine the AFH tool and published a final version for larger CDBG grantees on December 31, 2015, which would allow implementation to begin in earnest in 2016.

After some brief pauses to celebrate these major milestones, the team dove back in to work on developing AFH tools for PHAs and states as well as on drafting further guidance for grantees and planning for implementation and the first round of AFH submissions. 2016 was a sprint! By the end of the Obama administration, HUD had a final AFFH Rule and AFH tool for larger CDBG grantees in place, a first round of grantees who had worked on and submitted their AFHs in late 2016, and in-progress drafts of AFH tools for PHAs and states.

Phase 5—Stalled Out: Affirmatively Furthering Fair Housing in the Trump Administration (January 2017 through the Present)

The transition to a new administration in January 2017 proved challenging, and as of this writing, in early 2020, the future of AFFH is very uncertain. HUD published the AFH tool for states on March 11, 2016, but never finalized it. HUD then published the AFH tool for PHAs on January 13, 2017, under the condition that it would not get implemented until HUD issued guidance and data. Then, in 2018, HUD Secretary Ben Carson and the new HUD political leadership essentially halted the implementation of AFFH by suspending the tool that the rule requires grantees to use to complete their AFHs. The administration also announced that it would be undertaking a rule-making process to modify the AFH tool and the rule itself. Many of the key career staff involved throughout AFFH rule making and implementation became discouraged, and some left the agency altogether. Still, there was reason for some hope. The AFFH Rule and the AFH tool was released to the public, and a whole first round of grantees (many highlighted in this book; see Chapters 3 and 8) submitted completed AFHs by using the new rule and tool. They have overwhelmingly supported the new process and found it useful. As part of meeting their general AFFH obligations, some jurisdictions are conducting analyses and using a process that essentially mimics the rule. In January 2020, HUD issued a proposed rule, discussed in the Introduction and the Conclusion to this volume, that if finalized would reverse the core innovations of the 2015 AFFH Rule.

While the 2015 AFFH process is far from perfect, it is a big step in the right direction of affirmatively furthering fair housing. We hope that future administrations will pick it back up so our nation can actually equip communities with the tools and a framework to address barriers to fair housing and make investments to mitigate the effects of segregation. The suspension of the AFH tool was a serious setback, followed by HUD's rescission of the rule altogether. In reflecting on the development of the rule, we attempt to situate our deliberations at HUD within broader theories about how policy making operates. Finally, we end on an optimistic note by highlighting the major policy and practical innovations that we think stand out in the AFFH Rule—components that any future administration should build on in its efforts toward AFFH.

Theories of the Policy Process and Affirmatively Furthering Fair Housing

We noted at the beginning of this overview that Kingdon's policy streams approach partly helped explain the creation of the AFFH Rule: first, with significant changes in the politics stream with the election of President Obama, and, second, with a series of reports on the inadequacy of the AI process that helped bring attention to the need for policy change. But as our discussion of the internal negotiations at HUD has demonstrated, there was far less of a consensus on the policy solution itself.

We believe that several other theories of the policy process align with our experience of the internal process at HUD that led to the specific AFFH Rule. The resistance of various departments within HUD to the AFFH process, because of a perceived diversion of resources from their own departments, aligns well with a theory of institutional rational choice, with its emphasis on individuals acting out of their own self-interest; this theory seems to partly explain our difficulty in achieving consensus.[6] Indeed, the failures experienced in Phase 1 demonstrated the deeply held beliefs represented in the agency's different factions. To that end, the idea of an advocacy coalition framework (ACF), with its emphasis on competing groups vying with one another to achieve their policy ends, better captures the fiercely competitive nature of the process.[7] The launch of the AFFH Council in Phase 2 created a cross-HUD process and infrastructure for surfacing those conflicts regularly, as part of a slow process of finding compromise. Indeed, consistent with this perspective, the balanced approach ultimately endorsed in the AFFH process represented an example of compromise—not of core beliefs among these advocacy coalitions but of a policy learning around "secondary" aspects of the belief system of the groups involved. The ACF approach predicts that such policy-oriented learning is a slow process that requires years to develop—consistent with the glacial process of getting AFFH approved within HUD.[8] This framework seems to better explain our experience with the AFFH process than one focused on punctuated equilibrium, with long periods of stability followed by short periods of significant change.[9] Although the AFFH process represented a significant change, it was a drawn-out progression that mostly involved internal debate within the agency rather than a rapid transformation. Furthermore, as Chapter 3 discusses in its interviews with government officials, the AFFH Rule represented a more significant policy change than that predicted by incremental approaches to institutional change.[10]

Key Innovations of the Affirmatively Furthering Fair Housing Rule

Out of the arduous rule-making process emerged what we believe to be an innovative planning tool for local communities to address segregation and increase access to opportunity. Four key innovations lie at the heart of the rule's potential. First is its power as a planning tool, which begins with the provision of a standardized assessment mechanism that is then linked to grantees' investment plans. Second, for the first time, the rule defines the goal of AFFH and makes clear that access to opportunities that come with housing is at its core. The assessment tool adds concreteness to the concept of access to opportunity through its opportunity indices and analysis of racially and ethnically concentrated areas of poverty. Third, while the rule codifies the overall AFFH goal, it does not dictate local strategies; importantly, it explicitly embraces a both/and approach to the perennial tension between mobility and place-based strategies. And fourth, it embraces a more transparent and inclusive process by requiring robust community engagement as well as public provision of data with a standardized assessment framework.

Affirmatively Furthering Fair Housing as a Meaningful Planning Tool for Future Action

Most broadly, AFFH's approach to fair housing ties the process to bolder challenges through planning rather than solely through enforcement. HUD designed the AFFH Rule this way because of our theory of how communities would learn and respond—they would first use the AFH tool to identify fair housing barriers and develop an AFH with goals, incorporate concrete strategies in their subsequent HUD plans to address the goals set in the AFH, assess their progress in future AFHs, and then start the cycle all over again.

To better enable communities to learn during their assessment processes, HUD developed a standardized AFH tool, which essentially walked grantees through a set of analyses meant to support the jurisdiction's decision making about which goals to prioritize and which strategies to adopt to accomplish those goals. The AFH tool was meant to clarify what such an assessment should entail and address many of the concerns raised in the

GAO report and elsewhere, including specifying concrete goals that can be measured, along with timelines.

Critical to the AFFH process overall, the AFHs had to be submitted to HUD and then be referenced in subsequent plans submitted (the Consolidated Plan for jurisdictions and the PHA Plan for PHAs). This requirement created a direct link from the AFH analysis and proposed strategies to action—actual programmatic and investment decisions of participants. While the submission of both plans to HUD provided checks on this process, the expectation was that communities going through this process would genuinely learn during their assessments and that those lessons would shape their HUD plans and their actions.

The learning was meant to continue in each cycle. AFHs were required in advance of every major planning cycle (generally three to five years apart), and each AFH started by assessing progress on the goals and strategies from the prior assessment. Some strategies may not have been adopted or may not have had the intended effects, so those revelations would be part of the public process of again assessing how the community was faring as well as surfacing new issues and ideas.

Broadening the Analytical Focus: Access to Opportunity and Areas of Racially or Ethnically Concentrated Poverty

A number of novel elements of the AFH tool are particularly worth emphasizing for how they embodied HUD's commitment to making the AFFH Rule work as a *planning tool* for local communities. One of the most important was the explicit focus on access to opportunities that come with housing. Doing so harkened back to the original context of the Fair Housing Act, since its adoption was driven by the extreme disparities in opportunities that existed at the time. As noted, the Kerner Commission report connected many of those disparities to residential segregation and disparities in places. More recent research by Raj Chetty and his coauthors has confirmed that being raised in racially concentrated areas of poverty alters the life trajectory of residents, even today.[11]

Calling that out and focusing on the spatial aspect of opportunity were quite important to the rule. Physical separation within our society is integrally linked to inequality within our society; making progress on lessening inequality requires addressing this separation and the associated disparities in places.

The rule establishes the importance of opportunity in its clarification of the meaning of the AFFH mandate, which requires that jurisdictions take meaningful actions to "overcome patterns of segregation and foster inclusive communities free from barriers *that restrict access to opportunity* based on protected characteristics" [emphasis added].[12] The rule operationalizes "opportunity" within the AFH tool in two main ways. First, jurisdictions must assess disparities in a variety of opportunities typically accessed through neighborhoods, such as the quality of schools, access to public transit, and access to jobs. Second, jurisdictions are required to focus particular attention on areas of racially or ethnically concentrated poverty (R/ECAPs), areas of concentrated disadvantage that have historically provided the least access to opportunities.

While the link to opportunity and use of R/ECAPs became core to the rule, many fair housing staff and stakeholders were initially uncomfortable with this way of thinking about fair housing issues. The traditional fair housing stance does not incorporate a lens of concentrated poverty or opportunity. The AFH tool, however, directed communities to not only assess patterns of segregation but also attend to how those patterns might connect to disparities in neighborhood-based opportunities; the consideration of R/ECAPs required communities to consider where segregation may be having some of its most profoundly negative effects. This recasting highlights the emphasis of the AFFH Rule as a planning tool, used for prioritizing programmatic and investment efforts rather than solely for enforcing fair housing guidelines. It also provides the potential for the planning process to focus on nonhousing (and non-HUD) resources as part of a long-term strategy to improve spatial disparities across neighborhoods.

Locally Determined Priorities, Inclusive of Place-Based Reinvestment and Mobility

While the federal regulation sets the high-level goal of addressing residential segregation and disparities in opportunity, it does not prescribe any specific set of local strategies for achieving that goal. Communities are expected to have a data-informed and inclusive conversation and decide upon the right approach, given the local context. But we—HUD—were going to help them do it with the various components of the rule, including the AFH tool and the provision of data and technical assistance. This stance of HUD as a guiding partner is itself an innovation of the rule.

Nowhere was the tension between potential strategies more contentious than between place-based and mobility approaches (an issue discussed in more detail in Chapter 5). There is a lot of passion on both sides. Both groups point to the evidence showing the multiple negative consequences of living in segregated neighborhoods and areas of concentrated poverty. Advocates of mobility strategies say, "Let's get people out of those places with concentrated poverty." Their focus is on supporting households moving to areas that might provide better opportunities, particularly for economic advancement and for children. Advocates of redevelopment counter by asking, "Why should there be any places on the map characterized by such disadvantage? Why should we place the burden of moving—and all the disruption and isolation it can cause—on those who have been burdened most already?" The focus for this group is on investing in the neighborhoods to encourage economic mobility for their current residents.

What we tried to do through the regulation was to remain neutral in the mobility versus place-based debate, although this decision was hard-fought. The passions and tensions in the advocacy communities existed just as strongly among the HUD staff. It took a long time for everyone to get on board with a balanced approach that embraced place-based *and* mobility tactics. This balanced approach marked a sea change in the fight between people in the fair housing and community development camps. This multipronged approach said to HUD grant recipients that they should consider both approaches—addressing segregation by expanding access to areas of high opportunity and investing in neighborhoods to improve them as areas of opportunity for current residents. Jurisdictions need to enable mobility and decrease segregation, while also improving neighborhoods. They need to address nonhousing aspects of the neighborhoods that come with housing. That is one of the most critical things about this rule and makes it very different from what communities had been doing when they did their AIs.

We also hoped the AFFH Rule and AFH tool would produce some truly innovative strategies. When a community decided it wanted to adopt a strategy, such as increasing housing mobility, it was not obvious how exactly they would do it. Currently, there is not enough evidence to provide a menu of strategies that we know work in a given context. Although HUD provides some ideas based on the evidence of certain pilots, this rule is part of an important larger opportunity to tap into the creativity of hundreds or even thousands of communities across the country that are willing and able to try new things. We hoped communities would build on their local knowledge to find practical solutions that worked for their areas.

Empowering Inclusive Local Dialogue and Planning: Data and Community Engagement

The theory of how the AFFH process could truly move the needle on an issue as intractable as segregation rests on the apparatus the rule provides for a truly inclusive dialogue and process, in which data play a role in leveling the playing field.

At local community levels, all too often some people come with a lot more information than others, creating not only an uneven starting place for dialogue but also uneven power. Those with information can talk over others, particularly those groups whom they do not want to be part of the conversation. Because the data provided in the AFH tool were available to all, everyone was meant to have the chance to be fully informed and fully prepared to have a conversation. The common access to data should mean that when the public shows up and someone says something that is not right, individuals in the public who had access to the data could act as a correcting force by noting the disconnect. This kind of pause to correct things that are wrong does not happen nearly often enough in communities when plans or important investment decisions get made.

While nearly all the data provided in the AFH tool were already public, translating the data into readable maps and tables requires a level of sophistication and resources that many institutions, organizations—and certainly families—do not have. The AFH tool was meant to change that by creating an easy-to-use mapping system that conveyed the data in an easily digestible way for housing policy experts and novices alike.

Whether the form and ease are exactly correct is still an open question, but the logic is quite similar to that behind the Home Mortgage Disclosure Act (HMDA), the banking regulation that requires banks to provide publicly available information on every mortgage application they get and what happened to that application. Prior to the late 1970s, banks did not provide such data; hence there were no data to refute the claim by banks that they treated all individuals in the same manner. But the availability of HMDA data triggered a different conversation, in great part due to the use of those data by the advocacy community. The AFH tool armed advocates in the same way, enabling them to construct stories that were impossible to ignore and refute.

To enable the data to have this effect, the AFFH Rule requires a robust engagement process to ensure broad community participation, particularly from groups typically absent from local decision making. As part of the new process, jurisdictions must document their engagement strategies, post their draft AFHs publicly, and collect and respond to all public comments on the drafts in the AFHs they submit to HUD. This process includes explaining the rationale for not addressing specific comments in the content of the AFHs, much as federal agencies must address public comments in the rule-making process.

Robust, inclusive community engagement may be one of the most difficult components of the AFFH Rule to achieve, and several of the initial earliest AFH submissions to HUD in late 2016 may have fallen short. But evidence suggests that AFH submissions received before the suspension of the tool documented considerably more robust public engagement than did the AIs previously submitted by those jurisdictions.[13]

Final Thoughts

No new approach is flawless, and AFFH is no exception. HUD expected that the rule and its assessment tools would evolve as they were used, incorporating lessons on what was most and least useful. Indeed, the AFH tools themselves are subject to public comment and potential revisions every three years as part of the requirements of the Paperwork Reduction Act. But as HUD considers what revisions it may make to the Rule and tools, and as communities and future administrations think about building from the framework created, we continue to believe that the 2015 version of the rule has "good bones." It is a platform to build on, one that includes true innovations for creating a process that may be the start of really implementing the AFFH mandate of the Fair Housing Act, albeit fifty years late.

ENDNOTES

1. The Fair Housing Act of 1968 created this obligation for federal agencies undertaking housing and community development activities, and this obligation extends to how those funds are spent.

2. The specific congressional requester that triggered the GAO report is not delineated in its report.

3. U.S. Government Accountability Office, *Housing and Community Grants: HUD Needs to Enhance Its Requirements and Oversight of Jurisdictions' Fair Housing Plans (GAO-10-905)*, 2010, available at https://www.gao.gov/new.items/d10905.pdf.

4. Otto Kerner, *Report of the National Advisory Commission on Civil Disorders*, 1968, available at https://www.ncjrs.gov/pdffiles1/Digitization/8073NCJRS.pdf.

5. John W. Kingdon, *Agendas, Alternatives, and Public Policies* (Boston: Little Brown, 1984).

6. Elinor Ostrom, *Understanding Institutional Diversity* (Princeton, NJ: Princeton University Press, 2005).

7. Paul A. Sabatier, "Policy Change over a Decade or More," in *Policy Change and Learning: An Advocacy Coalition Approach*, ed. Paul A. Sabatier and Hank C. Jenkins-Smith (Boulder, CO: Westview Press, 1993), 13–39.

8. Paul A. Sabatier and Christopher M. Weible, "The Advocacy Coalition Framework: Innovations and Clarifications," in *Theories of the Policy Process*, ed. Paul A. Sabatier (Boulder, CO: Westview Press, 2007), 189–220.

9. Frank R. Baumgartner and Bryan D. Jones, "Agenda Dynamics and Policy Subsystems," *Journal of Politics* 53, no. 4 (November 1991): 1044–1074.

10. Kathleen Thelen, "Historical Institutionalism in Comparative Politics," *Annual Review of Political Science* 2, no. 1 (June 1999): 369–404.

11. For example, see Raj Chetty, Nathaniel Hendren, and Lawrence Katz, *The Effects of Exposure to Better Neighborhoods on Children: New Evidence from the Moving to Opportunity Experiment* (Cambridge, MA: National Bureau of Economic Research, May 2015).

12. 24 C.F.R. § 5.152. The rule explains that "meaningful actions" means "significant actions that are designed and can be reasonably expected to achieve a material positive change that affirmatively furthers fair housing by, for example, increasing fair housing choice or decreasing disparities in access to opportunity." Ibid.

13. Vicki Been and Katherine O'Regan, *The Potential Costs to Engagement of HUD's Assessment of Fair Housing Delay* (New York: NYU Furman Center, 2018), available at http://furmancenter.org/research/publication/the-potential-costs-to-public-engage ment-of-huds-assessment-of-fair-housing.

3

The Promise Fulfilled?

Taking Stock of Assessments of Fair Housing

Nicholas F. Kelly, Maia S. Woluchem,
Reed Jordan, and Justin P. Steil

The Department of Housing and Urban Development (HUD) created
the Affirmatively Furthering Fair Housing (AFFH) Rule to undo generations of policies that have left America's cities deeply segregated
and unequal. But as demonstrated by a half century of halting fair housing
progress and lack of enforcement of the Fair Housing Act's provision mandating that HUD and its grantees affirmatively further fair housing, the
prospects for real change even after the AFFH's Rule passage were unclear.
After years of effort at crafting the rule, its passage raised several pressing
questions. To what extent would municipalities resist efforts to reduce segregation and to increase access to place-based opportunities, or take meaningful steps to advance fair housing? Would HUD staff essentially ignore
these fair housing plans, as they had previous ones for decades, or would
they thoroughly review and provide municipalities with meaningful feedback? Would the new rule, so delayed, debated, and finally, as the previous
chapter demonstrated, pushed through with bureaucratic jiu-jitsu, live up
to its promise?

In this chapter, we examine the effectiveness of the AFFH Rule in helping jurisdictions craft policies that provide more equal access to place-based
resources and access to housing in areas rich with opportunities. With
limited private remedies to advance the AFFH provision in the courts, the
success of the rule before its suspension depended in large part on the enforcement system that HUD implemented. From October 2016 through
January 2018 (when HUD suspended the rule), 49 sets of HUD grantees,

representing 103 municipalities and public housing agencies from across the country, submitted plans to affirmatively further fair housing, called Assessments of Fair Housing (AFHs). In previous research, we have demonstrated that these plans represented a vast improvement on the Analyses of Impediments (AIs) previously required by HUD.[1] The AFFH Rule provided municipalities with relevant, locally tailored data; required municipalities to analyze and reflect upon those data; and asked municipalities to propose clear, realizable goals in response. This specificity stood in stark contrast to previous vague guidance on submitting AIs—plans that HUD rarely ever read and that did not require municipalities to demonstrate progress toward fair housing objectives. In the AFH process, HUD and other partners offered training to municipalities on how to successfully complete their fair housing plans under the new rule; reviewed every AFH to ensure that it fulfilled the standards required by the regulation; and refused to accept some substandard AFHs until municipalities made revisions.[2]

We collected all forty-nine AFHs that were reviewed by HUD before the Donald Trump administration suspended the AFFH Rule in January 2018—including the thirty-two that HUD accepted and the seventeen that HUD rejected. We then coded and analyzed these plans to identify the types of goals that the municipalities proposed. To examine the robustness of the plans, we determined whether the goals included (a) an objective supported by numerical metrics or milestones that would allow quantifiable evaluation of progress or (b) a new policy or program to accomplish that objective. Finally, we analyzed those data to understand which jurisdictions were more likely to submit fair housing plans with quantifiable objectives and to propose new policies to realize those objectives. We also sought to understand how they implemented the rule's "balanced approach" to housing mobility and place-based investments. Case studies of fair housing plans in Seattle, Washington; Temecula, California; Hidalgo County, Texas; and the Kansas City Metropolitan Area—including interviews with lead authors of all four of those plans—highlight the nuances of the AFFH Rule and the complexities that municipalities face when creating their fair housing plans.

Who Participated in the Assessment of Fair Housing Process?

The forty-nine municipalities that submitted AFHs varied along a number of metrics relevant to their responsibility to affirmatively furthering fair housing. HUD scheduled the due date for AFH submissions based on the due date for a municipality's Consolidated Plan. As a result, the municipalities that submitted AFHs were, if not quite randomly selected, then at least arbitrarily designated to submit their proposals before the rule's suspension. As Table 3.1 shows, these municipalities represented a broad swath of counties, cities, and towns from across the United States, from large counties (Los Angeles County) and big cities (Philadelphia) to small cities (Ithaca, New York) and small counties (Manatee County, Florida); from regional submissions (Kansas City) to smaller cities operating within a large fragmented metropolitan region (Somerville, Massachusetts). Table 3.1 also shows the range of levels of segregation within these communities, as measured by the Black-white dissimilarity and Latinx-white dissimilarity index, which indicates the proportion of a group that would need to move to create a uniform distribution. For this group of municipalities, the median Black-white dissimilarity index is 38, while the median Latinx-white dissimilarity index is 34. These medians among the AFH submitters can be compared to the national median Black-white dissimilarity score of 53 and the median Latinx-white dissimilarity score of 41.[3]

As discussed in the Introduction, Chapter 2, and Chapter 8 of this volume, the AFFH Rule relies on collaboration between the federal government and state and local governments. HUD's rule and the Assessment

TABLE 3.1. DISSIMILARITY INDICES OF MUNICIPALITIES THAT SUBMITTED ASSESSMENTS OF FAIR HOUSING ACCEPTED OR REJECTED BY THE U.S. DEPARTMENT OF HOUSING AND URBAN DEVELOPMENT

State	City	Black-White Dissimilarity Index	Latinx-White Dissimilarity Index
AK	Anchorage	34	25
AL	Mobile	53	31
AR	Jonesboro	33	28
AR	Springdale	24	31
AR	Rogers	17	34
CA	Los Angeles County	60	64
CA	Long Beach	57	59
CA	San Mateo County	55	51
CA	Cathedral City	29	43
CA	Paramount	26	21
CA	Pomona	25	41
CA	Moreno Valley	23	25
CA	Temecula	20	16
CA	Victorville/Apple Valley	16	12

(continued)

TABLE 3.1. (*Continued*)

State	City	Black-White Dissimilarity Index	Latinx-White Dissimilarity Index
CO	El Paso County	39	29
FL	Manatee County	46	42
GA	Savannah	44	30
GA	Sandy Springs	42	41
GA	Clayton County	29	34
IN	Hammond	36	22
KS	Lawrence	19	15
LA	New Orleans	68	41
LA	Jefferson Parish	56	33
MA	Somerville	30	39
MI	Washtenaw County	51	24
MO	Kansas City	62	47
NC	Wilmington	56	31
NC	Winston-Salem	51	48
NC	Greenville	36	25
NM	Santa Fe	21	37
NM	Rio Rancho	14	10
NY	New Rochelle	41	48
NY	Ithaca	25	18
OH	Hamilton	54	46
OH	Lake County	50	55
OR	Clackamas County	27	27
PA	Philadelphia	73	62
PA	Delaware County	64	26
PA	Dauphin County	47	35
PA	Chester County	46	49
SC	Horry County	38	32
SC	Richland County	38	34
TN	Nashville–Davidson County	50	49
TX	Hidalgo County	43	39
TX	Lewisville	22	35
VA	Harrisonburg	24	35
VT	Burlington	27	11
WA	Seattle	52	30
WA	Bellingham	16	23

Tool provide data, set out a broad framework for analysis, and ask localities to craft locally tailored goals based on that analysis. Planning scholars conducting research in other contexts have found that characteristics associated with successful future implementation include the factual basis of the plan, the presence of goals based on measurable objectives, and the specification of policies designed to achieve those goals.[4] To be effective, plan goals must be specific enough to be able to be tied to concrete actions, supported by a written commitment to carry out those actions, and include provisions for measuring progress. These include indicators of advancement, timelines for completing the required actions, and identification of the parties responsible for implementation.[5] Through the Assessment Tool, HUD provides municipalities with data as a starting point, requires them to analyze those data, and asks them to answer specific questions that HUD poses in the AFH Tool. The factual basis of the plans, therefore, has at least a shared baseline. There is significant variation, however, in the goals that municipalities put forth in their AFHs, the metrics they present to evaluate progress, and the new policies, if any, they plan to create to realize the goals. Accordingly, imperfect but consistently measurable proxies for plan quality or robustness among AFHs are commitments to measurable objectives or to the creation of new policies to implement goal objectives.

The presence of measurable objectives gives local residents and fair housing advocates clear benchmarks by which to hold local governments accountable for their progress on fair housing. A lack of measurable objectives, on the other hand, may indicate a conscious or unconscious effort to avoid accountability to either HUD or the public. Similarly, a new planned policy or program reflects an assessment of the obstacles to fair housing and an analysis of a specific, novel path to overcome that obstacle. Creating a new policy or program can involve the expenditure of political or financial capital by local government officials to secure its approval and allocate staff to execute it; officials are unlikely to provide those resources if they see it as a waste and unlikely to deliver results.[6] These two measures—whether a particular goal has a measurable objective and whether it represents a new policy—are the criteria by which we evaluate goals in the AFHs we analyze in this chapter.

The AFFH Rule is a form of meta-regulation that requires municipalities to develop a locally-tailored plan. As such, it allows municipalities significant leeway in shaping their plans.[7] Research on meta-regulation finds these types of regulations tend to be particularly successful when they have commitment from local stakeholders. We measure local commitment—which we expect to be associated with robust AFHs—first through local political ideology, which runs on a scale of –1 for most liberal and 1 for most conservative. Given the partisan divide on the AFFH Rule, we expect more

TABLE 3.2. DESCRIPTIVE STATISTICS ON MUNICIPAL CHARACTERISTICS

	Min.	Median	Max.
Population	30,720	193,637	10,105,722
Capacity			
Community Development Block Grant (CDBG) funding	421,205	1,627,663	38,807,208
CDBG timeliness	0	1.31	1.64
Political context			
Conservatism	−0.87	−0.12	0.52
Fair Housing and Equal Opportunity cases per million	63.57	339.34	1269.33
Average Fair Housing Initiatives Program organizations by state	0	3.33	16.67
Socioeconomic context			
Unemployment rate	0.03	0.067	0.13
Median household income	31,967	52,082	105,667
College graduates (%)	0.1	0.32	0.64
Heterogeneity and segregation			
Non-white–white dissimilarity	10	35	65
Black-white dissimilarity	14	38	73
Latinx-white dissimilarity	10	34	64
Asian-white dissimilarity	10	28	55
White non-Hispanic (%)	0.05	0.54	0.89
Black non-Hispanic (%)	0	0.09	0.68
Hispanic (%)	0.03	0.13	0.92
Asian non-Hispanic (%)	0.01	0.04	0.29
High-cost			
Median home value	82,400	197,200	917,700
Median gross rent	699	1004	1973
Vacancy rate	0.03	0.08	0.37
Share renters	0.22	0.44	0.74

liberal municipalities to express a greater commitment to it.[8] We also measure commitment through the strength of local nonprofit fair housing organizations funded by HUD's Fair Housing Initiatives Program (FHIP), given that fair housing is a low-salience issue and historically driven in part by these groups. Additionally, we examine the number of complaints alleging housing discrimination filed with HUD's Office of Fair Housing and Equal Opportunity (FHEO), given the importance in the past of these suits to force municipalities to act to address fair housing issues.[9] We also measure commitment by examining local socioeconomic conditions, which may shape fair housing efforts, as well as measures of heterogeneity and segregation that can influence the political context for creating policies to reduce racial disparities and demographic conditions.[10] Existing research has also found that greater capacity is associated with more rigorous compliance with meta-regulation.[11] As a result, we operationalize capacity by calculating the overall amount and efficient use of Community Development Block Grant (CDBG) funding as measured through HUD's "timeliness" measure in 2015 or 2016. We gather these data from the 2013–2017 5-Year American Community Survey, American Ideology project, and HUD.[12] We present summary statistics on these variables in Table 3.2.

Grantees vary widely across these measures of socioeconomic status, demographic composition, likely commitment, and estimated capacity. From large CDBG-funded cities (such as Philadelphia, with a CDBG allocation of more than $38 million) to smaller towns (such as Rogers, Arkansas, with a CDBG allocation of less than $500,000); from very conservative areas (such as Springdale, Arkansas, with a conservatism score of .42) to very liberal ones (such as New Rochelle, New York, with a score of −.53); from regions with low unemployment (such as Lewisville, Texas, at 4.2 percent) to small cities with high unemployment (such as Greenville, North Carolina, at 10.2 percent)—not only do these jurisdictions vary greatly in their level of segregation; they also range significantly in their demographic composition, from 89 percent white in Lake County, Ohio, to 4 percent white in Paramount, California.

What Did the Resulting Assessments of Fair Housing Look Like?

To evaluate the the AFHs, we build on the literature on plan quality by assessing fair housing goals in the AFHs in two ways. First, we code each goal in every assessment of fair housing in the forty-nine plans discussed here to evaluate whether the goal has a measurable objective, with a numerical metric or milestone presented to allow quantifiable evaluation of progress. Second, we examine whether the goal results in a new policy to achieve that objective. We also focus on a number of other substantive measures of the goals put forth in the fair housing plans—in particular, whether the goals advance place-based investments to reinvest in low-income communities or support promoting mobility for protected classes to access areas of greater

TABLE 3.3. CODING CATEGORIES

Categories	Coding Description
Metrics	
Measurable objective	Has a quantifiable metric.
New policy	Includes a specific new policy or program.
Place and Mobility	
Place-based	Involves investment in high-poverty neighborhoods or abandoned properties.
Mobility	Involves mobility strategies or targets high-opportunity neighborhoods.
Other Characteristics	
Affordable housing	Encourages the creation of affordable housing.
Public housing	References public housing residents or units.
Voucher	References housing voucher holders.
Zoning	References zoning or proposes zoning changes.
Displacement	References displacement or gentrification.
Regional	Calls for regional cooperation, coordination, or distribution.
Transportation	References improving public transportation or transit-oriented development.
Education	References improving schools or school performance.
Economic development	References workforce training, small business assistance, or job creation.
Environmental quality	References improvements to air and water quality, parks.
Disability	References access improvements, or discrimination or disparities based on disability.
Race or national origin	References discrimination or disparities based on race, ethnicity, or national origin.
Low-income	Targets or references the needs of low-income households.
Family status	References discrimination or disparities based on family status.
Age	Targets or references the elderly.
Fair housing education	Proposes fair housing education, outreach, or enforcement.
Homeownership	Seeks to increase homeownership or create income-restricted affordable homes.

opportunity. We also examine whether each goal falls into a variety of other categories, as illustrated in Table 3.3. Each goal can fall into multiple substantive categories and have quantifiable metrics or be considered a new policy. For example, the goal in Chester County, Pennsylvania, to encourage mobility among low-income residents living in areas of poverty by decreasing the number of voucher holders living in a high-poverty area from 43.9 percent to 39 percent would be coded as having a measurable objective concerning mobility and voucher holders.

In Table 3.4, we present the types of goals present in each plan and the number and share of those types of goals that contain a measurable

Goal Characteristic	Total goals	Goals with a measurable objective	Goals with a new policy	Goals with a measurable objective or new policy or both	% Goals with a measurable objective or new policy or both
TABLE 3.4. SHARE OF ASSESSMENT OF FAIR HOUSING GOALS CONTAINING MEASURABLE OBJECTIVES OR NEW POLICIES					
Affordable housing	255	94	22	109	43%
Fair housing education	148	33	7	39	26%
Disability	123	49	9	54	44%
Place-based	87	36	10	41	47%
Low-income	84	29	5	33	39%
Mobility	83	26	13	34	41%
Homeownership	81	43	6	46	57%
Voucher	76	23	5	25	33%
Economic development	73	23	4	27	37%
Transportation	61	7	5	10	16%
Race or national origin	54	17	7	20	37%
Public housing	54	14	2	15	28%
Zoning	50	9	14	21	42%
Regional	41	4	7	11	27%
Displacement	39	10	0	10	26%
Education	34	9	3	11	32%
Environmental quality	29	9	3	12	41%
Age	18	12	1	12	67%
Family status	6	2	0	2	33%

objective or include a new policy. Of the 857 goals in 49 AFHs in our sample, 255 of them address affordable housing, by far the most dominant focus area. Fair housing education and disability access are the next most common goals. On the other hand, homeownership and place-based goals are the most likely goal types to have measurable objectives. Zoning and mobility goals are the most likely to be accompanied by new policy efforts.

We next compare those municipalities that put forward goals with a large number of measurable objectives or new policies as compared to those that did not. Table 3.5 presents those municipalities that score in the bottom tercile according to these measures, with two or fewer goals meeting these criteria, compared to those in the top tercile, with six or more goals meeting these criteria. The only statistically significant difference between the two groups is the measure of Black-white dissimilarity, in which municipalities with more measurable objectives or new policies have higher levels of Black-white segregation than those municipalities with fewer measurable objectives or new policies.

To further test this relationship between municipal characteristics and goal characteristics, we estimate the relationship between the number of goals with a measurable objective or a new policy and measures of local context and capacity. In Table 3.6, we run four models to test the association of various municipal characteristics on a municipality's overall number of goals with a quantifiable metric or a new policy. In Model 1, we start with the one municipal characteristic that is significantly different in Table 3.5 and confirm that more segregated areas—those municipalities with larger Black-white dissimilarity indexes—have more measurable objectives and new policies in their AFHs. This association holds consistently across Model 2, where we control for municipal population. This model also reveals a statistically significant positive association between more populous municipalities and a larger number of quantifiable metrics and new policy goals. Model 3 adds measures of capacity, none of which show statistically significant relationships with measurable objectives or new policies. Model 4 adds other socioeconomic variables and finds a positive relationship between median household income and the continued significance of Black-white segregation with the number of measurable objectives or new policies in the fair housing assessments. The fact that this positive correlation between more segregated municipalities and more quantifiable goals and new policies persists after controlling for other relevant characteristics suggests that, according to at least one metric, the AFFH Rule was working as intended. Grantees with higher levels of segregation propose more concrete steps to reduce segregation and make access to place-based resources more equitable in their communities compared to those grantees with lower levels of segregation.

TABLE 3.5. T-TESTS TOP AND BOTTOM TERCILE FOR MEASURABLE OBJECTIVES OR NEW POLICIES

	Bottom tercile (*n* = 18)	Top tercile (*n* = 17)
Population	251,033	940,004
Capacity		
Community Development Block Grant (CDBG) funding	3,472,345	4,387,210
CDBG timeliness	1.11	1.35
Political context		
Conservatism	−0.15	−0.24
Fair Housing and Equal Opportunity cases per million	322.27	388.38
Average Fair Housing Initiatives Program organizations by state	7.15	4.9
Socioeconomic context		
Unemployment rate	0.071	0.072
Median household income	50,374	57,435
College graduates (%)	0.32	0.357
Heterogeneity and segregation		
Non-white–white dissimilarity	32	39
Black-white dissimilarity	35*	46*
Latinx-white dissimilarity	34	35
Asian-white dissimilarity	27	31
White non-Hispanic (%)	0.49	0.51
Black non-Hispanic (%)	0.13	0.23
Hispanic (%)	0.3	0.16
Asian non-Hispanic (%)	0.05	0.07
High-cost		
Median home value	202,966	279,476
Median gross rent	1,001	1,083
Vacancy rate	0.1	0.11
Share renters	0.47	0.44

* $p < 0.05$, ** $p < 0.01$, *** $p < 0.001$

Note: CDBG timeliness figures are available only for $n = 16$ of the bottom tercile and $n = 14$ of the top tercile.

TABLE 3.6. QUANTIFIABLE METRICS AND NEW POLICIES REGRESSED ON CITY CHARACTERISTICS

Ordinary Least Squares (OLS) Regression Results

	Model 1	Model 2	Model 3	Model 4
Black-White Dissimilarity Index	19.99**	15.73*	18.65*	18.02*
	(5.929)	(6.033)	(7.091)	(6.821)
Population (in millions)		1.418*	1.949*	1.883*
		(0.652)	(0.765)	(0.74)
Community Development Block Grant Funding (in millions)			−0.296	−0.276
			(0.198)	(0.202)
Conservatism			−3.286	−6.321
			(3.128)	(4.703)
Fair Housing and Equal Opportunity Cases (per million)			0.00328	0.00232
			(0.0047)	(0.0047)
Average Fair Housing Initiatives Program organizations by state			−0.0337	−0.291
			(0.166)	(0.199)
Percent unemployed				0.823
				(60.96)
Median Household Income (in thousands)				0.200**
				(0.0674)
Percent with College Degree				−14.23
				(12.92)
Percent White				−0.536
				(5.416)
Constant	−1.942	−0.981	−2.897	−7.438
	(2.485)	(2.433)	(2.985)	(8.551)
Observations	49	49	49	49
R^2	0.195	0.27	0.333	0.467

Standard errors in parentheses
* $p < 0.05$, ** $p < 0.01$, *** $p < 0.001$

In Table 3.7, we compare plans that have the most goals focused on place-based investments and support for mobility—what many HUD program participants believed were the core issues of the AFFH Rule—with plans that have the fewest such goals. Municipalities that submitted plans with more of these goals tend to have more CDBG funding (a function, in part, of their being large cities with comparatively high numbers of residents in poverty); be more ideologically liberal; and have a greater number of cases filed by HUD's FHEO office alleging discrimination in violation of the Fair

TABLE 3.7. T-TESTS TOP AND BOTTOM TERCILE FOR MOBILITY AND PLACE-BASED INVESTMENTS

	Bottom tercile (*n* = 17)	Top tercile (*n* = 19)
Population	212,169	953,208
Capacity		
Community Development Block Grant (CDBG) funding	1,436,945*	6,386,835*
CDBG timeliness	1.25	1.21
Political context		
Conservatism	−0.05*	−0.30*
Fair Housing and Equal Opportunity cases per million	249**	444**
Average Fair Housing Initiatives Program organizations by state	4.98	6.16
Socioeconomic context		
Unemployment rate	0.06	0.07
Median household income	58,187	59,759
College graduates (%)	0.34	0.37
Heterogeneity and segregation		
Non-white–white dissimilarity	28**	41**
Black-white dissimilarity	31**	48**
Latinx-white dissimilarity	33	40
Asian-white dissimilarity	24*	33*
White non-Hispanic (%)	0.54	0.51
Black non-Hispanic (%)	0.11	0.18
Hispanic (%)	0.25	0.21
Asian non-Hispanic (%)	0.05	0.07
High-cost		
Median home value	251,771	305,873
Median gross rent	1,065	1,104
Vacancy rate	0.09	0.1
Share renters	0.47	0.44

$p < 0.05$, $p < 0.01$, $p < 0.001$

Note: CDBG timeliness figures are available only for *n* = 16 of the bottom tercile and *n* = 15 of the top tercile.

Housing Act. As above, more segregated municipalities—as measured by not only Black-white dissimilarity but also non-white–white dissimilarity and Asian-white dissimilarity—have more goals focused on placed-based investments and on mobility than other municipalities.

We test this relationship more rigorously by estimating the relationship between the number of goals focused on mobility and on place-based investments and municipal characteristics, as seen in Table 3.8. The results in Models 1 through 4 indicate that a higher Black-white dissimilarity score is

TABLE 3.8. PLACE AND MOBILITY GOALS REGRESSED ON CITY CHARACTERISTICS

Ordinary Least Squares (OLS) Regression Results

	Model 1	Model 2	Model 3	Model 4
Black-White Dissimilarity Index	15.50***	14.47***	6.741	6.41
	(3.412)	(3.616)	(3.465)	(3.699)
Population (in millions)		0.343	0.00646	0.053
		(0.391)	(0.374)	(0.401)
Community Development Block Grant Funding (in millions)			0.245*	0.234*
			(0.097)	(0.11)
Conservatism			−1.46	−1.072
			(1.528)	(2.551)
Fair Housing and Equal Opportunity Cases (per million)			0.00863***	0.00911***
			(0.0023)	(0.00255)
Average Fair Housing Initiatives Program organizations by state			−0.0504	−0.0727
			(0.0812)	(0.108)
Percent unemployed				25.41
				(33.06)
Median Household Income (in thousands)				0.0163
				(0.0365)
Percent with College Degree				1.327
				(7.004)
Percent White				0.486
				(2.937)
Constant	−2.639	−2.407	−3.019*	−6.247
	(1.43)	(1.458)	(1.458)	(4.638)
Observations	49	49	49	49
R^2	0.305	0.316	0.585	0.592

Standard errors in parentheses
* $p < 0.05$, ** $p < 0.01$, *** $p < 0.001$

initially associated with more goals focused on mobility and place-based investments, but this relationship disappears once we control for the capacity of a municipality, measured by the value of local CDBG funding. The amount of CDBG funding—even when controlling for population—is positively associated with more goals focused on mobility and place-based investments. This connection suggests that the larger federal community development investment—allocated according to measures of population, share of population in poverty, and either share of overcrowded housing units or share of housing units built before 1940—is associated with more fair housing goals focused on increasing access to opportunity either through place-based investments or through support for mobility programs, when compared to those with lower levels of CDBG investment. In addition, the number of cases filed by HUD's FHEO office (at the county level, per million residents) is also a significant predictor of these place-based and mobility goals.

Case Studies

The forty-nine municipalities that submitted AFHs to HUD took varied approaches. Some, such as Hidalgo County, Texas, and Kansas City, Missouri, submitted regional plans to address fair housing, combining the work of several municipalities and housing authorities. Others, such as Temecula, California, focused on a narrow set of policy solutions and submitted an AFH with only four highly prescriptive goals. In this section, we examine four fair housing plans that vary along a number of relevant dimensions, but especially the capacity of the submitting grantees, in order to examine their varying approaches. We also conduct interviews with key staff working on those fair housing plans to understand the benefits and challenges they encountered with implementation. First, we examine Seattle, Washington, a city with substantial resources, that submitted a bold and creative initial assessment of fair housing. We then examine Temecula, California, a smaller city with less capacity that submitted a plan that was initially rejected and subsequently revised and accepted. We then examine two regional AFHs: one plan conducted by Kansas City, including five communities in total; and one by Hidalgo County, Texas, including eighteen housing authorities and municipalities. By examining variation within fair housing plans and by municipality type, we illuminate the diversity of municipal responses to the AFFH Rule.

Seattle: Building on a History of Racial Equity Work and Pursuing Fair Housing in a High-Cost City

Before embarking on the AFH process, Seattle was already engaged in extensive multi-agency collaborative work focused on racial equity and on affordable and fair housing. The AFH process provided an opportunity to reflect further on this existing work, to clarify how existing projects related to each other and to fair housing, and to cement many of these commitments in a single plan with goals and metrics. Seattle's extensive AFH also provides an illustration of how complex fair housing can be in high-cost cities where displacement is at the forefront of the minds of many working-class households, especially households of color, not segregation or integration. As Seattle's AFH emphasizes, in these high-cost contexts, anti-displacement work is a central strategy to advance integration, and the common conflations of mobility with integration and place-based investments with continuing segregation do not hold up.

Seattle's AFH stands as a robust encapsulation of the city's multipronged efforts to increase racial equity and includes important critiques of the federal AFFH Rule with suggestions for improvement to more effectively secure fair housing for future generations. The project represents a collaboration between more than a dozen departments, including the Seattle Housing Authority. While a regional collaboration with Seattle's frequent partner King County and its housing authority was considered, given the level of coordination already involved within the city, the city decided not to pursue a regional collaboration.[13]

In 2009, Seattle set out a series of public commitments through the creation of its Race and Social Justice Initiative. Out of this effort came several reports and smaller initiatives, including the Seattle 2035 Growth Management Plan, Seattle 2035 Growth & Equity: Analyzing Impacts on Displacement & Opportunity Related to Seattle's Growth Strategy, and the Mayor's Resolution 31577 committing to racial and social equity.[14] Seattle expands upon these plans in its AFH, using momentum gained over the previous years of work to tackle such issues as education, employment, and economic development. In addition to putting forward a strategy that reaches across multiple city agencies, the plan also effectively builds upon preexisting efforts to advance racial equity to highlight place-based policies as a powerful mechanism to combat inequity in the city. Staff in Seattle thus note that the AFH plays a useful role in helping bring together initiatives already underway:

> It gave yet another way to weave together many, many efforts from many departments and agencies that otherwise would be hard to find in one place, so that is one way in which I think it was a great tool. The report was able to show the many arenas in which fair housing issues have an impact. . . . We always looked at the Assessment of Fair Housing as an ongoing work plan. . . . [I]t was a way to get all those activities organized under one umbrella, and now it's a clearer check list for us.[15]

In contrast to some of the other forty-nine municipalities focusing more intently on mobility-based strategies, Seattle struggled with the tension between place-based investments in existing low-income neighborhoods and the implicit consequence of mobility-based strategies in contributing to ongoing neighborhood change. This tension reflects Seattle's approach to the AFH as just one aspect of a complex web of overlapping policies and legislative attempts to mitigate the history of white supremacy in the city. Seattle's staff critique the AFFH Rule, as follows:

> Members of Seattle's Race and Social Justice Equity Change Teams challenged HUD's prioritizing of integrated neighborhoods in high opportunity white communities as potentially biased toward the dominant culture in and of itself. Many communities struggling with the Assessment of Fair Housing will have to deal with a lack of consensus regarding placing high value on integrated communities while respecting individual choice to reside in communities of affinity whether by race, religion, immigrant status, or community history.[16]

Given this position, Seattle's AFH takes care to focus on a broad conversation about equity. The City of Seattle and the Seattle Housing Authority view the effort as a wide-reaching endeavor, writing that "it was difficult to ensure that the AFH was not limited only to impacts on vulnerable populations. It was necessary to remind agencies, stakeholders, and participants that the AFH is about inequity and potential discrimination regardless of income on a broader scope and scale than in prior planning."[17]

In Seattle, a high-cost city where gentrification and displacement are primary concerns, the struggle to balance place-based and mobility-based initiatives was particularly evident. As Seattle staff note:

> We want people to have a reasonable set of mobility options, but balanced with spending money in areas that aren't the poorest communities, or the communities that were racially and ethnically concentrated areas of poverty. Housing development work has traditionally been tied to trying to restore, reshape, rehab, and create homeownership opportunities in areas that are predominantly low and moderate income communities and therefore have higher percentages of people of color, people who are seniors, [and] people who have disabilities. . . . [W]e don't want to further segregate the city, but neither are we going to walk away from the very real, very serious issues of gentrification that are putting this enormous risk of displacement on certain neighborhoods of the city. . . . We are experiencing what San Francisco and

other major West Coast cities are experiencing. No one with average or lower incomes can afford to live here, and that is putting enormous pressure on the rental population.

The example of Seattle's AFH illustrates how in high-cost cities, anti-displacement efforts and affordable housing preservation investments are a crucial integration strategy. These place-based investments are increasingly essential to ensuring that residents of color, people who are disabled, and others have the opportunity to live in neighborhoods rich with public amenities and economic opportunities. These place-based investments in Seattle have the potential over the long term to be more effective at achieving the central goals of mobility strategies for access to opportunity than a mobility strategy could be, as central-city housing costs continue to rise. Seattle's plan also includes goals related to housing mobility, although without clear measurable objectives. For example, an explicit goal of Seattle's AFH focuses on providing more housing choices for families, for which the policy prescriptions range from funding larger units to offering financial assistance to families looking to live in higher-opportunity areas. These strategies are part of a greater effort to mitigate the dearth of properties available to larger households in Seattle's existing housing stock but are less structured than in some other jurisdictions' AFHs.

These mobility-related goals are part of a careful balance in Seattle's AFH between place-based and mobility goals. On the whole, Seattle makes a case for mobility to high-opportunity neighborhoods as a potential alternative to gentrification-induced displacement to high-poverty neighborhoods, a source of much community disruption in Seattle. Notably, the Seattle Housing Authority is also participating in the national "Creating Moves to Opportunity" project, an evaluation of its mobility interventions, with the Abdul Latif Jameel Poverty Action Lab.[18] These concurrent projects allow the city to fully absorb its work on Creating Moves to Opportunity into an effort that focuses on mobility as a tool for fair housing. Seattle also creates a number of goals focusing on place-based investments, particularly those that can improve housing quality and prevent displacement caused by gentrification. Seattle highlights a number of ways it is working to mitigate displacement by building medium-term affordability into the portfolios of high-displacement neighborhoods and by supporting low-income and marginalized individuals at risk of displacement. The place-based goals address a number of different areas of focus, including equitable access to schools, environmental justice, and affordable housing.

Seattle also uses its AFH to highlight some of the limitations of the process, in scope and in execution. Seattle's AFH challenges HUD on several of its metrics, including the widely used dissimilarity index, generally implemented to measure segregation but limited to measuring the geographic dispersion of only two groups at a time. In its AFH, Seattle notes that the metric's comparison of communities of color to white communities limits the city's ability to truly assess the diversity of its neighborhoods. As an example, its 2017 assessment cites a number of neighborhoods in which a diverse group of people of color are the majority (South Park, High Point, Rainier Valley, Pioneer Square, the International District, First Hill, and the Central Area), noting that just using a white–non-white dissimilarity measure does not reflect the diversity of many of the city's neighborhoods.[19]

Seattle pushes HUD to consider new measures in other parts of its AFH, including measuring Racially and Ethnically Concentrated Areas of Poverty (R/ECAPs). In particular, staff note that "changes in R/ECAP status can happen solely as an artifact of the large margins of error inherent in the American Community Survey (ACS) estimates used to test for R/ECAP status. This suggests a need to consider neighborhood demographic and socioeconomic conditions in a more holistic way that goes beyond ACS estimates."[20] In addition, given Seattle's articulation of a long-term strategy advancing racial equity, the city already has detailed knowledge of the data representing its communities. As described in its AFH, Seattle's engagement strategy was held up for four months due to an inconsistent inclusion of data "from the 1990, 2000, and 2010 Census regarding multi-racial individuals. This population represents approximately 5 percent of Seattle's total population. The lack of this data could potentially skew results for concentrations by race and ethnicity."[21] Seattle notes a number of other limitations to the AFH process. Given that Seattle is one of the first municipalities to submit an AFH, staff note that they did not receive the assessment of fair housing mapping and database tool until four months into the process.[22]

Despite these drawbacks, Seattle staff note that many parts of the AFH are immensely beneficial—namely, the value of the data and maps provided by HUD, which staff use in community meetings to create a "much richer dialogue" than would exist otherwise. The maps are particularly beneficial to the community process:

> To be completely cliché, a picture says a thousand words. . . . [W]e had two or three of the most key maps, mostly based on the racial and ethnic segregation and integration by neighborhood, made up into handouts and big billboards . . . and held these ice cream socials. And that was one of the most satisfying community engagement initiatives I've participated in in 35 years of being a public servant, because it was with people, the kids are sitting there making a mess on the end of the table, and having a great time, and their parents were relaxed. . . . We didn't ask them specific questions, we

just asked, "Can you take a look at this map and then give us your reaction?" And that led to some fairly extraordinary conversations, many of which are highlighted in the community engagement section of our plan. But if we hadn't had that tool, to some extent in a forced way, specifically looking at the effect of public and private actions on the demographics of our city, geographically displayed, there's no way . . . we could have gotten down to the level of information that we did, in a glance at a map. It took all this statistical stuff, and made it very plain English, and very direct.[23]

Seattle's staff note that by freezing the rule, HUD is preventing the city from tracking trends over time. This issue is particularly important because, as a result of the AFHs being submitted before HUD's suspension of the rule, Seattle is actually required to integrate its AFH goals into its Consolidated Plan and report on progress toward those goals. But without the updated data, Seattle's task becomes much more difficult. Staff in Seattle also note that HUD's freezing of the rule is creating a large amount of uncertainty about future work on the AFH Rule in terms of losing momentum around these issues and figuring out next steps. Also, in terms of implementation, Seattle notes that the AFH adds particular value around disability issues. As a result of the process, the rule gives departments the ability to raise those issues with more urgency.[24]

Overall, Seattle's AFH has a clear focus on racial equity and sets out meaningful goals to advance fair housing. The Seattle strategy addresses a balance between the place-based strategies that support vulnerable communities and the option to move to high-opportunity neighborhoods that individuals who experience poverty may also choose. The AFH illustrates how this balance is complicated in a high-cost city, where the significant need for place-based anti-displacement work could also be considered a strategy to promote integration and preserve neighborhood diversity. The fact that a high-capacity city such as Seattle finds HUD's data so useful—and argues for the need to bring the datasets back to allow for continued implementation of the AFFH Rule—speaks to the power of data and mapping in the AFH process to help governments have more impact within their communities.

Temecula: A Relationship with HUD Breeds Better Results

Temecula, California, was one of seventeen municipalities to receive a letter of "non-acceptance" from HUD. HUD's review of the AFH found that Temecula's initial submission in October 2015 had vague metrics that were occasionally beyond the jurisdiction's purview, prompting HUD to ask for a revision that Temecula submitted in January 2017.

Temecula's initial AFH features nine goals that are not clearly tied to the required analysis of the HUD-provided data. Goals in the AFH should be tied to contributing factors that affect the current state of fair housing in the jurisdiction authoring the plan—such issues as lending discrimination, land-use and zoning laws, or lack of regional cooperation. In the original AFH, some goals have contributing factors that are not supported by the analysis the city has conducted in the AFH, and the goals are framed in terms of regional programs that are not within Temecula's power to control. Temecula staff note that part of the reason for those vague goals is a lack of clarity about exactly what municipalities should include as part of their fair housing goals. As one staff member notes:

> We understood the necessity for the metrics, but what we had trouble communicating to them . . . was what is in our control, and what is out of our control. . . . [W]hat would happen to us if we didn't meet these metrics? We also didn't want to be overly optimistic, and then what if the market crashed again? And we had very little control over any of these things. They also could not tell us what would happen if we didn't meet these metrics.[25]

This question points toward a difficulty that a number of municipalities encounter in balancing the need for measurable, meaningful goals with actions that they can realistically achieve. Temecula staff also note that since HUD itself was also figuring out how to implement the AFH Rule during the process, writing the AFH led to an increased burden on staff time.[26]

HUD proposed a range of changes to Temecula's AFH after the initial submission, adding new and relevant contributing factors and focusing on goals and policies that were actually within the power of the Temecula City Council or city agencies to achieve. For example, Temecula's second draft removes goals addressing access and usage of the regional public transportation network. These revisions are not a statement about these goals' importance to fair housing but allow Temecula to focus on those aspects of the AFH that the municipality has the jurisdiction and resources to change. In an interview, Temecula staff note that they included that original goal because they thought the maps showed that transportation issues were an obstacle to achieving fair housing—but once HUD clarified the importance of focusing on actions within the city's control, they simply removed it.[27] This back and forth indicates that in some cases, municipalities trying in good faith to comply with the regulations had difficulty interpreting HUD's mandate.

HUD also urged Temecula to revise some original goals for more clarity, including such vague pronouncements as "Increase the affordable housing stock in the City."[28] In its revised goal, Temecula provides much more specificity, proposing instead an Affordable Housing Overlay "accommodating 2,007 affordable units for lower income households."[29] This careful look at the goals of the AFH led to a more robust and actionable set of aims in Temecula's revision, grounded in data, metrics, and realistic hopes of achievement. Each goal in Temecula's new AFH is followed by a detailed discussion, demonstrating the research behind the goal and the precedents that make pursuing this goal possible. In contrast to some other AFHs with a large number of goals, Temecula's final version has only four, which could make the plan more comprehensible to a broad audience and therefore more manageable to implement. Although they are targeted in their focus, Temecula staff put forth a number of measurable actions under those four categories.

Beyond the improvements to the AFH, HUD's technical assistance seemed to foster a positive relationship between HUD and Temecula.[30] City officials made great use of the technical assistance available to them through HUD, ultimately completing three rounds of revisions. Temecula staff indicate that the short time frame between revisions and an initial lack of mutual understanding about the requirements of the process led to some strain, but that overall they perceived the AFFH process as positive.

Temecula staff describe a few ways that this process facilitates future implementation. The AFH caused them to examine issues they would not have considered previously, including the strengths and weaknesses of their housing programs. Specifically, as with Seattle, their fair housing analysis revealed issues related to access for people with disabilities. They identified a need for more affordable housing for their special-needs residents. Similarly, the process pushed Temecula to complete an Americans with Disabilities Act transition plan.[31]

Hidalgo: A Wide Lens, a Less Effective Focus?

One innovation of the AFH process is to encourage regional collaborations between local jurisdictions. In the next two case studies, we examine two regional submissions. First, we examine Hidalgo County, Texas, a county on the U.S.-Mexico border with a median household income of $37,000 (one of the lowest among initial AFH submissions). As with Temecula, HUD initially rejected Hidalgo's submission. However, unlike Temecula, Hidalgo was still in the process of submitting a revision when HUD suspended the AFFH Rule. The first submission completed in October 2017 includes coordination between nineteen program participants, including fourteen housing authorities operating within the county. The community engagement efforts are robust, including about three hundred local stakeholders and organizations throughout the region, in addition to a survey of nearly six hundred community members representing all zip codes in Hidalgo County and several in-person community meetings. However, this incredibly wide net may have also contributed to the lack of specificity in Hidalgo's AFH that spurred the eventual request from HUD to submit a revised draft.

Although the AFH was submitted using Hidalgo County as the geographic boundary, the submission includes the efforts of the five entitlement communities in the McAllen-Edinburg-Mission Metropolitan Statistical Area (a geography defined by the Census as containing a significant population as well as adjacent communities connected to that population hub), including the Hidalgo County Urban County Program, and Cities of Edinburg, McAllen, Mission, and Pharr. Each of the five entities entered into a Collaborative Interlocal Agreement with the fourteen public housing authorities active within each of their jurisdictions. This regional partnership is not new to Hidalgo County; these particular entitlement communities have collaborated several times for other federal initiatives, including three previous Consolidated Plans. However, this particular effort is the first to include the Public Housing Authorities (PHAs), expanding their capacity to speak to issues of fair housing. Staff in the Hidalgo County Urban County Program explain that the housing authorities signed onto the proposal because of this history of regional collaboration and because it would reduce the regulatory burden, especially for small housing authorities with little staff support.[32]

Because the number of participants is so large—by far the largest participant cohort in any of the forty-nine submissions—a governing structure was created to coordinate efforts. Hidalgo County Urban County Program led the effort, with the cities of Edinburg, McAllen, Mission, and Pharr as well as the Housing Authorities of the County of Hidalgo, Edinburg, McAllen, Mission, and Pharr rounding out the executive committee. Each of the remaining nine housing authorities composed a "General Committee." To complete the work, Hidalgo County initiated a structure intended to meet the needs of each area of the AFH. Each committee member served on a number of subject-matter subcommittees, including education, transportation, poverty, disability and access, and others.

Hidalgo County's goals include affordable housing, infrastructure improvements, social services, economic development, and public facilities. However, the county fails to fully explain what interventions the collaboration aims to implement and how. For example, Goal #6 reads "To expand economic opportunities in Hidalgo County," yet the metrics and milestones remain vague, noting that participants would "support goals and projects identified within provider's long-term strategy," among other interventions.[33] Ultimately, Hidalgo County's AFH reflects competing interests: each of its nineteen parties has a particular commitment to the issues affecting that specific jurisdiction, leading to a lack of clarity about overall goals for the entire county.

An interview with staff reveals further reasons for vague metrics, which speak again to the conflicting incentives that municipalities face when developing fair housing goals, especially in a regional context. Staff note:

> Over the course of a year and a half of this project . . . there [were] 19 players involved, but three to four organizations were . . . almost nonexistent. And when [we were] drawing up our goals . . . we were very leery of putting those organizations on record, not knowing whether or not they're going to do their part. And if they didn't do their part, we felt, because this was a whole new document, we didn't know what the repercussions were, that if we had some participants not doing their part, how would that affect us, those that are doing their part. And that was unknown, and because that was unknown, we left it. We knew that there was going to be some clarification that was going to be required of us, and maybe we could work that out, but it didn't, and it got denied. . . . [T]hat's the backstory as to why our document didn't get approved.[34]

Within two months of their initial October 2017 submission, the Hidalgo County Collaborating Program Participants received a letter from HUD requesting specific revisions of the AFH "to meet the requirements under the AFFH rule." Although they were one of several to receive this notice to resubmit, they were one of only a small group of jurisdictions asked to submit a revision in late 2017. This initial letter was sent on December 12, 2017, but by January 5, 2018, it proved a moot point once HUD moved to suspend the AFFH Rule. As a result, the Hidalgo team never had the opportunity to work with HUD, as Temecula did, to improve its AFH.

Although Hidalgo County's revised AFH was stymied by federal policy changes, the letter still serves as an illustrative window into the aims of the program, particularly for those jurisdictions with such wide-ranging regional aspirations. In Hidalgo County's case, much of HUD's feedback focused on issues related to goal setting. Because the range of participants was so broad, they proposed goals that lacked specific and quantifiable metrics and milestones or responsible parties, thus making the goals much more difficult to enforce. HUD's revision letter to Hidalgo County recommends that the collaborative revise each goal to make it easier to evaluate and to ensure that the participants would actually reinforce fair housing throughout their individual geographies and the entire jurisdiction overall. Hidalgo

County's staff note that, had they been able to proceed with the AFH, they would have required those actors who had been absent from the process to actually implement the goals in their revised fair housing plan.[35]

Despite the arrested development of Hidalgo County's plan due to HUD's freezing of the AFFH Rule, staff there say the process was a vast improvement over the previous AI requirements. They note that they were able to learn a lot about their community through the local data they were required to collect as part of the process and through their community outreach. The rule freeze was therefore disappointing.[36]

Kansas City: An Ambitious Regional Plan

Like Hidalgo, Kansas City, Missouri, submitted a regional assessment. This regional collaboration included the five cities in the metropolitan area: Kansas City, Missouri; Kansas City, Kansas; Independence, Missouri; Blue Springs, Missouri; and Leavenworth, Kansas. This coalition built upon past engagement with the Mid-America Regional Council (MARC), the area's regional planning organization; the Regional Equity Network; and others. Notably, creating this plan entailed coordination across state lines. Yet despite such complex challenges of coordination, the partners were able to concentrate their efforts during the summer of 2016 and produce an ambitious and rigorous AFH, as measured by the number of goals with a quantifiable metric or new policy.

Kansas City's plan builds on a more established and robust regional planning body—MARC—than existed in Hidalgo County; indeed, MARC is the principal author of the plan. MARC staff explain that because of Kansas City's past regional collaboration, HUD urged it to again collaborate regionally in the AFH process.[37] Kansas City's regional focus enables the area to take a broad look at patterns of concentrated poverty and segregation. With this broad lens, it finds variation in patterns across areas of concentrated poverty in different parts of the region, noting that patterns of high concentrations of poverty are particularly severe in Kansas City, Missouri, and in Kansas City, Kansas. The other four cities within the regional AFH lack the same levels of segregation—a finding that could only have been recognized with a regional lens. Suburban areas in the region have the jobs and educational opportunities these cities lack—but without the public transit and affordable housing necessary to connect people to those opportunities. The fractured nature of school districts in the region and school residency requirements further reinforce racial disparities in opportunity.

Much as in Seattle, staff at MARC take issue with the definitions of R/ECAPs. In this case, staff find that many areas that fall slightly below the thresholds are, in fact, quite disadvantaged.[38] However, the staff believe that the AFH process was a vast improvement over the previous AI regime:

> The AI was very focused on looking at intentional acts of discrimination, and how to address those, where the AFH was really about institutional and historic racism, and the resulting consequences of those policies and actions, and what could communities do to help people get connected to economic and other opportunities. So, it was a much broader view of the problems that people in urban places face—well, and even suburban places—and how to help, what policies communities could take . . . to address them.[39]

Even more than its regional analysis, Kansas City's fair housing goals are particularly noteworthy for their clarity. First, Kansas City divides its goals into multiple sections that emphasize the importance of fair housing work at the local and regional levels. In its "local goals" section, each of the five participating cities focuses on specific AFFH measures unique to the locality. Then, in the "regional goals" section, the collaborative puts forward specific measures that apply across all the program participants and that try to forge greater regional equity, such as working with local housing authorities to explore a regional approach to using vouchers, including a regional housing locator service; creating model zoning codes that all the smaller city participants could implement to increase their housing stock; developing incentive policies to create more affordable housing in higher-opportunity areas; and better connecting transit with affordable housing and employment centers.

For example, the first regional goal in Kansas City's plan is to "expand the use of Community Development Financial Institutions and New Market Tax Credits in neighborhoods with concentrations of persons in protected classes and low income residents." This strategy involves convening the Local Initiatives Support Corporation, AltCap, other sources of capital, MARC, and the participating localities to develop a plan of action. This type of convening across municipalities and sectors is a powerful example of how municipalities can use the AFH as a convening tool to start collaborations. By specifying the jurisdiction responsible for each goal, Kansas City's AFH makes tracking progress and ensuring accountability much more likely.

Overall, Kansas City has twenty-three goals with quantifiable metrics or new policies—an indication of a potentially rigorous fair housing plan. Even so, staff note that a number of the communities outside Kansas City have very modest goals, even those related to initiatives they are already undertaking. Staff note this circumstance occurs because they were advised not to include goals that they could not begin to implement within five years. This highlights again the conflicting incentives facing municipalities in setting up goals, especially in a regional context. Kansas City, like Hidalgo County, has a regional plan for which some lower-capacity, less-motivated municipalities contributed less-ambitious goals. Unlike Hidalgo County, Kansas City's carefully designed AFH, with separate regional and local goals, yields ambitious, quantifiable regional objectives even as it exposes some variation in the robustness of local goals.

Kansas City's goals tend to be placed-based but also include mobility efforts, attempts to create mixed-income communities, goals to combat displacement, and zoning changes. Staff note that the push for place-based initiatives came from the community engagement process:

> It struck me as naive on HUD's part, that suggesting that people who lived in disadvantaged areas, that if we could figure out how to move them to areas of opportunity, they would do better. Their children would do better, they would have better access to jobs, and other crime-free neighborhoods. So, all of that seems like it might make sense, but we did 25 public meetings, and in many of them people said, "We don't want to move. We like our neighborhood; we just wish it were better. We wish it were safer, we wish our housing stock was better. We wish there were better community services, but we don't necessarily want to move." I remember one meeting in particular. You probably noticed, but we have an East-West dividing line along the street called Troost, which was historically, Blacks lived to the East, and whites to the West. There were folks who would say, "Well, I would move West of Troost, but I would not move across the state line, which is only about two miles away, to Johnson County, Kansas, where the opportunities might be even better." So, they wanted to stay near their community. Somehow, we need all communities to be healthy, and that means lifting up the disadvantaged communities to the standard of the opportunity.[40]

In the long run, MARC staff view the AFFH as the first step in a long-term process to educate the public and shift the opinions of wealthy households around fair housing issues—to demonstrate "that affordable housing doesn't lead to a disaster in your community if you accept low-income people." They also note that, separate from the AFH process, a movement around affordable housing and access to opportunity has been growing in Kansas City that could support further implementation in the future.

In terms of ways to improve the AFFH process, Kanas City staff cite funding to go along with the AFFH mandate as a key improvement that could be made. Funding would have been preferable to technical assistance, in their view. They also recommend allowing communities to use their own data instead of HUD's where they are more helpful. This perspective varies from that of other municipalities discussed in this chapter, which welcomed HUD's data even as they supplemented them with local data. Regarding implementation, MARC also pointed toward the importance of how the AFH is incorporated into the Consolidated Plan process. MARC staff note that they are tracking progress on regional goals but not on the local goals of each community.[41] However, staff note that the localities are keeping track of local implementation because the AFFH Rule requires reporting to HUD in their Consolidated Plans.[42]

Kansas City's AFH shows that it is possible to develop an ambitious regional fair housing plan. It also reveals how high-capacity cities may interpret the AFH document differently but still develop equally thoughtful assessments of fair housing. Seattle's document, as noted above, spends far more time than Kansas City's discussing fair housing in the context of its broader racial equity work. The Kansas City regional AFH has less discussion of racial equity and social inclusion than Seattle's but is more focused on specific measurable objectives in its fair housing goals. Both plans are carefully thought out and include ambitious, measurable objectives related to furthering fair housing, and both were accepted by HUD. The very different approaches in these AFHs exemplify the latitude that the AFFH Rule gives grantees to shape fair housing plans according to their own local needs. These and the rest of the AFHs suggest that one of the main reasons that the Trump administration cited for rolling back the AFFH Rule—that it limits local flexibility—is not accurate. On the contrary, we observe municipalities setting out goals to fulfill the AFFH Rule in ways that suit their particular municipal needs.

Looking Forward

Overall, we find that the municipalities put forward a range of creative goals to affirmatively further fair housing, including measurable objectives and innovative new policies intended to make access to place-based resources, such as high-performing schools or access to jobs, more equitable. For many municipalities, the AFFH process began by engaging in a lengthy series of community engagements that helped produce these original fair housing goals. Some municipalities initially failed to meet the AFFH Rule's standards but then worked with HUD to improve their plans. Although this process was not perfect in all cases, overall, the municipalities' staff members we spoke with reported positive experiences with the rule and disappointment in HUD's action to freeze it. The oversight from HUD and the technical assistance that this agency and other nonprofit organizations provided speak to the importance of these continuing oversight and technical assistance roles. Certainly, there is room for improvement in the AFFH Rule, as likely would be the case with any new major federal requirement. Our conversations with municipalities' staff members engaged in the AFH process speak to ways in which the rule could be improved in the future, were it to be reinstated, as do subsequent chapters in this book. Contrary to HUD's justifications for suspending it, overall, the AFFH Rule in the first forty-nine submissions appears to be an important starting point for creating meaningful action plans that focus on positive, measurable results. Future research is needed to determine how effective these plans are at guiding municipalities to implement these policy changes.

Indeed, despite federal retrenchment, many municipalities have been proceeding voluntarily with their own AFHs. From New York City to Dallas to Denver to Boston, cities are continuing to fulfill the promise of the AFFH Rule. Future research could focus on how cities are responding to this regulatory uncertainty and the variations we see in these self-driven AFH processes. It also raises questions for academics and practitioners about how best to support these efforts and encourage more municipalities to participate.

Our research has made us hopeful for the future of efforts to affirmatively further fair housing. After a half century of virtual inaction at the local level to combat entrenched patterns of segregation and racial inequality, many of the municipalities we studied are making concerted efforts to take steps toward real change for their residents. We find that many municipalities have risen to the occasion to produce innovative goals to increase access to opportunity in their communities. We hope this chapter provides an evidence base for policy makers in the future looking to revive the 2015 AFFH Rule or perhaps adopt some form of the AFH in their own communities.

ENDNOTES

1. Justin P. Steil and Nicholas F. Kelly, "The Fairest of Them All: Analyzing Affirmatively Furthering Fair Housing Compliance," *Housing Policy Debate* 29, no. 1 (2019): 85–105, available at https://doi.org/10.1080/10511482.2018.1469527.

2. Justin P. Steil and Nicholas F. Kelly, "Survival of the Fairest: Examining HUD Reviews of Assessments of Fair Housing," *Housing Policy Debate* 29, no. 5 (2019): 736–751, available at https://doi.org/10.1080/10511482.2018.1524444.

3. "Residential Segregation Data for U.S. Metro Areas," available at https://www.governing.com/gov-data/education-data/residential-racial-segregation-metro-areas.html.

4. William C. Baer, "General Plan Evaluation Criteria: An Approach to Making Better Plans," *Journal of the American Planning Association* 63, no. 3 (1997): 329–344; Philip R. Berke and Steven P. French, "The Influence of State Planning Mandates on Local Plan Quality," *Journal of Planning Education and Research* 13, no. 4 (1994):

237–250; Philip Berke and David Godschalk, "Searching for the Good Plan: A Meta-analysis of Plan Quality Studies," *Journal of Planning Literature* 23, no. 3 (2009): 227–240; Philip R. Berke, "Enhancing Plan Quality: Evaluating the Role of State Planning Mandates for Natural Hazard Mitigation," *Journal of Environmental Planning and Management* 39, no. 1 (2010): 79–96.

5. Baer, "General Plan Evaluation Criteria," 1997; Berke and Godschalk, "Searching for the Good Plan," 2009.

6. Focusing on new policies is not a perfect metric, in that it overlooks municipalities that are already implementing existing, effective fair housing policies (see Chapter 5). We nevertheless believe that new policies created to achieve AFFH goals are still a relevant indication of a more robust AFH, one in which the process of creating it has generated new approaches to furthering fair housing. Another reason why we might believe that new policies are indications of strong plans: given the historic lack of enforcement of fair housing, it would be reasonable to expect many jurisdictions undergoing the AFH to discover fair housing issues for which they do not yet have policy solutions.

7. Cary Coglianese and Evan Mendelson, "Meta-Regulation and Self-Regulation," in *The Oxford Handbook on Regulation*, ed. Martin Cave, Robert Baldwin, and Martin Lodge (Oxford: Oxford University Press, 2010), 146–168.

8. Gabe Rubin, "Democrats Laud HUD's Fair-Housing Rule, Republicans Try to Block Funding," *Morning Consult*, July 10, 2015, available at https://morningconsult.com /2015/07/10/democrats-laud-huds-fair-housing-rule-republicans-try-to-block-funding/.

9. Michael H. Schill and Samantha Friedman, "The Fair Housing Amendments Act of 1988: The First Decade," *Cityscape: A Journal of Policy Development and Research* 4, no. 3 (1999): 57–78; Robert G. Schwemm, "Overcoming Structural Barriers to Integrated Housing: A Back-to-the-Future Reflection on the Fair Housing Act's Affirmatively Further Mandate," *Kentucky Law Journal* 100 (2011): 125–176; John Yinger, "Sustaining the Fair Housing Act," *Cityscape: A Journal of Policy Development and Research* 4, no. 3 (1999): 93–106.

10. Steil and Kelly, "The Fairest of Them All."

11. Sharon Gilad, "It Runs in the Family: Meta-regulation and Its Siblings," *Regulation and Governance* 4, no. 4 (2010): 485–506.

12. Chris Tausanovitch and Christopher Warshaw, *American Ideology Project*, 2015, available at http://www.americanideologyproject.com.

13. City of Seattle and Seattle Housing Authority.

14. These documents from Seattle's Race and Social Justice Initiative are available at https://www.seattle.gov/rsji; see also, 2017 City of Seattle and Seattle Housing Authority Joint Assessment of Fair Housing, available at: https://www.seattle.gov/housing /data-and-reports.

15. Debra Rhinehart, strategic adviser, Department of Human Services, interview, November 15, 2019.

16. Ibid.

17. City of Seattle and Seattle Housing Authority.

18. "Creating Moves to Opportunity | The Abdul Latif Jameel Poverty Action Lab," available at https://www.povertyactionlab.org/na/cmto.

19. City of Seattle and Seattle Housing Authority.

20. Rhinehart interview.

21. City of Seattle and Seattle Housing Authority.

22. Rhinehart interview.

23. Ibid.

24. Ibid.

25. Lynn Lehner, Temecula, interview, November 5, 2019.

26. Ibid.

27. Ibid.

28. U.S. Department of Housing and Urban Development, "Response to Temecula, CA Regarding Revision of AFH," November 30, 2016.

29. City of Temecula, "City of Temecula: Final Assessment of Fair Housing," report (City of Temecula, September 2016).

30. Ibid.

31. Lehner interview.

32. Steven de la Garza, Hidalgo County Urban County Program, interview, November 26, 2019.

33. Hidalgo County, "Hidalgo County, Texas Regional Assessment of Fair Housing," 2017.

34. Garza interview.

35. Ibid.

36. Ibid.

37. Marlene Nagel and Frank Lenk, Mid-America Regional Council, interview, November 25, 2019.

38. Ibid.

39. Ibid.

40. Ibid.

41. Ibid.

42. Ibid.

Protests

4

Affirmatively Furthering Fair Housing

Are There Reasons for Skepticism?

HOWARD HUSOCK

It is not difficult to understand the motivations of the federal Affirmatively Furthering Fair Housing (AFFH) Rule. Notwithstanding two generations of anti-discrimination "fair housing" policy enforcement, the minority poor in the United States continue to be disproportionately concentrated, residentially, in disadvantaged neighborhoods. This circumstance, in turn, can influence adult access to employment and, perhaps more significantly, limit access of disadvantaged children to the higher-performing schools found in more affluent communities.[1] The AFFH Rule itself emphasizes the latter point, stating as a normative goal that "no child's ZIP code should determine her opportunity to achieve." What distinguishes the AFFH Rule from historic fair housing strategies or anti-discrimination efforts is its obligatory nature for communities that accept Department of Housing and Urban Development (HUD) funding. As HUD puts it, "The final rule helps to facilitate communities relying on local knowledge and local decision-making to determine best strategies for meeting their fair housing *obligations* at the local level—including making place-based investments to revitalize distressed areas, or expanding access to quality affordable housing *throughout* a community" [emphasis added].[2]

Using the leverage of federal funding to support the construction of affordable housing (meaning subsidized, whether directly or indirectly) in relatively high-income communities and to use such housing to deconcentrate poverty is strong medicine, to be sure. A new generation of social science research, however, suggests that such an approach holds the promise of successfully addressing social problems—including, for instance, race-linked housing patterns and minority access to good public schools—that have long seemed intractable. As HUD has stated, in reference to covered jurisdictions:

> The approach provided by this rule is intended to make program participants better able to evaluate their present environment to assess fair housing issues such as segregation, conditions that restrict fair housing choice, and disparities in access to housing and opportunity, identify the factors that primarily contribute to the creation or perpetuation of fair housing issues, and establish fair housing priorities and goals.[3]

This chapter acknowledges and reviews recent research that provides support for an AFFH approach before going on to express skepticism about it. My skepticism disputes neither the findings nor (in any major way) the methodology of the relevant research. Rather, I question the practicality of bringing AFFH policy to scale, in part because of the difficulty of tailoring policy such that those most likely to benefit are those targeted by the program. I take the view that, notwithstanding its name, affirmatively furthering fair housing is less about "fair housing"—in terms of nondiscrimination, equal opportunity, and racial/ethnic integration—and more about a model to improve the life chances, and the prospect of upward mobility, for those who participate in the program; in other words, zip code should not define prospects. The arguments that follow express skepticism especially in this context. Specifically, I raise questions concerning the program's implicit but, I argue, central assumptions: that little can be done to ameliorate conditions in disadvantaged zip codes and that "deconcentration" of their residents should be prescribed. The chapter puts such an approach in the context of past public policies that, I argue, have undermined the social and physical capital of lower-income neighborhoods, undermined minority asset building, and, in effect, resisted the idea, endorsed here, that poor neighborhoods can be good neighborhoods—conditioned, crucially, on the provision of public goods in the form of a full range of effective public services.

Affirmatively Furthering Fair Housing Rationale and Related Evaluation Research

The research findings that have provided support for AFFH-type policy have not, to be sure, examined the effects of the AFFH Rule itself, the final version of which was promulgated by HUD only in mid-2015 and implemented only briefly before its suspension. Rather, they are based in studies of the experimental HUD program Moving to Opportunity for Fair Housing (MTO), which, between 1997 and 2005, offered randomly selected households in high-poverty public housing projects the opportunity to move to low-poverty neighborhoods through the use of housing vouchers that allowed for rental of housing with private landlords, with rent capped at 30 percent of household income. Research based on evaluation of the MTO program has taken a variety of forms over the past decade, and recent positive results have emerged only over time, after a first round of studies observed only modestly positive effects, if any. Jeffrey Kling, Jeffrey Liebman, and Lawrence Katz found, for instance, in 2005, that "housing mobility by itself does not appear to be an effective anti-poverty strategy—at least over a five-year horizon. The MTO demonstration program was motivated by theories and non-experimental empirical results suggesting that there would be large economic gains from moving to lower-poverty neighborhoods." However, they "found no consistent evidence of treatment effects on adult earnings or welfare participation. Whether economic gains begin to appear in the longer run, particularly among MTO children, remains to be seen."[4]

Other research has found that significant housing market distortions that disadvantage those not participating in the program cannot be ruled out. A 2015 study concludes that increases in the number of voucher holders may drive up rents such that they conform to the amount the voucher covers—to the potential detriment of lower-income, nonvoucher households.[5]

Skeptical accounts have, however, given way to new research that shows more positive results. Recent work by Raj Chetty, Nathaniel Hendren, and Lawrence Katz has led to significant enthusiasm for an MTO-style deconcentration approach. Using a longitudinal analysis, they find that MTO offers important long-term promise. Specifically, they conclude that the children of MTO participant households earn significantly more as young adults than would otherwise have been expected. They write:

> Moving to a lower-poverty neighborhood significantly improves college attendance rates and earnings for children who were young (below age 13) when their families moved. These children also live in better neighborhoods themselves as adults and are less likely to become single parents. The treatment effects are substantial: children whose families take up an experimental voucher to move to a lower-poverty area when they are less than 13 years old have an annual income that is $3,477 (31 percent) higher on average relative to a mean of $11,270 in the control group in their mid-twenties.[6]

Another analysis that also draws on MTO may help explain such findings: "As households move from high-poverty to low-poverty tracts via the MTO rent subsidy, their rent falls and their child value-add rises." Consequently, "policy-makers can significantly affect child outcomes as long as housing vouchers directly target high-value-added neighborhoods."[7] Even voucher holders who were not part of the MTO experiment are said to be likely to choose neighborhoods with better schools when they have children reaching school age.[8] Morris Davis, Jesse Gregory, Daniel Hartley, and Kegon Tan go on to suggest that "large-scale adoption" of voucher-based programs could have such positive effects.[9] The AFFH Rule would seem to be a first step in such a direction.

Methodological Reasons for Skepticism

Nonetheless, even if one accepts the findings of Chetty, Hendren, and Katz as persuasive about the potential value of poverty deconcentration on the MTO model, some skepticism is still in order. First, it is worth noting that in the MTO program, although public housing residents were randomly selected for the offer of housing vouchers that would allow them to move to higher-income neighborhoods, the moves were entirely voluntary. Thus, the assumption that these same households would not have thrived in public housing—or ultimately stayed—is open to question. In addition, on an implementation level, serious questions exist about the practicality of a scaled-up AFFH-type program. Chetty, Hendren, and Katz note that

> the same moves [to higher-income neighborhoods] have, if anything, negative long-term impacts on children who are more than 13 years old when their families move, perhaps because of the disruption effects of moving to a very different environment. The gains from moving fall with the age when children move, consistent with recent evidence that the duration of exposure to a better environment during childhood is a key determinant of an individual's long-term outcomes.[10]

It is hard, however, to imagine a federal program for which eligibility, for instance, would be limited to narrow population bands (typically, aid programs are based on household income) or that requires quick and ongoing adaptation to market conditions (e.g., adjusting rents such that they do not distort the nonsubsidized market).

Practical Reasons for Concern

Further, it is important to keep in mind that, notwithstanding the relatively large magnitude of federal spending on housing choice vouchers (at $19 billion annually, its appropriation exceeds that of cash public assistance, for instance), it is not an entitlement program and thus does not serve all those households that would qualify simply on the basis of income. Robert Collinson, Ingrid Ellen, and Jens Ludwig[11] estimate that of 19 million renters with incomes below 50 percent of area median, only 4.6 million receive any form of federal housing assistance, and 2.2 million of these receive housing vouchers. Thus, only one in four of those eligible currently receive housing assistance.[12] Expansion to serve the universe of the income-eligible could thus require nearly $100 billion annually or more.[13] One must conclude that scaling up the program to serve the universe of low-income households, as well as to make it possible for the recipients to be dispersed to higher-income neighborhoods, is extremely unlikely. Indeed, Congress has consistently declined to support relatively small budget increases for the program, such as one proposed by the Barack Obama administration to increase the voucher budget to $21.2 billion.[14]

The Unwritten Rules of the Housing Market

Moreover, such extensive intervention in the lives of individual low-income households and in higher-income neighborhoods must work against powerful and perennial tides in the socioeconomic character of the housing market. First, low-income households may not prefer to move to low-poverty areas, in which they would be atypical. As Ellen observes, "Social ties also likely play a role in potentially limiting the neighborhoods considered by voucher households. If people choose to locate near family and friends, and disadvantaged individuals tend to have disadvantaged social networks located in higher-poverty neighborhoods, then this may restrict where voucher families look for housing."[15] Low-income households, in other words, may value other aspects of neighborhood life, such as proximity to religious institutions and family members, even more than school-system quality.

Further, large-scale dispersion of low-income households to higher-income neighborhoods must be considered in the context of historic residential housing patterns and choices, which are largely shaped by socioeconomic status. This informal but powerful system has long been recognized by scholars. P. H. Rees observes that "socioeconomic status is a universal sorting principal in American cities."[16] Michael White notes, further, that residence is related to a household's sense of status: "Educational attainment and occupation are good overall indicators of a neighborhood's status. The level of income, correlated with these two characteristics, is the most direct indicator of a household's ability to 'purchase' status, or at least purchase a residence in what is regarded as a high status neighborhood."[17] Put another way, one's residence is not just a means to purchase a package of publicly provided amenities; it is regarded as evidence of achievement and accomplishment. Indeed, community residents may well not regard the quality of life in their community as neither immutable nor inevitable nor as evidence of "privilege."

Communities whose services are viewed by the AFFH Rule as appropriate to be shared may be viewed by residents as the result not simply of affluence but of ongoing community effort: school board oversight, parental involvement, code enforcement, policing. Communities, in the context of such local control, expect new entrants to share such values and to contribute to what may be voluntary efforts; capacity to afford to buy or rent in a community is seen as a marker of such capacity.

Although discrimination based on race and ethnicity arguably require efforts, such as the AFFH Rule, its effects can be overemphasized. As Anna Hardman and Yannis Ioannides write:

> For the vast majority of U.S. households, neighbors' incomes and other characteristics are the market-driven outcome of individual choices. Households' tastes for housing space, quality and access to jobs and amenities, together with their incomes and assets, define demand for housing types and locations. Prices set in the housing market determine what housing units and neighborhoods households can afford.[18]

Nor is it obvious that a public interest in more racially and ethnically diverse neighborhoods—what can be understood as an expanded version of fair housing, as judged by intracommunity racial and ethnic diversity—is best served by government-initiated interventions designed to achieve such an outcome. As Herbert Gans observes in his classic 1967 book about postwar American suburbanization, *The Levittowners*, "Experience with residential integration in many communities, including Levittown, indicates that it can be achieved without problems when the two races are similar in similar socio-economic level and in the visible cultural aspects of class."[19] Indeed, backlash toward AFFH-style interventions can transcend race, as in the case of Westchester County, New York, where an AFFH-style HUD initiative (sparked by a lawsuit) designed to encourage the construction of subsidized housing in affluent areas has stirred controversy. A self-identified African American resident of one higher-income community observed: "As an African-American who happily resides in one of the aforementioned towns targeted for this deplorable lower income housing, I am appalled at this decision to reward those individuals who . . . chose the easy way out instead of dedicating oneself to hard work. . . . My wife and I worked hard to be able to purchase a home and PAY TAXES in one of these towns, just like everyone else who resides in them."[20] This is just one person's comment, of course. However, I have encountered similar attitudes in conducting magazine reportage in the south suburbs of Chicago, where voucher holders were relocating to middle-class African American neighborhoods and where local political leaders expressed reluctance to accept such households.[21]

Is Relocation Necessary? The Flaws of Environmental Determinism

It is crucial, however, not to focus narrowly on the implementation flaws of the AFFH Rule in considering how housing markets can best serve those of modest means. One must consider its crucial—and, in my view, faulty—underlying assumption: that low-income neighborhoods cannot be "good neighborhoods" and that government-led intervention must seek, in effect, to rescue such households (especially because of the future prospects of their children) through relocation. Again, the AFFH Rule is less about non-discrimination and more about improving the life chances of those potentially relocated. The impracticality of such an effort at a grand scale begs the bigger question of how best to lay the groundwork for the largest numbers of lower-income households to enjoy a high quality of life and hope, plausibly, for a path of upward mobility for themselves and their children. In my view, this goal requires, as a practical matter, a commitment to providing the highest-possible-quality public goods for low-income neighborhoods—that is, the places where most poor households actually live. And it requires an appreciation of the flaws of a long history of choosing other approaches that have not turned out well.

Work such as Chetty, Hendren, and Katz's compares the fates of members of low-income households who move to more affluent communities with those who remain "behind," if you will, in comparison communities—such as public housing. It is important to appreciate the profound, and relevant, irony of such a comparison. For although public housing projects would become associated with crime, disorder, and long-term poverty, that was hardly the goal or the vision of their original, idealistic proponents. For its Depression-era advocates, public housing was viewed in terms not dissimilar from those of current-day advocates of the AFFH Rule: a new, safe, sanitary, bright environment in which low-income children would thrive. Privately built low-income neighborhoods were branded as slums—and were implicated in social ills. In regard to the original public housing authorizing legislation, John Bauman writes that "the Wagner-Steagall bill enunciated a national housing policy: to provide federal aid for the eradication of slums, and 'for decent, safe and sanitary dwellings for families of low-income . . . for the reduction of unemployment and the stimulation of business activity.'"[22] Nor was the improvement conceived of as merely a physical upgrade. Alexander von Hoffman describes the view that one's surroundings can shape and improve one's character as "environmental determinism," a doctrine he sees as one with deep roots:

> A long tradition of environmental determinism inclined Americans to see the nation's slums and ghettos as a great source of the violence. Since the nineteenth century, the belief that one's living environment can shape one's character and behavior had motivated numerous reform efforts—for public schools, recreational areas, and especially housing. . . . From the idea that the ghetto environments were the source of many ills, it was but a small step to the solution of new and better homes for the lower classes.[23]

The response to this dream that failed has been to identify flaws that might be fixed, whether caused by high-rise design[24] or due to a presumed lack of income mixture.[25] Increasingly elaborate forms of financing and subsidy, such as the low-income housing tax credit and inclusionary zoning, have sought to guarantee income-group mixture, on the assumption that such an environment will somehow help uplift those of lower incomes.

The AFFH Rule falls squarely in this long Progressive—and, I would argue, naïve—tradition. Although it is framed as a housing integration strategy, it is clearly designed—first and foremost—to improve the life chances of potential participants. Racial integration is a useful rationale that allows the program to avail itself of settled case law and federal regulatory authority. But language such as that which asserts that one's zip code should not be one's destiny clearly has in mind the goal of improving life chances, not seeking racial integration as an end in itself.

Its underlying assumptions, however, ignore the possibility that, with the right package of public goods, low-income neighborhoods with widely dispersed ownership and modest housing types can be good neighborhoods—that is, springboards for upward mobility—as they surely have been in the past. In other words, a more fully realized community development strategy—to use HUD parlance—might be more effective and inspire less resistance. One cannot, of course, overlook the fact that municipal governments have, historically, failed to provide the sorts of public goods that make for healthy neighborhoods—and they should be pressured, not least by their own citizens, to do so. But ignored too is history that indicates that "slums" were unjustly maligned and can be seen as having offered a better chance for asset building and upward mobility than the generations of subsidized housing that have been undertaken—best symbolized by the establishment, in 1965, of HUD, a new federal agency dedicated to this purpose.

The Overlooked History of Privately Provided Affordable Housing

For what might be called a counter-history of American slums, one can look to such investigations as *Slums of the Cities*, issued by the federal Commissioner of Labor Statistics in 1892, and *Immigrants in Cities*, issued by the U.S. Immigration Commission in 1907. Notably, the 1894 report, in which canvassers assessed conditions, found that in poor neighborhoods in sixteen cities (including New York, Philadelphia, and Chicago), although individual baths and toilets were rare, "there was no greater sickness prevailing in the districts canvassed than in other parts of the cities involved, and while the most wretched conditions were found here and there, the small numbers of sick people discovered was a surprise to the canvassers."[26] (Notably, a key public good, widely supplied in this era, was the public bath.[27]) Surprising too is the finding that "the earnings of the occupants in the slum districts canvassed are quite up to the earnings of the people generally and at large."[28] In other words, New York's Tenement Museum's latter-day characterization of tenement housing as memorializing the "urban log cabin"—that is, a starting point for gradual improvement—is not misplaced.[29]

By the time of the 1907 Immigration Commission report, it was not clear that physical conditions in areas designated as slums were nearly as bad as the retrospective stereotype. The commission reported that 80 percent of the homes studied were kept in either good or fair condition.[30] To the extent that conditions were substandard, the commission pointed the finger less at private owners than at local government: "The neglected appearance of many of the streets is a result of indifference on the part of public authorities."[31] Nor was housing beyond the means of low-income households—a common concern today. In 1909, another federal investigation, this one by the President's Home Commission, found that the lowest-income households surveyed in the District of Columbia paid a reasonable percentage of their incomes for housing—indeed, far less than the 30 percent that would later be considered a gold standard: "The average family, with an income of $500 or less per annum, expended about $6 per month for rent, this item constituting about 21 percent of the total family income."[32]

Significantly, low-income neighborhoods in the pre–public housing, pre-subsidy era were not, as legend would have it, dominated by a few powerful absentee landlords: "A very large proportion of families living in houses owned by some member of the family are seen to have one, two, or three tenements to a house."[33] An analysis of the 1892 data indicates, for instance, that in Chicago, of 1,439 residential structures in the area surveyed, 397 were occupied by their owners. Just as important, however, is the fact that many of these were multifamily structures—including seventy-three two-family, sixty-eight three-family, and fifty-one four-family homes. As a result, of 3,484 renter (non-owner) households, 1,042, or 29.8 percent, lived in buildings in which resident-owners also lived.[34] Many tenants were also themselves resident-landlords, since boarders were common.[35] Moreover, it is quite possible that some resident-owners owned additional, nearby property. This was a neighborhood, one can infer, in which owners would have been immediately accountable for the upkeep of the premises and in which tenants would feel a responsibility of good behavior, less they face eviction. A social as well as an economic compact was in force. Owners held a valuable asset; tenants could see the example of owner-occupants and aspire to own a similar asset. Both economic and social capital was being accumulated in what outsiders viewed as slums. Such were the worlds that were blithely swept away by such housing reformers as Catherine Bauer, who cleared the way for public housing in which owners were replaced by a distant management and ownership was public. Worse, the failure of the reform model has led to the belief that "concentrated poverty," by its nature, makes for an undesirable neighborhood. The AFFH Rule is inspired directly by such a view.

Dispersed ownership of modest dwellings—including minority group member ownership—continued, in fact, until, in some cases, actual clearance for public housing occurred. Consider, for instance, the St. Louis neighborhoods that were cleared to make way for the later-infamous Pruitt-Igoe public housing project, itself demolished only two decades after it was built. Federal census data from 1950, five years before the construction of the Pruitt portion of the project and six years before Igoe, are revealing. An examination of St. Louis Census tract 11-A, which was 98 percent Black, reveals that 21 percent of all housing units (828 of 3,696) were the property of "nonwhite owners."[36] In addition, the Census data show that, although there were just 721 single-family units, there were 828 owner-occupied units—meaning that at least 107 owners could be found in two-family through five-family buildings. Thus, as in nineteenth-century Chicago, many tenants rented from on-site owners. The numbers were not dissimilar in Census tract 21-B, which was 96 percent Black. At least 23 percent of all dwelling units had an owner present, and almost all (460 of 480 owner-occupants) were Black. The numbers for both neighborhoods are below the citywide average—34 percent owner-occupants and 41 percent of structures with an owner present—but not dramatically so. Notably, in the case of tract 11-A, the percentage of owner-occupants (21 percent) exceeds that of an adjacent, predominantly white neighborhood (18 percent). One finds, further, that rents in tract 11-A ($27.71 per month) were lower than the citywide median ($28.55) and lower than in one adjoining, predominantly white neighborhood ($33). Rents were lower than the citywide median in tract 21-B as well ($21.85 per month), although higher than in a nearby white neighborhood ($17.53). What were residents getting for their money, though? In 1950, 28 percent of all dwelling units across St. Louis had either "no private bath" or were deemed "dilapidated." In 11-A, that figure was 30 percent. It was much higher in 21-B (56 percent), which was closer to that in an adjoining, overwhelmingly white neighborhood (44 percent). Poor sides of town existed in the St. Louis of 1950, in other words, that were white and Black.

One could argue that such numbers demonstrated the need for racially integrated public housing on a large, Pruitt-Igoe–type scale. But that argument would rest on the faulty assumptions of environmental determinists: that physical conditions should be the main gauge of the health of a community; that left to themselves, such conditions would be a permanent feature of urban life; and that the only steps that could make life better were demolition and relocation. Further, these assumptions clashed sharply with the views of those who began to critically examine "urban renewal" as early as the late 1950s and early 1960s, including the sociologist Gans. In his landmark book *The Urban Villagers*—an appreciation of Boston's tenement West End district, based on research he conducted shortly before its demolition to make way for high-rise apartments—Gans writes, "The federal and local housing standards which are applied to slum areas reflect the value pattern of middle-class professionals [who] place greater emphasis on the status functions of housing than does the working class."[37] Gans is not unalterably opposed to slum demolition and its replacement with publicly provided housing, but he is the first to express skepticism about just how bad areas branded as slums really were. He writes in *The Urban Villagers*:

> Existing physical standards have so far failed to make a distinction between low-rent and slum housing. . . . Slums should be eliminated but low-rent structures must be maintained, at least in the absence of better housing for people who want, or for economic reasons must maintain, low rental payments and who are willing to accept high density, lack of modernity and other inconveniences as alternative costs.[38]

But even by middle-class standards, the assumptions behind public housing—the conditions of which would become the benchmark for MTO and, by extension for the AFFH Rule—ignore a great many things, notably including the fact that ownership is, by definition, not an option in public housing and that asset ownership can lay the foundation for gradual movement up and out of poorer neighborhoods. Here lies what can be termed a "snapshot fallacy": that the conditions observed at a given moment are permanent unless policy makers act. But the conditions for improvement were not absent in the poor Black neighborhoods of 1950 St. Louis.

Home values in Tract 11-A, for single-family units, were relatively similar to the citywide average ($8,026, compared with $9,220), suggesting the possibility of upward mobility for owners and sales to tenants, who might follow the owners up the housing ladder. And even in the pre–civil rights era, 24 percent of St. Louis Blacks (37,500 of 153,766) lived in majority-white neighborhoods of what was, in its social and racial mores, very much a Southern city, at a time when Jim Crow remained firmly in place in the United States. Private housing markets can disperse households based on their income and ability to pay, and they were starting to do so in the St. Louis of 1950. Rather than allow that process to take its course, public housing helped create a publicly subsidized Black ghetto and froze it in place for decades. Residents couldn't become property owners and, with rents set low, lacked the financial incentive to get out. Those providing private, low-income housing (including many Black property owners) would, moreover, have logically found it difficult or impossible to compete against the government. Indeed, a good case can be made that African Americans were particularly disadvantaged by public housing because its advent and growth coincided with their migration from the rural South to the urban North.

One can argue, of course, that this sad history provides the rationale for compensating minority families in some way. The policy question, however, is not whether some intervention in low-income minority communities is justified but, rather, what sort of investments might actually improve matters for as many residents as possible.

What Affirmatively Furthering Fair Housing Overlooks: What Upward Mobility Requires

The neglected idea that low-income neighborhoods with modest homes could lay the foundation for upward mobility was, in fact, understood by some, even in the Progressive era. In their classic 1911 book *Zone of Emergence*, Albert Kennedy and Robert Woods, settlement house leaders in Boston's South End, observe:

A noticeable thing about the zone is the amount of property in the hands of immigrant people. Nearly 50 percent of the small dwellings and three-family tenements are in the hands of one-time immigrants in relatively humble circumstances.

This real estate is mortgaged to a large share of its value but it stands as a symbol that the newcomers are taking possession of the land. Ownership of property is one of the surest indications that emergence is emergence, indeed.[39]

Thus, Woods and Kennedy, in contrast to such housing reformers as Edith Elmer Wood and Catherine Bauer, who emerged in the 1920s and 1930s, implicitly understand that the *process* of upward mobility ("emergence") was itself integral to upward mobility itself. The steps that lead a household to a "better" neighborhood—work, savings, marriage—were, and are, encouraged by the private, socioeconomically stratified private housing market. It is thus that the so-called better neighborhoods are formed in the first place. By this logic, the process of doing what is required to move to a better neighborhood, then, is as important as relocation itself. Promoters of the AFFH Rule fail to understand this.

This, then, is an argument that the AFFH Rule—and the vision of assisting those of lower incomes through dispersion to higher-income neighborhoods—is yet another ill-advised response to what might be termed the original sin of public housing, at least as implemented over time, for which we continue to identify difficult and elaborate antidotes. If not through AFFH, however, how should we proceed in an effort to improve the life chances of low-income household members?

Poor Neighborhoods as Good Neighborhoods

The answer, broadly, begins with abandoning the idea that low-income neighborhoods cannot be good neighborhoods—that is, communities that lay the groundwork for upward mobility and can be desirable places to live in their own right. The pessimistic view that this is not possible was actually central to the original vision of HUD as a federal agency. In 1966, the inaugural HUD undersecretary, Robert Wood, told the National Association of Social Workers that "the historic role of the city has deteriorated badly. In some city neighborhoods, blight and poverty have gone hand in hand for generations, and the slum is no longer a way station. . . . [T]he bus has stopped running to the suburbs and the poor are increasingly insulated from the larger society."[40] This assertion looks absurd, in retrospect. Nonetheless, HUD took the approach of what might be called "gilding the ghetto"—replacing privately owned housing with either public housing or subsidized housing owned by large, politically connected private or nonprofit owners.[41]

Such initiatives would, again, have competed with private, low-income owners, helping undermine their capacity to accumulate assets and move out and up. The right approach—then and now—was not to emphasize housing quality but, rather, to take steps to provide the high-quality public goods associated with "better" neighborhoods: good schools, safe streets, clean parks and playgrounds, reliable public transit. It is here where our emphasis must lie today, rather than with what are likely to be quixotic attempts of the minority poor to move to more affluent neighborhoods.

Amy Wax captures well the choice regarding public education, a key service for advocates of the AFFH Rule:

> Two approaches in particular have received wide popular attention and strong professional advocacy for addressing inequalities in K–12 education. Both are motivated by a genuine desire to make headway against racial and economic inequalities in learning and achievement, and to improve prospects for disadvantaged children. The first seeks to reduce the number of high-poverty schools, which tend to be segregated both by class and race, by dispersing students from poor families to schools with predominantly middle-class or affluent students. The hope is that low-income students will acquire the habits, focus, and academic discipline of their classmates, as well as benefit from a more rigorous and orderly environment. So-called "income integration" initiatives have gained traction in a number of public-school districts nationwide. The second type of effort is directed at drastically altering the character of the schools disadvantaged students attend. So-called "no excuses" K–12 charter programs create a high-intensity, demanding, all-encompassing atmosphere designed to work a comprehensive improvement in poor students' academic outcomes, as well as their outlook, habits, and behavior.[42]

Wax expresses concern not only about the practicality of the dispersal model but about how it could lead to race and class tensions, not unlike what Gans observes regarding neighborhood integration. In expressing a preference for the "no excuses model," she says:

> The no-excuses alternative . . . is better equipped to negotiate the tensions between uplift models and progressive commitments, and to deal with the persistence of race and class differences. Such schools educate mainly low-income students, which renders socioeconomic disparities less salient. The important comparisons are not to better-off students, but to similar children educated in

less-demanding settings. The goal is maximum improvement rather than impossible equalization. Because students and teachers need not constantly confront inequalities that are the product of larger social forces, the embrace of active acculturation can proceed without apology to beneficiaries or benefactors.

She is far from alone in taking the view that public charter schools, especially, show positive results in educating disadvantaged populations and do so without geographic relocation of their households. As David Leonhardt has written in the *New York Times*, "Many charters have flourished, especially in places where traditional schools have struggled. This evidence comes from top academic researchers, studying a variety of places, including Washington, Boston, Denver, New Orleans, New York, Florida and Texas. The anecdotes about failed charters are real, but they're not the norm."[43]

Beyond the specific issue of education for the disadvantaged, the emergence of a new and effective model for this crucial public good reminds us that, since the founding of HUD—the agency that eventually begat the AFFH Rule—a series of other effective policies to improve the quality of life in low-income neighborhoods in a number of ways have emerged. Public safety, notably, has been improved drastically as the result of so-called public order (aka "broken windows") policing, such that crime rates in many cities (notably New York) have been sharply reduced. There is dispute as to which specific strategies aimed at crime prevention and reduction have been most effective, but few dispute that nonexogenous factors (i.e., specific new law enforcement approaches) play a role.[44] In other words, we have learned that we are not helpless to reduce crime in low-income neighborhoods. Business improvement districts, through which neighborhood commercial enterprises band together in a formal legal structure that takes steps to complement public services, have proven to be a means through which private business interests effectively take responsibility for the safety and upkeep of neighborhood shopping districts.[45] Private support for park maintenance (through so-called park conservancies) has improved this crucial amenity, either by directly assisting with maintenance in parks in low-income areas (for instance, Brooklyn's Prospect Park) or by freeing public funds that would have been devoted to park maintenance in higher-income neighborhoods that can attract philanthropic support.

One can argue, of course, that the opportunity to move to a higher-income neighborhood with a superior set of public goods should be at least one of the options available to residents of lower-income neighborhoods. However attractive such an approach might be for some people, at least in theory, it is my view that it is an approach that is neither practical (on a large scale) nor one that sends a constructive message about the steps that are required for true upward mobility—anymore than one's hitting the lottery sends a constructive message about how as many people as possible can lift their incomes.

Broadly, then, the experimental character of the AFFH Rule as well as its practical challenges, coupled with promising new means to improve the quality of life in low-income neighborhoods, means that this is not the time to give up on the possibility implied by HUD's original mission: taking steps to make sure that poor neighborhoods are good neighborhoods. The approach of affirmatively furthering fair housing risks being a course of most resistance, while failing to touch the lives of the majority of the poor.

ENDNOTES

1. Douglas S. Massey, *Categorically Unequal: The American Stratification System* (New York: Russell Sage Foundation, 2007), 110–112.

2. Department of Housing and Urban Development (HUD), Final Rule, Affirmatively Furthering Fair Housing, *Federal Register*, July 16, 2015.

3. Ibid., Executive Summary.

4. Jeffrey R. Kling, Jeffrey B. Liebman, and Lawrence F. Katz, "Experimental Analysis of Neighborhood Effects," *Econometrica* 75, no. 1 (2007): 83–119.

5. Michael D. Eriksen and Amanda Ross, "Housing Vouchers and the Price of Rental Housing," *American Economic Journal: Economic Policy* 7, no. 3 (August 2015): 154–176.

6. Raj Chetty, Nathaniel Hendren, and Lawrence F. Katz, "The Effects of Exposure to Better Neighborhoods on Children: New Evidence from the Moving to Opportunity Experiment," *American Economic Review* 106, no. 4 (April 2016): 855–902.

7. Morris A. Davis, Daniel A. Hartley, Jesse Gregory, and Kegon T. K. Tan, "Neighborhood Choices, Neighborhood Effects and Housing Vouchers," Working Paper Series (Federal Reserve Bank of Chicago, January 11, 2017), 29, 43, available at https://ideas.repec.org/p/fip/fedhwp/wp-2017-02.html.

8. Ingrid Gould Ellen, Keren Mertens Horn, and Amy Ellen Schwartz, "Why Don't Housing Choice Voucher Recipients Live Near Better Schools? Insights from Big Data," *Journal of Policy Analysis and Management* 35, no. 4 (2016): 884–905.

9. Davis et al., "Neighborhood Choices, Neighborhood Effects and Housing Vouchers," 43.

10. Chetty, Hendren, and Katz, "The Effects of Exposure to Better Neighborhoods on Children."

11. Robert A. Collinson, Ingrid Gould Ellen, and Jens Ludwig, "Low-Income Housing Policy," in *Economics of Means-Tested Transfer Programs in the United States*, ed. Robert A. Moffitt, vol. II (Chicago: University of Chicago Press, 2016), 59–126.

12. G. Thomas Kingsley, "Trends in Housing Problems and Federal Housing Assistance," Urban Institute, October 2017, available at https://www.urban.org/sites/default/files/publication/94146/trends-in-housing-problems-and-federal-housing-assistance.pdf.

13. Ibid.

14. Office of Management and Budget, "Agency Fact Sheet, FY 2017 Executive Budget," n.d., available at https://portal.hud.gov/hudportal/documents/huddoc?id=ProposedFY17FactSheet.pdf.

15. Ingrid Gould Ellen, Michael Suher, and Gerard Torrats-Espinosa, "Neighbors and Networks: The Role of Social Interactions on the Residential Choices of Housing

Choice Voucher Holders," 2016, quoted in Ingrid Gould Ellen, "What Do We Know about Housing Choice Vouchers?" *Regional Science and Urban Economics* 80 (2020): 1–5.

16. P. H. Rees, *Residential Patterns in American Cities* (Chicago: University of Chicago, Department of Geography, 1979).

17. Michael J. White, *American Neighborhoods and Residential Differentiation* (New York: Russell Sage Foundation, 1988).

18. Anna Hardman and Yannis M. Ioannides, "Neighbors Income Distribution: Economic Segregation and Mixing in Urban Neighborhoods," *Journal of Housing Economics* 13 (2004): 368–382.

19. Herbert J. Gans, *The Levittowners: Ways of Life and Politics in a New Suburban Community* (New York: Random House, 1967).

20. Comments posted in response to Sam Roberts, "Westchester Adds Housing to Desegregation Pact," *New York Times*, August 10, 2009, sec. N.Y. / Region, available at https://www.nytimes.com/2009/08/11/nyregion/11settle.html.

21. Howard Husock, "Let's End Housing Vouchers," *City Journal*, Autumn 2000, available at https://www.city-journal.org/html/let%E2%80%99s-end-housing-vouchers -12152.html.

22. John F. Bauman, "Catherine Bauer: The Struggle for Modern Housing in America, 1930–1960," in *The Human Tradition in Urban America*, ed. Roger Biles (Lanham, MD: Rowman and Littlefield, 2002), 164.

23. Alexander von Hoffman, *Calling Upon the Genius: Housing Policy in the Great Society, Part Three* (Joint Center for Housing Studies, Harvard University, March 2010), available at https://www.jchs.harvard.edu/sites/default/files/w10-6_von_hoffman.pdf.

24. Oscar Newman, *Defensible Space: Crime Prevention through Urban Design* (New York: Macmillan, 1972).

25. Douglas S. Massey and Nancy A. Denton, *American Apartheid: Segregation and the Making of the Underclass* (Cambridge, MA: Harvard University Press, 1993).

26. U.S. Commissioner of Labor Statistics, "Slums of the Cities," 1892, 19.

27. Marilyn Thornton Williams, *Washing "the Great Unwashed": Public Baths in Urban America, 1840–1920* (Columbus: Ohio State University Press, 1991).

28. Ibid., 2.

29. This description can be found on the website of WNET, public television, available at https://www.thirteen.org/tenement/logcabin.html.

30. U.S. Immigration Commission, *Immigrants in Cities: A Study of the Population of Selected Districts in New York, Chicago, Philadelphia, Boston, Cleveland, Buffalo, and Milwaukee* (Washington, DC: 1911 U.S. Immigration Commission, 1911), 560.

31. Ibid., 5.

32. The President's Homes Commission, *Report of the Committee on Improvement of Existing Houses and Elimination of Insanitary and Alley Houses* (Washington, DC: President's Homes Commission, 1909), 288.

33. U.S. Commissioner of Labor Statistics, "Slums of the Cities," 86.

34. Ibid., 588.

35. Ibid., 121.

36. U.S. Department of Commerce, Bureau of the Census, St. Louis, Missouri Census Tracts, Table 3, Characteristics of Dwelling Units by Census Tracts, 52.

37. Herbert J. Gans, *The Urban Villagers: Group and Class in the Life of Italian-Americans* (New York: Collier Macmillan, 1982), 309.

38. Ibid.

39. Albert J. Kennedy and Robert Woods, *The Zone of Emergence: Observations of the Lower Middle and Upper Working Class Communities of Boston, 1905–1914* (Cambridge: Massachusetts Institute of Technology Press, 1969), 39; Leonard S. Rubinowitz and Elizabeth Trosman, "Affirmative Action and the American Dream: Implementing Fair Housing Policies in Federal Homeownership Programs," *Northwestern University Law Review* 74, quoted in Howard Husock, "Rediscovering the Three-Decker House," *Public Interest* (Winter 1990): 53.

40. Robert Wood, "Obligations of an Affluent Society" (May 27, 1966), quoted in Cato Institute, "The Inherent Flaws of HUD," Policy Analysis (Cato Institute, December 22, 1997), 5.

41. Howard Husock and Tom Sheehan, "Making Money on the Ghetto," *Boston Phoenix*, July 8, 1975.

42. Amy Wax, "Educating the Disadvantaged," *National Affairs*, Spring 2017, 4.

43. David Leonhardt, "Opinion | School Vouchers Aren't Working, but Choice Is," *New York Times*, January 20, 2018, sec. Opinion, available at https://www.nytimes.com /2017/05/02/opinion/school-vouchers-charters-betsy-devos.html.

44. New York Police Department, "The Historic Reduction in Crime Rates in New York, 1990–2014," n.d.; See also Hope Corman and Naci Mocan, "Carrots, Sticks, and Broken Windows," *Journal of Law and Economics* 48, no. 1 (April 1, 2005): 235–266.

45. Goktug Morcol, Lorlene Hoyt, Jack W. Meek, and Ulf Zimmermann, "Business Improvement Districts: Research, Theories, and Controversies" (London: CRC Press, 2008), available at https://www.crcpress.com/Business-Improvement-Districts-Research -Theories-and-Controversies/Morcol-Hoyt-Meek-Zimmermann/p/book/9781420045765.

The Fair Housing Challenge
to Community Development

Edward G. Goetz

Since the 1960s, community development organizations have been investing in new and rehabilitated housing in high-poverty neighborhoods. Nonprofit organizations, including community-based organizations, and some for-profit developers specializing in affordable housing have for years been supported by regional and national financial intermediaries (e.g., the Local Initiatives Support Corporation [LISC] and Enterprise Community Partners) and the public sector in developing subsidized, low-cost housing in disadvantaged neighborhoods. In recent years, fair housing advocates have posed a strong challenge to community developers regarding the effectiveness of place-based housing and neighborhood initiatives. According to this challenge, community development efforts are, at best, ineffective in reversing long-standing trends of decline in disadvantaged neighborhoods and, at worst, counterproductive to those objectives and to the cause of racial equity. Some fair housing activists have advocated instead for a set of spatial strategies to address racial equity that they insist are more consistent with the mandates of the Fair Housing Act.

The fair housing challenge to community development is about housing policy and how best to achieve racial equity more generally. The equity question revolves around whether integration is a necessary precondition for racial justice. Many insist on the imperative of integration and the necessity of pursuing integration to fully address contemporary issues of racial injustice.[1] These advocates routinely enlist studies on the effects of neighborhood characteristics on individual outcomes to show the importance of spatial inequality and the need for integration.[2] Two elements of this literature are particularly relevant to fair housing advocates. First is the core assertion that neighborhood conditions play a central role in determining life chances and that people of color have been disproportionately consigned through discrimination and other mechanisms to disadvantaged neighborhoods that maintain and perpetuate social, political, and economic inequalities. The second important element of the argument is that significant public action has contributed to these patterns of spatial injustice.

This second element of the argument in particular is relied upon to justify a public policy response, arguing that the public sector has some responsibility to right the wrongs to which it has so directly contributed. Dispersal of subsidized housing and households and deconcentration of poverty have been the dominant approaches that fair housing advocates deem necessary to achieve integration and racial justice. Community development efforts that continue to locate subsidized housing in disadvantaged communities of color contribute to the problem, not to the solution.

These views contrast with those who question the necessity, or even the advisability, of integration and who distinguish between segregation (the spatial pattern of racial clustering) and the "diverse social factors that contribute to bringing it about or maintaining it."[3] According to this argument, our efforts should focus not on rearranging people into different neighborhoods but rather on addressing the factors that produce spatial and racial inequalities. Integration into white-dominated neighborhoods (the only type of integration that whites, as a rule, tolerate) entails what Mary Pattillo calls a "celebration of Whiteness."[4] Furthermore, the fair housing argument for integration is generally justified by the desire to provide access to the same opportunities that are available to whites in predominantly white neighborhoods. Philosopher Tommie Shelby thus argues that integration reinforces "the symbolic power that whites hold over blacks by encouraging whites to see their relationships with blacks not as intrinsically valuable forms of interracial community but as an avenue for blacks to share in (not abolish) white privilege."[5]

Yet there is no necessary connection that leads from an acknowledgment of the problem of spatial inequity to integration as a solution. Just as reasonable a response is what Iris Marion Young calls the movement of resources rather than of people.[6] How do these competing visions of racial equity play out in housing policy debates between fair housing advocates who emphatically offer the integrationist approach and community development organizations whose work focuses on neighborhood improvement?

Two Movements

The fair housing and affordable housing/community development movements are largely separate projects. Fair housing advocacy emerged out of the racial desegregation efforts of the mid-twentieth century.[7] As noted in Chapter 1, most of its early political actions were focused on opening communities and housing submarkets to African American occupancy. The community development movement arose later and focused on conditions within disadvantaged—and often racially segregated—inner-city neighborhoods. Political scientist Mara Sidney, one of the few scholars to study the two movements side by side, points out that despite baseline agreements on issues of social justice, very little collaboration occurs between advocates in the two camps. She writes, "Fair housing groups do not typically partner with the affordable housing movement in local movements for regional justice," and "national fair housing policy has produced a population of local fair housing groups that have trouble developing allies and do little to mobilize the public behind their cause. . . . At the same time, for a variety of reasons, affordable housing advocates may not perceive fair housing or civil rights advocates as natural allies."[8] This division has meant that the two movements have largely developed in isolation from each other. Although both are concerned with housing conditions for low-income people and people of color, they operate largely independently.

This separation is duplicated within the bureaucracy of the federal agency charged with affordable housing and fair housing implementation—the U.S. Department of Housing and Urban Development (HUD). Fair housing officials within HUD regard themselves and their objectives as marginalized within an agency that prioritizes the development of affordable units over the pursuit of integration or desegregation. Even worse, they report "deeply entrenched opposition" within HUD to initiatives that would further fair housing objectives.[9]

Separate Agendas

Although both movements have core concerns that center on housing justice, they have largely separate agendas. The fair housing movement sees itself as the watchdog over implementation of the Fair Housing Act. HUD's relative lack of commitment to enforcement and lack of sufficient resources devoted to enforcing fair housing have meant that enforcement is often accomplished through the private litigation strategies of fair housing advocates. The Fair Housing Act is seen by experts as having two objectives—equal access (the elimination of discrimination) and integration.[10] As many have pointed out, equal access is process-oriented, with the goal of all having equal treatment in housing transactions.[11] Integration, on the other hand, is outcome-oriented, with the objective of racially mixed communities. Fair housing activists pursue both objectives and perceive a significant overlap between the two. Freer choice in housing markets for people of color is expected to lead to a number of outcomes, including the spatial outcomes of desegregation and integration.

Fair housing activism is not limited to monitoring private actions in the housing market. The Fair Housing Act obligates the federal government to operate its housing programs in such as a way as to "affirmatively further" fair housing goals. This mandate has led to fair housing advocacy related to whether public programs of housing assistance are themselves discriminatory or in any way not serving the goal of integration. Thus, fair housing litigation efforts may frequently target public agencies, alleging that the implementation of their programs creates, maintains, or perpetuates patterns of racial segregation. It is at this point that the fair housing movement comes into conflict with the efforts of affordable housing activists and community developers.

Community development advocates approach questions of racial justice from a different perspective. The movement focuses on building economic and political capacity within disadvantaged neighborhoods to deal with the material and political needs of those communities. Community developers work in disadvantaged neighborhoods, applying an ever-dwindling variety and number of resources to the task of revitalizing disadvantaged areas and providing affordable housing that is safe and well run for people with limited incomes. Their work is concentrated in low-income neighborhoods of central cities in an attempt to counter or to replace the limited private- and public-sector investment in those communities.

Affordable housing is a key element of community development activities. Affordable housing is valued for its own sake, for the stability it provides to lower-income families, for the improvement in living conditions that it represents for many families, and for the money that it saves low-income families that can then be used for other necessities. Affordable housing is also valued for the physical upgrading that it typically represents for disadvantaged neighborhoods.

When, as is often the case, affordable housing developers are community-based, nonprofit developers, they may also enrich their housing with social services that are supportive of lower-income families. Community ownership of real estate is also valued as a means of building capital, allowing community ownership of assets, discouraging more exploitative and external control of the neighborhood, and being more responsive to the development agenda of residents rather than speculative capital markets. According to the model, any profits from such housing are kept "within the community" by being reinvested locally to produce other benefits for residents.

Fair housing activists increasingly object to the housing focus of community development organizations. The associate director and staff attorney for the Fair Share Housing Center of New Jersey, for example, filed a lawsuit against the state of New Jersey, claiming that the "case challenges the notion that more or new affordable housing in cities is fundamentally helpful for revitalization. In fact, building affordable housing in the cities has no net revitalizing effect at all."[12] They see such actions as perpetuating patterns of racial segregation, and they object to the continued development of such housing in communities of color. Indeed, to the extent that community developers rely on public resources to provide affordable housing in low-income neighborhoods, their actions are sometimes indistinguishable, according to fair housing advocates, from the type of discriminatory public policies that have contributed to segregation and concentrations of poverty in the past. For this reason, one fair housing writer characterizes community developers as the "poverty housing industry"—a phrase calculated to conjure images of a large-scale, impersonal constellation of actors who profit from the provision of housing to poor people.[13] To some fair housing advocates, then, the very work of community development must be curtailed to reorient housing subsidies to neighborhoods with better opportunity structures, so that the residents of assisted housing can also benefit from resource-rich neighborhoods and avoid the detrimental effects of low-income neighborhoods.

The Three Stations of Fair Housing Spatial Strategy

The fair housing movement has, over the past two decades, generated an ever-more-aggressive spatial strategy with the aim of achieving greater integration. This strategy has generated within the movement more frequent criticism of community development. Indeed, the relations between the two movements have worsened to the point that several "mediation" efforts have been attempted by national foundations, tracts have been written on both sides attempting to explain and resolve the tension, and lawsuits have been initiated against affordable housing practices.[14]

The distinction between the equal access and integration objectives of fair housing has become more pronounced as the spatial strategies of the movement have evolved.[15] In fact, it is possible to identify three stations of fair housing spatial strategy that represent an increasingly aggressive approach to achieving integration goals: (1) opening exclusionary communities, (2) preventing further segregation, and (3) dismantling existing low-income communities of color.

Each of these strategies is an extension of the movement's reach—that is, the progression is an accumulation of strategies, not the replacement of earlier methods with new ones. The second and third stations, in particular, produce tension between fair housing and community development. There is no conflict between fair housing and community development advocates in the pursuit of nondiscrimination—that is, equal access. The debate between the two positions arises only in relation to the spatial strategies of fair housing.

1. Opening Exclusionary Communities

In its early stages, from the 1940s through the 1960s, the fair housing movement focused primarily on "opening" housing markets and providing equal access to all communities regardless of race or ethnicity. Thus, the movement began with calls to open white neighborhoods and the suburbs to non-white families. Policy initiatives in this station have been of four types: (1) the expansion of various housing subsidy programs to increase low-cost housing production in the suburbs; (2) the elimination of land-use regulations that have the effect of excluding lower-income housing in suburban communities; (3) the elimination of private deed restrictions and covenants and other discriminatory private-sector actions within the housing market, such as steering, that have had the effect of creating and maintaining neighborhood color lines; and (4) voluntary "mobility" programs that facilitate the movement of families into predominantly white or lower-poverty neighborhoods.

Policies in this station include fair-share regional housing approaches, for example, that establish concrete goals for affordable housing development for all communities within a region in an effort to enhance the spread of affordable housing options, to diversify predominantly white communities, and ultimately to enhance the housing options of very-low-income people and people of color.[16] In some locations, higher levels of government have been given review powers over local land-use decision making when those decisions have prevented affordable housing developments from going forward.[17] Some jurisdictions have used "inclusionary housing" programs that require or incentivize private developers to build a number (or percentage) of affordable units in exchange for approving a market-rate housing development proposal.[18] Finally, such mobility programs as Moving to Opportunity for Fair Housing (MTO) have provided portable housing voucher subsidies to families to make moves to neighborhoods with more whites and/or less poverty.

On these issues and about these policies, there is general agreement between fair housing and community development advocates. Indeed, members of both camps would point to the need for greater efforts to build affordable housing in those communities where it does not yet exist in large numbers. Although there is no conflict between the two movements on this question, a lack of sufficient resources devoted to affordable housing makes it impossible to meet housing needs in exclusionary communities and in disadvantaged neighborhoods. Thus, conditions of resource scarcity, which are more or less a permanent aspect of affordable housing policy, position community development and dispersion as competing goals.

2. Preventing Further Segregation

Fair housing advocacy, however, quickly expanded beyond opening exclusionary communities to incorporate efforts to mitigate the development or perpetuation of racially defined housing submarkets. Programs of this sort, which mark the second station of fair housing's spatial strategy, have come in two varieties: (1) "impaction" rules that limit the production of subsidized housing in neighborhoods that are already considered segregated or poverty-concentrated and (2) "integration maintenance" programs that manage and limit the entry of minority families into communities to establish and maintain prescribed integration levels.

The second station of fair housing spatial strategy is fundamentally different than the first by virtue of the fact that the policies utilized *place the burden for integrating on members of the protected class.* These policy approaches work by limiting housing choices for members of the protected class so as to avoid concentrations or resegregation. Because of this, impaction and integration maintenance programs were among the first that brought the fair housing movement into conflict with affordable housing/ community development objectives. Impaction rules limit the amount of subsidized housing in disadvantaged areas, leaving families who might have benefited from subsidized housing and do not wish to move to predominantly white neighborhoods without it. It is arguable even that impaction rules limit the overall amount of assisted housing because of the great resistance to subsidized housing by residents who already live in the areas that integrationists find acceptable.

The decision in *Shannon v. HUD* (1971), for example, was an early demonstration of the intent of the fair housing movement to prevent further ghettoization by restricting the placement of subsidized housing in disadvantaged neighborhoods and of the court's interpretation of the Fair Housing Act as authorizing such action. The case resulted in the development of "siting restrictions" that required HUD to have in place a method of judging the impact of a proposed development on the pattern of racial occupancy in the affected neighborhood. More recently, the objective of preventing further segregation has surfaced in criticisms of the Low-Income Housing Tax

Credit (LIHTC) program. Community development advocates chafe under these siting restrictions, which they claim limit their ability to effectively address the housing needs that exist in disadvantaged neighborhoods.

So-called integration maintenance programs worked by limiting the access of disadvantaged groups to communities or to housing developments to maintain a degree of racial diversity deemed appropriate by program designers. Access by disadvantaged groups was limited to prevent the racial turnover of these neighborhoods and resegregation of disadvantaged families. The courts have since ruled that such limitations are unconstitutional, and these programs no longer exist.

3. Dismantling Existing Low-Income Communities of Color

The third station of fair housing's spatial strategy is the dissolution of existing communities in the name of desegregation. As such, it is the most interventionist of the three stations. This strategy is most prominent in a series of desegregation lawsuits pursued by fair housing attorneys in the 1980s and early 1990s. The settlements reached in a number of cities resulted in the demolition of public housing projects, the shift of housing subsidies into housing choice vouchers, and the displacement and relocation of public housing residents. The third station of fair housing's spatial strategy is also reflected in the demolition and redevelopment of public housing through the federal HOPE VI program and other forms of subsidized housing through the Choice Neighborhoods Initiative. While many of the residents of these public housing developments welcome the chance to move, the universal nature of the approach (usually involving demolition of housing and displacement of all residents) virtually ensures the displacement of many who do not. Some residents, typically very-low-income African Americans, not only object to their forced displacement but actively protest it.[19] To the extent that these efforts involve the involuntary displacement of lower-income families and relocation to other neighborhoods, this strategy also generates opposition from affordable housing advocates.

Origins of the Tension

The tension between integration and community development is as old as federally assisted housing for lower-income families. Within ten years of its introduction, the public housing program, the nation's oldest form of subsidized housing for low-income households, prompted debate within the community about where such housing should be built and whether its primary effect was to provide much-needed housing for the community or to perpetuate patterns of residential segregation.[20]

As the civil rights movement of the 1950s and 1960s progressed, many activists within the community, including several mainstream civil rights organizations, such as the Congress of Racial Equality (CORE) and the Student Nonviolent Coordinating Committee (SNCC) began to advocate less for integration and more for the development of political and economic capacity within communities. Leaders from Malcolm X to Stokely Carmichael were suspicious of integration and regarded it to be a hollow prospect. Malcolm X thought integration "a deception"—a kind of political sleight of hand that diverted attention from more fundamental questions of power. He believed that integration was "another tool of the oppressor, one that retained the basic inequalities in society."[21] As the 1960s wore on, the alternative ideas of power and community control increasingly challenged the integrationist message of the mainstream civil rights movement.[22]

The community development movement emerged out of the tumult of the 1960s and the attempts to fashion new solutions to the problems of American ghettos. Community Development Corporations (CDCs) were created by federal legislation in the 1960s as a means of combining political goals of community control on the one hand with ownership and control of economic and financial assets on the other. The CDC approach was seen as an alternative to the top-down methods of urban renewal and that program's repeated failure to produce sufficient affordable housing on cleared sites. CDCs were, according to John T. Baker, "efforts of leaders within low-income, predominantly black communities to create institutions through which residents of low-income communities could exercise control over important social, political, and economic resources both within and beyond the boundaries of their communities."[23] Laura Hill and Julia Rabig call CDCs "one of the Black freedom movement's most enduring legacies."[24]

The choice between "gilding the ghetto" on the one hand and integrating on the other became the framing question for American urban policy by the end of the 1960s. Facing a fourth consecutive summer of ghetto rioting in America's cities, President Lyndon Johnson in 1967 appointed a National Advisory Commission on Civil Disorders. It was charged with examining the scale of rioting that had been occurring since 1964 and determining the causes and possible means of preventing future disorders. The commission positioned its work within the framework of the two prevailing ideas about how to deal with conditions in communities: ghetto enrichment and residential integration.

The relative merits of these strategies were more and more the subject of debate within the fair housing movement by the end of the 1960s; the question of whether to work to improve ghetto areas was on the agenda within the housing rights movement as it never had been before.

Movement historian Juliet Saltman notes that the National Committee Against Discrimination in Housing (NCDH) newsletter, *Trends*, contained an average of thirty-seven references to integration in each issue in 1956. By 1970, the average issue included the term only twice.[25] In its place was a growing emphasis on revitalizing the ghetto and discussion of the merits of multiple strategies. The debate consumed the movement for several years. As Saltman recounts:

> The Chicago national conference in 1971 revealed a deep concern with this issue, as indicated in the summary of the proceedings. Debate, which was never resolved, included the following points: 1) The desirability of dispersing the ghetto as opposed to extending equal opportunity in housing; 2) whether the focus should be on improving the quality of housing everywhere rather than anything else; 3) should the goals be strengthening and rebuilding the ghetto as opposed to open housing; and 4) to what degree do the goals, however defined, extend to groups other than negroes.[26]

Open housing activists frequently conceptualized the debate as being between integration on the one hand and greater choice and access to housing on the other. While understanding the terms of this tradeoff, open housing advocates often found it difficult to make a choice. Saltman describes local open housing activism across the country and its ambivalence about this issue. She reports on activists in Denver who worked "to provide every citizen of the metro area freedom of choice but in practice they encouraged everyone to make integrative moves." In Los Angeles, she reports, "the immediate goal was to allow people out of the ghetto, but the long-term goal was related to freedom of choice," while in Seattle, activists prioritized desegregation while the director indicated that the intent was "first, last, and always, a free and meaningful choice in housing for everyone everywhere."[27]

The question has persisted in many forms since then. Several housing policy developments throughout the 1970s, 1980s, and 1990s have reflected this basic debate. The question of where to place assisted housing produced court rulings and the introduction of siting restrictions for HUD housing in the 1970s.[28] Important legal decisions established the expectation that HUD would consider the place impacts of the siting of affordable housing developments to reduce the overconcentration of such projects in minority and low-income neighborhoods. Yet the issue remained contentious because HUD and local actors insisted that such housing provided neighborhood-based benefits to disadvantaged areas, and thus a blanket policy of dispersing such housing would have the effect of depriving low-income neighborhoods of much-needed capital investment and housing resources.[29]

The operation of some integration maintenance programs put the distinction between housing access and integration into stark relief. These programs, operated by local fair housing organizations, were initiatives aimed at preserving racial diversity in communities where it already existed and at keeping communities that had diversified from resegregating through a combination of white flight and the in-migration of people of color. Integration maintenance programs are usually undertaken by previously white communities to manage the changing racial composition of their populations to maintain a desired mix. Such management includes "discouraging additional black occupancy" in neighborhoods that have a preferred level of integration,[30] which is typically just below the percentage of people of color that would induce white families to move out. As such, the programs incorporated the notion of a tipping point (the percentage of people of color within a neighborhood that would trigger white flight).[31] In some cases, integration maintenance programs have included incentives for white families to remain in a community that is changing or have consisted of attempts to attract white in-movers. In these instances, the programs work by attempting to influence the residential choices of families. Whether it is by discouraging further entry into neighborhoods or incentivizing whites to move in, sociologist Harvey Molotch characterizes these efforts as "competing for whites."[32] The normative standard for integrated neighborhoods in these programs is the white neighborhood, and integration means attracting a few, but not too many, people of color, while trying "to maintain a physical environment conducive to middle-class white residency."[33]

One type of integration maintenance program, however, worked by more actively limiting housing access by people of color to limit their numbers within a community to a prescribed level. Once again, the overriding concern in these quota-based approaches was the imperative to avoid activating white fear and prejudice and thus avoid creating white flight and racial turnover. By restricting housing opportunities for people of color to an approved percentage within a predominantly white community, these programs involved a form of purposeful discrimination in the service of integration when families of color were denied housing opportunities on the basis of their skin color. Quota-based integration management programs rather starkly revealed the potential conflict between the fair housing goals of choice and access on the one hand and the achievement and maintenance of integration on the other. Such programs, as William Wilson and Richard Taub point out, "violate[d] the letter of the 1968 Fair Housing Act by limiting the housing options of racial minorities."[34] They also violated many local housing ordinances, thereby forcing some communities to modify their nondiscrimination ordinances to allow such action.[35]

Contemporary Conflict

The Spatial Distribution of Tax-Credit Housing

The debate between community development and integration has surfaced in contemporary times in several ways. One of the most notable is the concern over the geographic distribution of low-income tax-credit housing. Fair housing advocates argue that the program is being operated in ways that perpetuate segregation by placing too many units in minority and high-poverty neighborhoods. Thus, the tax-credit controversies are examples of the second station of fair housing spatial strategy, a concern with preventing further segregation.

The LIHTC program operates by providing tax credits to investors in subsidized housing. Public agencies with responsibility for implementing the program develop Qualified Allocation Plans that set out the guidelines for distributing tax credits to developer applicants. These Qualified Allocation Plans allow the states to build into the program ancillary policy objectives by incentivizing certain types of developments, such as those near transit facilities, or projects with energy-saving designs, for example. In fact, the federal legislation requires that Qualified Allocation Plans incorporate additional selection criteria, including whether the project serves populations with special housing needs, provides for eventual tenant ownership, or is energy-efficient.[36] The statute indicates that Congress intended the LIHTC program to serve many policy objectives and that it wanted states to have some flexibility in prioritizing them.

The statute requires that preferences be given to projects that serve the lowest-income tenants, that provide assisted housing for the longest period of time, and that are located in distressed neighborhoods (so-called qualified census tracts) and contribute to "a concerted community revitalization plan."[37] Qualified census tracts are defined in the law as tracts with either a poverty rate greater than 25 percent or in which more than 50 percent of households have incomes at or below 60 percent of the area's median income. The qualified census tract requirement is, in effect, a congressional directive to use the LIHTC program to support community development projects in disadvantaged neighborhoods.

The qualified census tract requirement is the provision of the law that is most widely opposed by fair housing advocates because of the incentive it provides for development in disadvantaged neighborhoods. As fair housing attorney Elizabeth Julian argues, "When the LIHTC program was created, the legacy of segregation in prior housing programs for low-income people was ignored in both the statute and the regulatory process."[38] Frequently, LIHTC implementation is criticized for ignoring the second clause of the qualified census tract requirement: that the housing built in disadvantaged neighborhoods be tied to a "concerted community revitalization plan." That is, LIHTC projects in qualified census tracts are criticized for being one-off projects that only have the effect of locating affordable, subsidized units in a high-poverty neighborhood rather than being part of a larger community development effort. Revision of the qualified census tract requirement is a standard recommendation in assessments of the LIHTC program.[39]

Legal challenges in New Jersey, Texas, Connecticut, and Minnesota have contested the allocation of tax credits, alleging that the program's implementation has unnecessarily and unlawfully concentrated units in disadvantaged neighborhoods.[40] The New Jersey case was filed with the aim of forcing "a ruling from the Court that would prevent any LIHTC allocations in high-poverty, predominantly minority census tracts."[41] The plaintiffs strongly challenged the idea that building tax-credit housing in central-city neighborhoods had any potential to revitalize the community. The Fair Share Housing Center of New Jersey asserted that the case "challenges the notion that more or new affordable housing in cities is fundamentally helpful for revitalization. In fact, building affordable housing in the cities has no net revitalizing effect at all."[42]

Affordable housing developers responded by arguing that the position of the plaintiffs in the New Jersey case, one that would limit LIHTC housing in core neighborhoods, was the equivalent of "condemning poor people to awful living conditions while claiming to fight on their behalf."[43] In the end, the court ruled in favor of the defendants, upholding the New Jersey Qualified Allocation Plan. Since then, however, the state has changed its allocation plan in the direction advocated for by fair housing activists and now includes more incentives for development in "opportunity neighborhoods."[44]

Texas Department of Housing and Community Affairs v. The Inclusive Communities Project

In Texas, the Inclusive Communities Project, a fair housing advocacy group based in Dallas, filed suit in March 2008, alleging that the tax-credit projects in the Dallas metro area were being "disproportionately located in the slum and blighted neighborhoods."[45] Although the case began as a challenge to the allocation of tax credits in Texas's Qualified Allocation Plan, it eventually reached the Supreme Court on the question of whether claims based on the disparate impact of a policy were actionable under the Fair Housing Act. Disparate impact claims do not require proof of intent to discriminate but instead require proof that a policy led to an adverse and disparate impact on one or more of the protected classes in the Fair Housing Act and that a less discriminatory alternative policy is available. In the summer of 2015, the Supreme Court ruled in favor of the Inclusive Communities Project and established that disparate impact claims were in fact cognizable under the Fair Housing Act.

The Supreme Court did not, however, rule on the substance of the Inclusive Community Project's case against the state of Texas. The court reaffirmed the validity of multiple policy objectives in the operation of housing policy. It reasoned that "from the standpoint of determining advantage or disadvantage to racial minorities, it seems difficult to say as a general matter that a decision to build low-income housing in a blighted inner-city neighborhood instead of a suburb is discriminatory, or vice versa."[46] Furthermore, noted the court, "If the specter of disparate-impact litigation causes private developers to no longer construct or renovate housing units for low-income individuals, then the FHA [Fair Housing Act] would have undermined its own purpose. . . . And as to governmental entities, they must not be prevented from achieving legitimate objectives."[47] The decision clearly acknowledges community development and puts it on equal footing with dispersal. The decision holds that "disparate-impact liability mandates the 'removal of artificial, arbitrary, and unnecessary barriers,' not the displacement of valid governmental policies. . . . The FHA is not an instrument to force housing authorities to reorder their priorities."[48] The court continues, "It would be paradoxical to construe the FHA to impose onerous costs on actors who encourage revitalizing dilapidated housing in our Nation's cities merely because some other priority might seem preferable."[49] Thus, the Supreme Court decision in the case affirms the legitimacy of disparate impact claims but leaves intact the central debate between the competing policy objectives of integration and community development.

After the case was sent back to the trial court, however, the Inclusive Communities Project lost when the district court ruled that the plaintiffs had not proven that a specific policy in the Texas Qualified Allocation Plan was the direct cause of the spatial and racial disparities in the location of tax-credit projects in the Dallas region.[50] The interpretation of the ruling by practitioners, however, is what will actually determine its impact. One policy blog written shortly after the ruling maintains that "it is highly likely that developers and advocates of traditional community development will need to meet much higher standards for showing how current and future minority residents would benefit from revitalization."[51] The writers, both affiliated with the Urban Land Institute, a national organization of real estate and land-use professionals, go on to aver that "community developers may face more concerted legal opposition to their housing activities as well."[52]

Some evidence suggests that governmental officials also see the court's ruling as a directive to shift strategies away from investment in the urban core. Two months after the decision, for example, an official with the Georgia Department of Community Affairs said, "If the end result [of the agency's practices] is that we are primarily building in high minority areas with no access to community resources, then we need to make changes in the Qualified Allocation Plan [of the tax-credit program]."[53] If this interpretation prevails, the early net effect of *Texas DHCA v. The Inclusive Communities Project* will be a victory for the spatial strategy of fair housing advocates at the expense of community development.

Affirmatively Furthering Fair Housing

Finally, as discussed throughout this volume, HUD under the Barack Obama administration also acted to codify the affirmatively furthering fair housing provision of the 1968 Fair Housing Act. The provision to "affirmatively further" fair housing requires that in addition to regulating the actions of the private sector in housing, the federal government must ensure that its own programs and its own actions further fair housing goals. This clause has been interpreted to apply directly to federal actions implementing housing programs (for example, governing the siting of federally subsidized housing to ensure that the placement of subsidized units does not maintain or enhance patterns of segregation) and, more indirectly, to apply to the use of federal housing and community development funds by state and local governments.

The affirmatively furthering fair housing provision establishes the obligation on the part of the federal government to ensure that local governments spend federal housing and community development funds in accordance with fair housing goals. As a result, the Obama administration issued the Affirmatively Furthering Fair Housing (AFFH) Rule in 2015. Specifically, it strengthens the requirements for local governments to assess local fair housing issues and to incorporate fair housing goals into local plans of action by laying out steps for analyses of local housing conditions. While being designed as a way to analyze spatial inequities and create housing programs to combat segregation, the AFFH Rule reiterates the agency's dual focus by noting the legitimate "role of place-based strategies . . . to improve conditions in high poverty neighborhoods, as well as preservation of the existing affordable housing stock . . . to help respond to the overwhelming need for affordable housing."[54] Still, on balance, the AFFH Rule limits the notion of acceptable community development to rehabilitation (nothing is said about new development in impacted neighborhoods) and warns against a sole reliance on development in disadvantaged neighborhoods when the chance to develop in opportunity neighborhoods exists.

As for action steps, however, the AFFH Rule requires only the completion of an analysis and the preparation of a housing approach that would be consistent with local conditions. The 2015 AFFH regulations were hailed by fair housing advocates as an important step in extending the effectiveness of the Fair Housing Act. Given the backlash during the Donald Trump administration against the rule, however, it is as yet undetermined whether it will lead to a generalized shift in local policy away from meeting housing needs in central-city neighborhoods and toward a greater emphasis on dispersal and integration. The regulations do not resolve the issue related to the relative importance of equal access and integration in Title VIII.

The words of Obama's HUD secretary, Julián Castro, confirm that the agency did not intend for the AFFH Rule to endorse integration over community development:

> I agree with folks who say that, just because these neighborhoods are distressed and they're minority neighborhoods, that [doesn't mean] we shouldn't invest in them. We should invest in them. We shouldn't forget about them. They do have value. And so, we can't just have a policy of trying to get people out. There are a lot of people who don't want to move, and we have to improve their neighborhood, too.[55]

These words are similar to another statement of Castro's in late 2015. After endorsing the idea of moving people to "opportunity" neighborhoods, he noted, "At the same time, you can't forget about the distressed areas and investing in the older urban core neighborhoods." Government, he said, cannot "forget about folks who also want to live [in central neighborhoods], where they have lived forever. That's their home, that's where they want to be. If you gave them a choice to go somewhere else they wouldn't because they want to live there."[56]

The Trump administration, while hostile to the AFFH Rule, has had less to say about how it would approach the tension between fair housing and community development.

Conclusion

The aggressive spatial strategy of fair housing, a strategy that emphasizes integrated settlement patterns, has led to heightened levels of tension with community development and affordable housing efforts directed at lower-income, minority neighborhoods. The spatial strategy of fair housing, however, has the potential to create tensions with other policy objectives as well.

Federal initiatives in sustainability and transportation policy, especially efforts to coordinate transportation and housing investments, present fair housing activists with the same concerns.[57] The logic of coordinated investment and transit-oriented development, another periodic goal of the federal government, suggests that affordable housing should be present where transit service levels are high. The problem, for fair housing advocates, is that transit service is often greatest in central-city areas with high concentrations of poverty that they find inappropriate for more affordable housing investment.

HUD's development of the Location Affordability Index (LAI) similarly presents fair housing advocates with concerns. The LAI measures the combined housing and transportation costs in a neighborhood, providing a more complete understanding of the true cost of living in any given area than is provided by traditional housing affordability measures. Whether it is used to determine how housing programs affect the transportation costs of assisted families or where to place assisted housing to minimize transportation costs, the LAI highlights the advantages of locating affordable housing in core areas that are well served by transit. This feature is alarming to fair housing groups, who call the LAI an "inappropriate tool for siting new low-income housing" and have opposed transit-oriented development plans that call for affordable housing along transit lines because of fears that locating assisted housing by transit lines would perpetuate segregation.[58] In fact, fair housing activists worry that HUD and the Department of Transportation overemphasize the importance of housing cost and transit access; they urge policy makers to instead "recognize the additional variables greatly impacting household costs and quality of life."[59]

Fair housing advocates frequently criticize the development of affordable housing in disadvantaged neighborhoods as a "path of least resistance." Such an argument suggests that affordable housing is placed in low-income neighborhoods because these neighborhoods lack the resources to effectively oppose such housing. Thus, developers and agencies go where they have a higher likelihood of success, and a reinforcing pattern of spatial concentration of subsidized units ensues. Ironically, the second and third stations of the fair housing spatial strategy outlined above also follow paths of least resistance. Integrationists who focus their strategy on stopping or reducing affordable housing development in disadvantaged neighborhoods capitalize on antipathies toward subsidized housing shared by policy makers and middle- and upper-income citizens. It is typically not difficult to enlist opposition to subsidized housing, especially with an argument that certain places have too much of it. Indeed, as I have pointed out elsewhere, the logic of opposition to affordable housing in the core actually provides a rationale for opposition in exclusionary areas.[60] Defining subsidized housing as a community problem only reinforces the resistance of white middle- and upper-income communities.

Similarly, at the third station of fair housing spatial strategy, integrationists who pursue the demolition of public housing and the dispersal of low-income communities also trade on these attitudes. Additionally, however, the third station of fair housing spatial strategy also activates the considerable self-interest of landowners, developers, and local officials who benefit from the demolition of public housing and the economic and land-use transitions that follow.

Convincing some elected officials and property owners that they have received too much subsidized housing is not so difficult a task, especially compared to the difficulties involved in convincing other officials in exclusionary communities that they need to produce more of such housing. When fair housing integrationists add their voices to the array of interests already opposed to subsidized housing, they follow a path of least resistance. While they may succeed in convincing some officials and activists that their communities are being taken advantage of, these efforts do nothing to get housing built in exclusionary communities. What fair housing integrationists repeatedly fail to demonstrate is how shutting off subsidized housing in the core, or demolishing it, will necessarily reduce opposition to the production of subsidized housing in exclusionary communities.

When fair housing integrationists move to restrict affordable housing in certain communities and try to discourage or limit occupancy in certain neighborhoods, they assert the primacy of integration over other housing goals, such as equal access. In so doing, they offer a stylized reading of the Fair Housing Act that privileges integration over access. The legislative history of fair housing, the language of the act itself, and subsequent actions by the courts and Congress do not support a privileged position for integration.

Furthermore, efforts to date in engineering integration have perforce accommodated white intolerance at all stages. Although levels of white segregation exceed those of other groups, efforts to break up segregated communities have focused on the demolition and redevelopment of communities of color. The very definition of integration itself tends to be that level of minority occupancy that whites will tolerate, such that program administrators work to limit the reconcentration of people of color in new communities. The reluctance on the part of the courts, policy makers, and fair housing integrationists to burden the white community with the obligation of integration is a central fact of integration efforts in the United States. As a result, our efforts to integrate typically come at the expense of communities of color, through the manipulation or restriction of housing choice, or via the denial of needed community development funding.

Fair housing advocates would do better to direct their activism toward those communities that resist subsidized housing rather than toward those that build it. We know that in the United States, the wealthy are more segregated than the poor, and that whites are more segregated than people of color. The fair housing movement should return to advocacy that forces open the communities that exercise exclusionary tactics.

ENDNOTES

1. Elizabeth Anderson, *The Imperative of Integration* (Princeton, NJ: Princeton University Press, 2010); Florence Roisman, "Constitutional and Statutory Mandates for Residential Racial Integration and the Validity of Race-Conscious, Affirmative Action to Achieve It," in *The Integration Debate: Competing Futures for American Cities*, ed. Chester Hartman and Gregory Squires (New York: Routledge, 2009), 67–84.

2. Ingrid Gould Ellen and Margery Austin Turner, "Does Neighborhood Matter? Assessing Recent Evidence," *Housing Policy Debate* 8, no. 4 (January 1, 1997): 833–866; Robert J. Sampson, Jeffrey D. Morenoff, and Thomas Gannon-Rowley, "Assessing 'Neighborhood Effects': Social Processes and New Directions in Research," *Annual Review of Sociology* 28, no. 1 (2002): 443–478.

3. Tommie Shelby, *Dark Ghettos: Injustice, Dissent, and Reform* (Cambridge: Harvard University Press, 2016), 39.

4. Mary E. Pattillo, "The Problem of Integration," *The Dream Revisited*, January 20, 2014, available at http://furmancenter.org/research/iri/essay/the-problem-of-integration.

5. Shelby, *Dark Ghettos*, 70.

6. Iris Marion Young, *Inclusion and Democracy* (Oxford: Oxford University Press, 2002).

7. Juliet Saltman, *Open Housing: Dynamics of a Social Movement* (New York: Praeger, 1978).

8. Mara S. Sidney, "Fair Housing and Affordable Housing Advocacy: Reconciling the Dual Agenda," in *The Geography of Opportunity: Race and Housing Choice in Metropolitan America*, ed. Xavier de Souza Briggs (Washington, DC: Brookings Institution Press, 2005), 266–286.

9. National Commission on Fair Housing and Equal Opportunity, *The Future of Fair Housing: Report of the National Commission on Fair Housing and Equal Opportunity* (National Commission on Fair Housing and Equal Opportunity, 2008).

10. Alexander Polikoff, "Sustainable Integration or Inevitable Resegregation: The Troubling Questions," in *Housing Desegregation and Federal Policy*, ed. John Goering (Chapel Hill: University of North Carolina Press, 1986), available at https://www.questia.com/library/105726029/housing-desegregation-and-federal-policy; Charles E. Daye, "Whither 'Fair' Housing: Mediations on Wrong Paradigms, Ambivalent Answers, and a Legislative Proposal," *Washington University Journal of Law and Policy* 3, no. 1 (January 1, 2000): 241–294; Robert W. Lake and Jessica Winslow, "Integration Management: Municipal Constraints on Residential Mobility," *Urban Geography* 2, no. 4 (October 1, 1981): 311–326; Leonard S. Rubinowitz and Elizabeth Trosman, "Affirmative Action and the American Dream: Implementing Fair Housing Policies in Federal Homeownership Programs," *Northwestern University Law Review* 74 (1979): 491–616; Sidney, "Fair Housing and Affordable Housing Advocacy."

11. Daye, "Whither 'Fair' Housing."

12. Robert Neuwirth, "Renovation or Ruin: Is the LIHTC Program Promoting Segregation?" *Shelterforce*, September 1, 2004, available at https://shelterforce.org/2004/09/01/renovation-or-ruin/.

13. Myron Orfield and Will Stancil, "Why Are the Twin Cities So Segregated?" *Mitchell Hamline Law Review* 43, no. 1 (2017): 2.

14. Edward G. Goetz, *The One-Way Street of Integration: Fair Housing and the Pursuit of Racial Justice in American Cities* (Ithaca, NY: Cornell University Press, 2018).

15. Ibid.

16. Justin D. Cummins, "Recasting Fair Share: Toward Effective Housing Law and Principled Social Policy," *Law and Inequality: A Journal of Theory and Practice* 14, no. 2 (1996): 53.

17. Sharon Krefetz, "The Impact and Evolution of the Massachusetts Comprehensive Permit and Zoning Appeals Act: Thirty Years of Experience with a State Legislative Effort to Overcome Exclusionary Zoning," *Western New England Law Review* 22, no. 2 (January 1, 2001): 381.

18. Nico Calavita, Kenneth Grimes, and Alan Mallach, "Inclusionary Housing in California and New Jersey: A Comparative Analysis," *Housing Policy Debate* 8, no. 1 (January 1997): 109–142.

19. Antonio Raciti, Katherine A. Lambert-Pennington, and Kenneth M. Reardon, "The Struggle for the Future of Public Housing in Memphis, Tennessee: Reflections on HUD's Choice Neighborhoods Planning Program," *Cities* 57 (September 2016): 6–13; Amy L. Howard and Thad Williamson, "Reframing Public Housing in Richmond, Virginia: Segregation, Resident Resistance and the Future of Redevelopment," *Cities* 57 (September 2016): 33–39.

20. Preston H. Smith II, *Racial Democracy and the Black Metropolis: Housing Policy in Postwar Chicago* (Minneapolis: University of Minnesota Press, 2012); James Q. Wilson, *Negro Politics: The Search for Leadership* (Glencoe, IL: Free Press, 1960); St. Clair Drake and Horace R. Cayton, *Black Metropolis: A Study of Negro Life in a Northern City* (Chicago: University of Chicago Press, 1970).

21. James Tyner, *The Geography of Malcolm X: Black Radicalism and the Remaking of American Space* (New York: Routledge, 2006), 79.

22. Peniel E. Joseph, ed., *The Black Power Movement: Rethinking the Civil Rights—Black Power Era* (New York: Routledge, 2006).

23. John T. Baker, "Community Development Corporations: A Legal Analysis," Valparaiso University Law Review 13, no. 1 (1978): 55.

24. Laura Warren Hill and Julia Rabig, eds., *The Business of Black Power: Community Development, Capitalism, and Corporate Responsibility in Postwar America* (Rochester, NY: Boydell and Brewer, 2012), 9.

25. Saltman, *Open Housing.*

26. Ibid., 310–311.

27. Ibid., 125.

28. *Shannon v. HUD*, 436 F. 2d 809 (3d Cir. 1970).

29. Goetz, *The One-Way Street of Integration.*

30. Harvey Luskin Molotch, *Managed Integration: Dilemmas of Doing Good in the City* (Berkeley: University of California Press, 1972).

31. Lake and Winslow, "Integration Management"; Molotch, *Managed Integration.*

32. W. Dennis Keating, *The Suburban Racial Dilemma: Housing and Neighborhoods* (Philadelphia: Temple University Press, 1994).

33. Molotch, *Managed Integration*, 101.

34. William Julius Wilson and Richard P. Taub, *There Goes the Neighborhood: Racial, Ethnic, and Class Tensions in Four Chicago Neighborhoods and Their Meaning for America* (New York: Knopf Doubleday Publishing Group, 2011), 179.

35. Lake and Winslow, "Integration Management."

36. The full list of selection criteria that Qualified Allocation Plans must include is "project location, housing needs characteristics, project characteristics, including whether the project includes the use of housing as part of a community revitalization plan, sponsor characteristics, tenant populations with special housing needs, public housing waiting lists, tenant populations of individuals with children, projects intended for eventual tenant ownership, the energy efficiency of the project, and the historic nature of the project." Internal Revenue Code §42 (m)(1)(C).

37. Internal Revenue Code §42 (m)(1)(B)(ii). The qualified census tract incentive was added to the program by amendment in 1989.

38. Elizabeth K. Julian, "Recent Advocacy Related to the Low-Income Housing Tax Credit and Fair Housing," *Journal of Affordable Housing and Community Development Law* 18, no. 2 (2009): 185–192.

39. Jill Khadduri, *Creating Balance in the Locations of LIHTC Developments: The Role of Qualified Allocation Plans* (Washington, DC: Poverty and Race Research Action Council and Abt Associates, February 2013), available at http://www.prrac.org/pdf/Balance_in_the_Locations_of_LIHTC_Developments.pdf; Casey Dawkins, "The Spatial Pattern of Low Income Housing Tax Credit Properties: Implications for Fair Housing and Poverty Deconcentration Policies," *Journal of the American Planning Association* 79, no. 3 (July 3, 2013): 222–234.

40. In re: Adoption of 2003 Low Income Housing Tax Credit Allocation Plan, 848 A. 2d 1, 5 (N.J. Super. Ct. App. Div. 2004). Another suit was filed in 2002 by the Connecticut Civil Liberties Union against the state allocating agency in Connecticut on the basis of the segregatory impact of the LIHTC program in the Hartford metropolitan area, *In Re: Declaratory Ruling on Connecticut Low Income Housing Tax Credit Program*; see the brief description in Keren M. Horn and Katherine M. O'Regan, *The Low Income Housing Tax Credit and Racial Segregation* (New York: Furman Center for Real Estate and Public Policy, 2011); *The Inclusive Communities Project, Inc., v. The Texas Department of Housing and Community Affairs*, complaint filed March 28, 2008, in the U.S. District Court, Northern District of Texas, Dallas Division, 3:08-CV-546-D, 12; Housing Discrimination Complaint: *Metropolitan Interfaith Council on Affordable Housing, et al. v. State of Minnesota, et al.*

41. James A. Long, "The Low-Income Housing Tax Credit in New Jersey: New Opportunities to Deconcentrate Poverty through the Duty to Affirmatively Further Fair Housing," *Annual Survey of American Law* 66, no. 1 (May 12, 2010): 54.

42. Neuwirth, "Renovation or Ruin."

43. Ibid.

44. Ingrid Gould Ellen and Keren Horn, *Effect of QAP Incentives on the Location of LIHTC Properties: Multi-Disciplinary Research Team Report* (Washington, DC: U.S. Department of Housing and Urban Development, 2015).

45. *The Inclusive Communities Project, Inc., v. The Texas Department of Housing and Community Affairs*, 546 U.S. 12 (2015).

46. Ibid.

47. Ibid.

48. Ibid.

49. Ibid.

50. Julieta Chiquillo, "After Supreme Court Victory, Dallas Nonprofit Loses Racial Bias Suit against Texas Agency," *Dallas News*, August 31, 2016, available at https://www.dallasnews.com/news/dallas/2016/08/31/supreme-court-victory-dallas-nonprofit-loses-racial-bias-suit-texas-agency.

51. Stockton Williams and Maya Brennan, "A New Landscape of Housing Access and Opportunity," *Urban Land Magazine*, November 30, 2015, available at https://urbanland.uli.org/economy-markets-trends/new-landscape-housing-access-opportunity/.

52. Ibid.

53. Anna Simonton, "What a Fair Housing Victory in the U.S. Supreme Court Means for Atlanta | Atlanta Progressive News," *Atlanta Progressive News*, September 19, 2015, available at http://atlantaprogressivenews.com/2015/09/19/what-a-fair-housing-victory-in-the-u-s-supreme-court-means-for-atlanta/.

54. "Affirmatively Furthering Fair Housing," *Federal Register* 9 (January 14, 2020): 2041–2061.

55. Shelterforce Staff, "Interview with HUD Secretary Julián Castro," *Shelterforce*, February 4, 2016, available at https://shelterforce.org/2016/02/04/ishelterforce_i_exclusive_interview_with_hud_secretary_julian_castro-2/.

56. Melissa Harris-Perry, "Julian Castro on Public Housing in New Orleans," *Melissa Harris-Perry* (MSNBC, August 30, 2015), available at https://www.msnbc.com/melissa-harris-perry/watch/julian-castro-on-public-housing-in-new-orleans-516027971685.

57. See Edward G. Goetz, "Sustainable Fair Housing? Reconciling the Spatial Goals of Fair Housing and Sustainable Development in the Obama Administration," in *Urban Policy in the Time of Obama*, ed. James DeFilippis (Minneapolis: University of Minnesota Press, 2016); Edward G. Goetz, "The Fair Housing Tightrope in the Obama Administration: Balancing Competing Policy Objectives of Fair Housing and Locational Efficiency in Assisted Housing," *Journal of Urban Affairs* 37, no. 1 (February 2015): 53–56.

58. Philip Tegeler and Hanna Chouest, "The 'Housing + Transportation Index' and Fair Housing," *Poverty and Race* (2011); available at https://prrac.org/the-housing-transportation-index-and-fair-housing/; Oak Park Regional Housing Center, "Affirmatively Furthering Fair Housing and the Center for Neighborhood Technology's H+T Affordability Index," February 2012, 7.

59. Oak Park Regional Housing Center, "Affirmatively Furthering Fair Housing and the Center for Neighborhood Technology's H+T Affordability Index," 2.

60. Edward G. Goetz, "The Politics of Poverty Deconcentration and Housing Demolition," *Journal of Urban Affairs* 22, no. 2 (June 2000): 157–173.

Prospects

6

Gentrification, Displacement, and Fair Housing

Tensions and Opportunities

Vicki Been

The Fair Housing Act's requirement that the secretary of the Department of Housing and Urban Development (HUD) administer HUD's programs in a manner "affirmatively to further the policies" of the act,[1] which came to be referred to as the "Affirmatively Furthering Fair Housing (AFFH)" requirement was an unusual congressional acknowledgment that just ending discrimination is not enough. Instead, affirmative steps are necessary to undo the horrendous legacy that more than a century of policies and practices by governments, businesses, and private individuals to segregate cities, suburbs, and towns across the United States have imposed upon generations of African American and Latinx individuals.[2] The Fair Housing Act thus mandates that the government must take affirmative measures to undo the pernicious segregation that has resulted from its past actions and thereby begin to correct the many injustices that have resulted from that segregation.[3] Those injustices range from unequal access to good schools, job opportunities, healthy environments, and neighborhoods with low crime and other essential services and amenities to persistent (and growing) gaps between the wealth of whites and African Americans and Latinx individuals.[4]

But how exactly local governments should go about dismantling residential segregation is not a simple matter, especially in growing cities, where many formerly affordable neighborhoods that had large shares of racial or ethnic minorities in their populations are becoming gentrified. For the purposes of this chapter, I define "gentrification" as unusual increases in housing costs in low-income neighborhoods over a sustained period of time. The complexities of how to achieve fair housing as neighborhoods change have spurred decades of debate about place-based versus people-based housing assistance.[5] The many thoughtful comments submitted during consideration of the AFFH Rule,[6] and in the debates over regulations regarding HUD's application of disparate impact standards[7] and its Small Area Fair Market Rent Rule,[8] also reveal the nuanced difficulties of the issues that fair housing goals raise.

Of course, complexity can be the refuge of people who prefer the status quo or of those too timid to take a stand until all uncertainty is resolved. But even among those who earnestly want to reduce inequality and achieve diverse and thriving neighborhoods for all in their communities, the dilemmas posed by the obligation to affirmatively further fair housing in the context of gentrification make efforts to introduce effective policies fraught with dangers—of unintended consequences, legal challenges to well-intentioned judgment calls, and criticism from stakeholders who view the dilemmas differently or fail to see the nuances of the debate.

This chapter seeks to make the challenges of fair housing in the context of gentrification more concrete, with the hope that getting beyond abstract arguments will help encourage more productive thinking about how local governments can reduce segregation in gentrifying neighborhoods fairly, in ways that will not result in resegregation in the years to come, and, given the limited resources that local governments have, in the most cost-efficient ways possible. To be concrete, I must ground the discussion in actual neighborhoods, and I have chosen to focus on neighborhoods in New York City because the affordable housing crisis there is especially pronounced, gentrification and fair housing debates are particularly sharp, and the city already has adopted many of the anti-displacement tools that other jurisdictions are now considering.[9] The first section seeks to put the questions in context by providing a brief overview of the affordable housing crisis in New York City. The second section gives a summary of some of the main strategies the city has chosen to address that crisis and the opposition to those strategies that has arisen. The third section outlines the hard questions about how best to achieve fair housing in growing cities that the opposition to the city's proposals (as well as the thoughtful comments of proponents) raises and explores some of those questions with concrete examples of how they might play out in particular neighborhoods. The chapter concludes by exploring how the assessments of fair housing required by the 2015 AFFH Rule, although now no longer required,[10] might provide an opportunity to make progress toward resolving the difficult issues that the previous section discusses.

Putting the Questions in Context: New York City's Affordable Housing Crisis

Gentrification can occur even when population is declining and there is an apparent surplus of housing, as a particular neighborhood becomes desirable for people with higher incomes than those of existing residents.[11] But the fair housing challenges that gentrification raises are particularly acute when the lack of affordable housing makes new development desirable, and that development either raises fears of gentrification in existing low-income neighborhoods or raises concerns that low-income neighborhoods are not getting their fair share of investment in public services and amenities because development is going elsewhere. It is helpful to start, therefore, by situating questions about gentrification in the broader context of the lack of affordable housing that is plaguing many cities.

New York City, like so many cities and towns across the country, is facing a significant crisis of affordability. The city's renters and those who seek to purchase homes in New York City face enormous pressures caused primarily by four significant factors: (1) the city's housing stock does not appear to be keeping up with demand; (2) middle- and upper-income households are increasingly seeking housing in the neighborhoods close to the central business and cultural districts; (3) for most of the years since the mid-2000s, wages have been stagnant or have even declined, while rents consistently have increased; and (4) the number of New Yorkers living at or near the poverty line far outstrips the number of apartments rented at rates affordable to those households.

The City's Housing Stock Is Not Increasing Enough to Meet Demand

New York City has a population of about 8.3 million people as of July 2019. At the beginning of the 2010 decade, it grew at rates higher than the city had seen since the 1920s,[12] but the city has experienced population declines in the last few years because of declining international immigration.[13]

The city's housing production also has grown: there were about 260,000 more housing units in the city in 2016 than in 2000.[14] As significant as that production was, however, it has to be viewed in context: while the housing stock grew by 8.2 percent during those years, the adult population grew by 11 percent, and the number of jobs in the city grew by 16.5 percent.[15] Further, housing production has slowed in recent years: between 2001 and 2008, before the Great Recession, housing production was 25 percent higher on average than in the post-Recession period between 2009 and 2018.[16] In addition, population growth is not the only source of demand for housing;

some housing is purchased or rented by people who are not residents of the city.[17] People who are homeless or living in overcrowded or substandard apartments also require additional housing options. As a result, vacancy rates remain low, and the share of housing affordable to the city's low- and moderate-income households fell significantly between 2000 and 2016. All those measures suggest that more housing is needed, especially for the households in the city with moderate or lower incomes.[18]

Demand for Housing in Cities Like New York by Middle- and Upper-Income Households Has Grown

Households with incomes in the top 40 percent of the U.S. income distribution were the only households who were more likely to live in higher-density neighborhoods in 2014 than they were in 2000.[19] In New York City, households making more than $200,000 in income per year grew from 6.2 percent of the population in 2010 to 8.3 percent in 2016.[20] While the number of resident and nonresident wealthy buyers in the city is smaller than the media attention to those buyers would suggest, and their demand for luxury apartments may have peaked, they undoubtedly affect what gets built and the price of housing in the city.[21] Indeed, the New York University (NYU) Furman Center recently showed that the median renter in newly constructed units in the city had a household income that was one-third higher than the median income of all other renters and that the gap between the rents in new units and those in all other units has grown substantially in recent years.[22]

Rents Have Increased Far Faster Than Wages

One result of inadequate supply is that rents have gone up significantly— almost 20 percent between 2006 and 2016 in constant dollars.[23] But the city's median income, like the nation's, declined or stagnated between 2008 and 2014, as shown in Figure 6.1. While median income has increased since then, increases in rent have far outpaced increases in renter income since 2006, as shown in Figure 6.2.

The Number of Low-Income Households Far Outstrips the Number of Affordable Apartments

The number of New York City households with especially low incomes also increased during this period. Indeed, New York City has a larger number of people living in poverty in the 2011–2015 period than it has had since at least 1970.[24] More than 37 percent of all renter households in New York

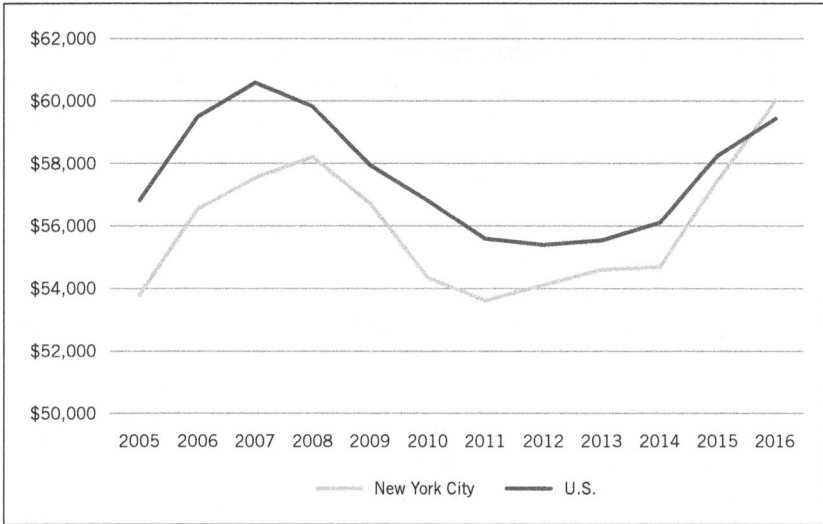

Figure 6.1. Inflation-adjusted median household income (2017$). *(Sources: American Community Survey; NYU Furman Center)*

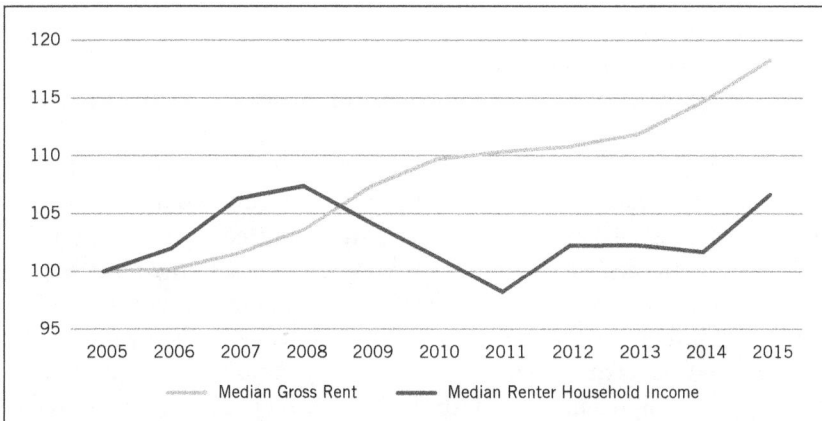

Figure 6.2. Index of real median gross rent and real median renter income, New York City (Index = 100 in 2006). *(Sources: American Community Survey; NYU Furman Center)*

City earned incomes in 2016 that would be considered either "very low income" or "extremely low income" by HUD's standards. That means that the city has more than 1.2 million households with incomes between $0 and $40,800 for a family of three.[25] But the city had only about 515,000 housing units in 2017 with rents affordable to households in those income categories.[26] That number includes all public housing, other subsidized housing, all unsubsidized but rent-regulated housing, and all unregulated market-rate housing rented for less than $999 per month. Further, the number overstates the supply available to those lowest-income households, because some of the units are rented to households with higher incomes that could afford units that rent for more.

Addressing the Affordable Housing Crisis

In sum, New York City's population, and its low-income households, are increasing faster than the supply of housing, especially housing affordable to the lowest-income households. This situation means that more people are competing for existing housing, and, in that competition, wealthier people are able to outbid poorer people. Because some of the housing going to wealthier people is in neighborhoods that have been home to many low-income households, gentrification results.

Indeed, in 2016, the NYU Furman Center assessed all fifty-five subborough areas in New York City to identify low-income neighborhoods (those with a median income below the city's median in 1990) in which rents had increased between 1990 and 2010 faster than the average rate for the city as a whole. Using that definition, its assessment showed that fifteen low-income neighborhoods were gentrifying.[27]

The city laid out its strategies for addressing the need for additional affordable housing in 2014 in *Housing New York: A Five-Borough, Ten-Year Plan* and updated and expanded those strategies in late 2017.[28] Mayor Bill de Blasio committed to building or preserving two hundred thousand units of housing by 2024 (later expanded to three hundred thousand units by 2026).[29] As of the end of March 2020, the city had financed the construction of 49,818 new homes and had preserved the affordability of another 114,386 for at least several more decades ("preserving" means financing rehabilitation or investments in the buildings and apartments as needed and entering into regulatory agreements with the owners to keep the homes affordable for the current occupants, restrict future rent increases, and require future tenants to meet income-eligibility standards). Of those 164,204 homes, 44 percent are affordable to households meeting HUD's definition of "extremely low" and "very low" income households (those making 50 percent or less of the HUD-determined area median income [AMI]).[30]

The strategies to achieve more affordable housing are multifaceted. In 2016, the city passed the most rigorous mandatory inclusionary program of any large city in the nation. It requires all new development resulting from rezonings or other land-use actions that significantly increase development capacity to make 20 to 30 percent of all the homes developed permanently affordable to a range of extremely low, low, and moderate incomes.[31] The city also passed Zoning for Quality and Affordability, a comprehensive effort to remove regulatory barriers and reduce the cost of construction for affordable and senior housing, to allow a wider range of senior housing, and to improve first-floor retail and community facility spaces so that streets are more inviting and lively.[32]

The city also is reviewing the zoning in a number of neighborhoods, with an eye toward increasing the density of the neighborhoods while also investing in infrastructure, schools, parks, job-training opportunities, and other necessary improvements in neighborhoods that have traditionally been left behind. Some neighborhoods can increase density through infill construction on underused properties, but to allow growth in other neighborhoods often requires a comprehensive neighborhood rezoning, along with considerable investments in infrastructure, schools, parks, and other neighborhood needs. The first such comprehensive community redevelopment plan was adopted in 2016 in East New York, one of the city's poorest neighborhoods. The investments resulting from the rezoning are bringing $250 million to the neighborhood and paying for a new school, improvements to six neighborhood parks, major street and safety improvements, significant water and sewer improvements, an enhanced industrial development zone, and extensive job-training efforts. At least half of the six thousand new housing units planned are expected to be affordable, and 40 to 45 percent of those affordable homes will be targeted to households making between $23,000 and $39,000.[33]

The Resulting Fair Housing Dilemmas

The city's efforts to rezone for growth in East New York and other neighborhoods have faced considerable pushback.[34] Advocates and existing residents in neighborhoods where rezonings have been proposed worry that new housing in the neighborhoods will lead to displacement of low-income residents,[35] and have called for no upzonings, upzonings that only allow affordable housing, or a variety of measures that they argue may help prevent displacement and harassment.[36] The city has had a wide range of anti-displacement programs in place for years and recently began providing legal assistance to low-income tenants facing eviction, along with assistance to help homeowners stay in their homes.[37] Nevertheless, tenant advocates are calling for additional measures ranging from special no-harassment districts to community land trusts.[38] Opposition also revolves around the incomes that the new affordable housing being built should target: some advocates argue that the affordability levels should mirror the existing incomes of the community.[39] Some also oppose the proposed rezonings because they claim that the areas being studied are home to more of the city's poor and its racial and ethnic minorities than neighborhoods that the city is not considering for such rezonings.[40] In addition, some opponents question whether adding more market-rate housing to the city is desirable and are skeptical that increasing supply actually affects the affordability of housing.[41]

This troubling combination of concerns and arguments raises four main questions about the meaning of fair housing in gentrifying neighborhoods. First, the criticism of the city's selection of neighborhoods in which it may propose comprehensive rezonings and community development investments presents fundamental challenges to traditional place-based investments. On the one hand, enabling growth in neighborhoods that have been left behind in terms of investment and redevelopment could help promote integration if new residents are of different races, ethnicities, or incomes than existing residents. In addition, promoting comprehensive community redevelopment in those areas might help redress prior neglect, discrimination, and segregative or expulsive land-use policies. Indeed, failing to promote development in neighborhoods ignored in the past may be discriminatory. On the other hand, revitalization might be associated with further segregation of racial or ethnic minorities if it is accompanied by displacement or if the neighborhood subsequently moves from predominantly minority to predominantly white. Further, because growth always brings costs as well as benefits, growth in neglected neighborhoods may unfairly burden the very people who have already suffered from government and private discrimination.

A second set of questions concerns how governments can prevent displacement while also affirmatively furthering fair housing. One manifestation of that tension arises in discussions about how state and local governments should target the incomes to be served through subsidized housing to integrate those neighborhoods. On the one hand, targeting homes to those incomes currently prevalent in the neighborhood may further concentrate poverty and (because of the correlation between poverty and racial segregation) perpetuate existing segregation. On the other hand, especially if the subsidized housing is a small share of the new housing expected in the neighborhood, targeting incomes higher than the current population's may be less immediately effective in preventing displacement than targeting the incomes of existing residents vulnerable to displacement. Another concern is whether tools for preventing displacement will promote or slow down integration and increase or decrease movement to higher-opportunity neighborhoods. Do anti-displacement tools, such as tenants' right-to-purchase programs, preferences used in the allocation of new subsidized housing, or rent regulation that extends tenancies beyond what they would otherwise likely be, have the effect of perpetuating segregation if they enable or even encourage current residents to stay in a neighborhood that is currently segregated? Or do those tools help create stably integrated neighborhoods and reduce the likelihood of displacement that disproportionately affects minority families?

A third set of questions, closely related to issues about the fair housing implications of anti-displacement tools, concerns how cities should promote mobility while also respecting people's desire to stay in their current neighborhoods. Do efforts to promote mobility unfairly put the burden of integration on those who have suffered the most from segregation? Where is the line between encouraging people to take advantage of opportunities to move to different neighborhoods and deterring them from remaining in their existing neighborhood or punishing them for doing so? The debates over how HUD's Small Area Fair Market Rent rule would affect tenants in low-vacancy cities began to surface these issues, but they will require much more thought as efforts to encourage mobility increase.[42] Similarly, they point to the need for the thoughtful design of mobility programs to address the challenges that people face in moving away from social and other networks.[43]

The fourth set of questions, related to the first, is how to assess the effects that zoning changes, neighborhood investments, and even building forms have on the segregation or integration of a neighborhood. It is relatively easy to conclude that, for example, zoning that allows only single-family homes will result in a less diverse neighborhood than zoning that allows multifamily and single-family developments. It is another matter to determine whether height limits of eight stories rather than ten,[44] proposals to uniformly upzone areas around transit stations,[45] inclusionary housing programs that allow off-site provision of the affordable housing,[46] uniform limits on density that leave room for significant growth in only some neighborhoods,[47] or historic preservation of some neighborhoods[48] will promote, deter, or have no effect on integration.

Those are difficult questions that require thought and debate at a more concrete level than discussions about gentrification, or even about fair housing, typically entail. To illustrate how concrete discussions may help us move toward better discussions about such dilemmas, the following sections ground the first two sets of questions in specific neighborhood contexts. I leave for another day more extensive analysis of the last two sets of questions and discussion of an overarching fairness framework that could guide comprehensive resolution of all the questions I have raised.

Distributing the Benefits and Burdens of Growth

Answering the first set of questions demands that we have an underlying theory about how to fairly distribute the burdens and benefits of growth. Development may bring "eyes on the street," jobs, and the customer base necessary to support retail, community organizations, transit, and culture. It is appropriate, or perhaps even mandatory, for cities to invest in infrastructure where they are seeing growth, so growth naturally brings with it new facilities and services. But growth also brings change, risk, the possibility of greater congestion, and other disadvantages.

So, how should those benefits and burdens be distributed? Surely it is wrong to deny the benefits of investment to neighborhoods in which a particular racial, ethnic, religious, or other group protected by the Fair Housing Act constitutes a large share of the population—that denial is what prompted the municipal service disparity legal challenges of the 1970s[49] and the environmental justice cases challenging disparities in cleanup of polluted sites and the siting of hazardous facilities that began in the 1980s and 1990s.[50] Indeed, the lack of investment in some neighborhoods is part and parcel of "expulsive zoning"[51] and is rooted in the sorry history of unequal government support for mortgage financing, roads, and other investments in predominantly white suburbs that contributed to the residential segregation that mars our metropolitan areas today.[52]

But putting aside for a moment questions of displacement, if new growth is now targeted to some neighborhoods, along with service and facility investments, are the burdens that will accompany that growth unfair? How do we even measure whether a neighborhood is being asked to grow? Do we compare a proposed density to the density that is there now or to the maximum density that the community has seen in the past? And how do we compare the growth asked of different neighborhoods? If the primarily white or wealthy areas of a city are also areas of high density, as they are in at least some of the cities seeing significant gentrification, have those neighborhoods already accommodated their fair share of growth, or must they be asked to take the same amount of growth as areas that didn't grow in the past (and does that depend on the reasons those areas didn't grow)?[53]

More broadly, what should a fair distribution of land-use changes to allow (or disallow) additional capacity look like?[54] Must the growth be evenly distributed over every neighborhood (however defined) in the jurisdiction (however defined)? In New York City, for example, should each of the city's 59 community districts be required to accommodate at least 1/59 of the projected growth? Or should every neighborhood be required to accommodate an increase in the share of its population at least equal to the expected growth rate of the jurisdiction as a whole?

How should the distribution of growth relate to market demand? What role should other factors, such as environmental concerns, proximity to the central business district or other job centers or amenities, land assembly challenges, and the cost of building in different places, play in determining where growth should be encouraged?[55]

Current debates in New York City over the Chinatown neighborhood's calls for rezonings to limit building heights and controversies over the towers being built at the edge of Chinatown in lower Manhattan provide a concrete example of these issues.[56] With the growth discussed earlier, Queens and Staten Island are at their all-time population highs, the Bronx is close to its historic 1970 high of nearly 1.5 million, and Brooklyn is near or over its historic 1950 high of more than 2.7 million people.[57] Although Manhattan is growing, its population is still more than 680,000 below its 1910 peak, and the population density of the Lower East Side/Chinatown was 10 percent lower in 2010 than it was in 1970.[58] So it may be fair to ask at least some neighborhoods in Manhattan to accept more growth. On the other hand, the fact that some neighborhoods in the city (such as those in Staten Island and in some parts of Queens and Brooklyn) have historically been lower density should not necessarily mean that those neighborhoods should be able to lock in that privilege.[59]

Or consider East New York, which was rezoned in 2016. The area studied as part of the rezoning had twenty thousand fewer people than at its historic high of sixty-six thousand in 1950.[60] The neighborhood suffered in the years it lost population, so that by 2016, the surrounding community district had a poverty rate of 28.4 percent, and only 24.5 percent of the fourth-grade students in its public schools performed at grade level in math proficiency tests.[61] The area is now growing faster than the borough of Brooklyn as a whole but was not considered to be gentrifying as of 2015.[62] Was the rezoning to allow another approximately six thousand homes (enough for about sixteen thousand people) unfair, given the neighborhood's distressed conditions and large share of low-income households, or was it necessary to better resource the neighborhood and to help prevent pressure on the existing housing stock as the area deals with the already increasing demand?

More generally, Figure 6.3 shows a map of the changes in residential density in New York City since 1970. There are stark differences in growth or depopulation by neighborhood, and those differences may correlate in various ways with race, ethnicity, and poverty. How should that data inform our thinking about the fairness of which neighborhoods should be asked to accommodate the city's growth? What should those differences suggest about which neighborhoods should be prioritized for investment?

Preventing Displacement without Perpetuating Segregation

To illustrate the problem of how efforts to prevent displacement may pose challenges to achieving fair housing goals, consider Washington Heights/Inwood in Upper Manhattan. The area is gentrifying[63] and was rezoned

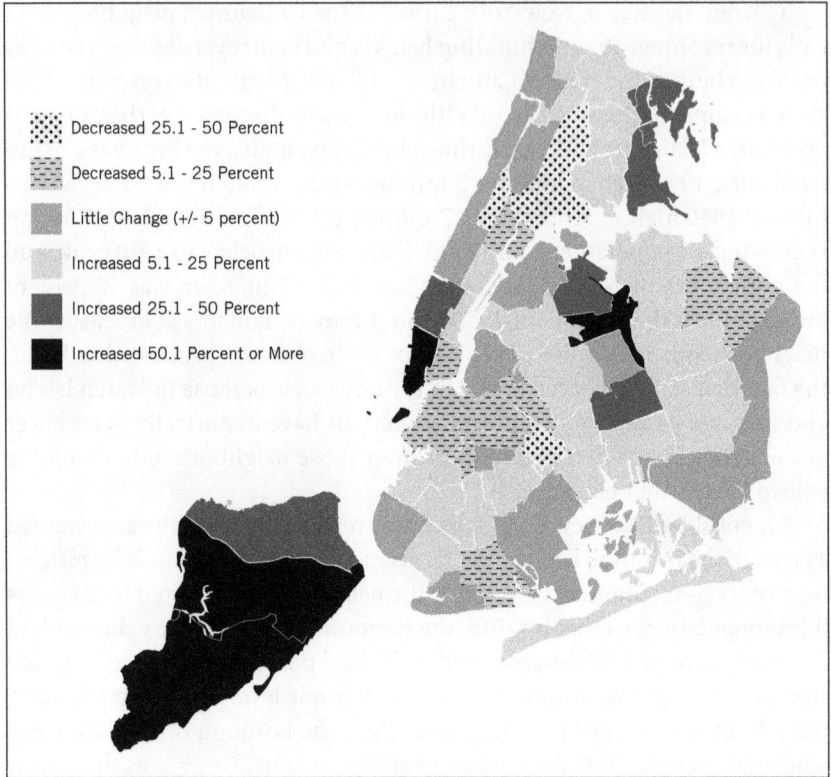

Decreased 25.1 - 50 Percent

Decreased 5.1 - 25 Percent

Little Change (+/- 5 percent)

Increased 5.1 - 25 Percent

Increased 25.1 - 50 Percent

Increased 50.1 Percent or More

Figure 6.3. Change in population density, 1970–2010. *(Sources: U.S. Census Bureau; Neighborhood Change Database; NYU Furman Center)*

for additional capacity on underused commercial land near the Harlem River.[64] Figure 6.4 shows that between the 2000 Census and the 2012 to 2016 American Community Survey, household income shifted: the share of households in the very lowest income categories remained stable, but the share of those with moderate incomes fell, and the share of the population with higher incomes increased. One way to prevent displacement, of course, is to ensure that new housing development includes affordable housing. But should that affordable housing be targeted to the very-lowest-income households—those making less than $40,000 per year—when the share of those households is stable and higher than the share of low-income households in the city as a whole? Or should policy makers aim the subsidized housing toward the households that are making $40,000 to $60,000 (and whose share of the population is decreasing)? If the city targets only the very lowest incomes for the affordable housing, would that perpetuate the concentration of poverty? Given the relationship between poverty and race and ethnicity, and given that much of the current population is

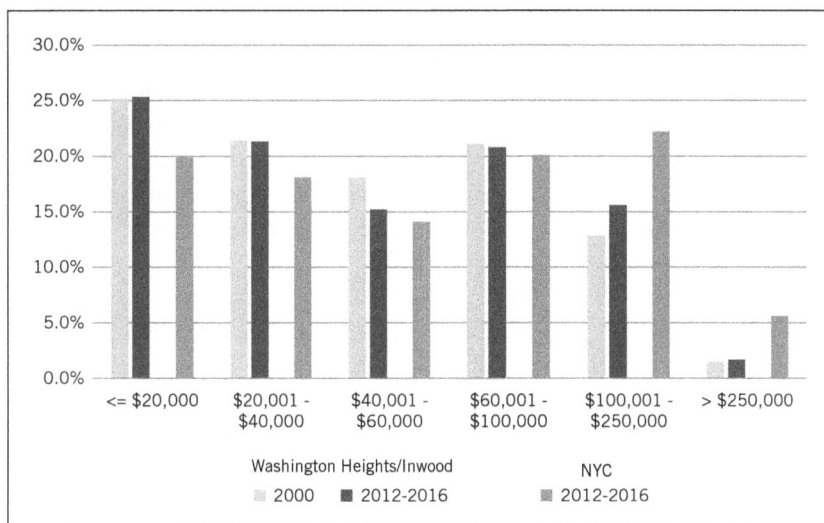

Figure 6.4. Washington Heights/Inwood household income distribution (2017$). *(Sources: American Community Survey; NYU Furman Center)*

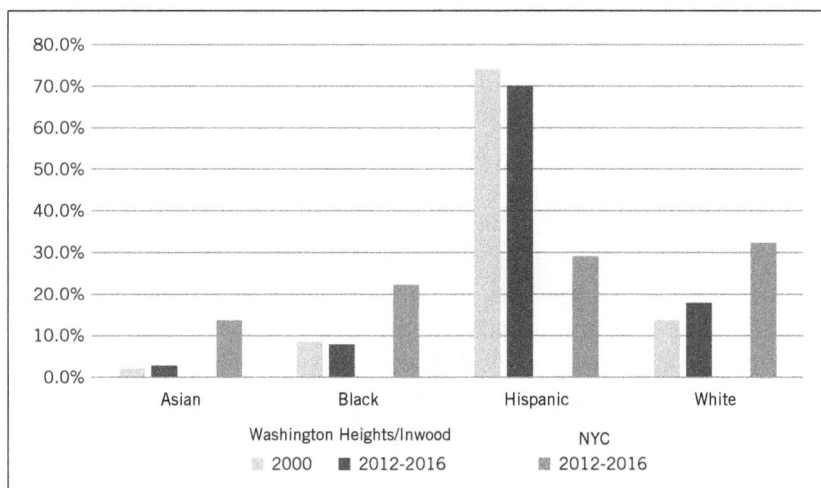

Figure 6.5. Washington Heights/Inwood racial and ethnic composition. *(Sources: American Community Survey; NYU Furman Center)*

Latinx, as shown in Figure 6.5, would targeting only the very lowest incomes perpetuate segregation? Or, given the trend toward a higher share of white residents, is it imperative that the city do everything it can (including targeting the incomes of the lowest-income current residents) to help Black and Brown people stay in (or even move to) the neighborhood to keep it from becoming disproportionately white?

It is important to keep in mind that the lowest-income households may be the most rent-burdened and the most at risk of displacement, but they also may already be in public housing or privately owned but subsidized housing with protections that limit their rents to a percentage of their income and prevent evictions except in narrow circumstances. It may be that the people most at risk of any displacement that might occur are people in the low- and moderate-income categories rather than people in the extremely- and very-low-income categories.

Another way to allow people to stay in a neighborhood even if their current housing becomes unaffordable is to grant priority for neighborhood residents in the allocation of affordable housing provided in the area. New York City's new affordable housing typically is made available to eligible applicants through a lottery, with priority for up to half of the units given to eligible residents of the community district in which the new housing is located.[65] A version of that community preference has been in place since the early 1980s. New York's preference has been challenged under the Fair Housing Act,[66] and HUD rejected at least one other city's initial proposal to adopt preferences to address the problem of displacement and fear of displacement on the grounds that the preference proposed might have a disparate impact by race.[67]

Some have suggested that the preference should be limited to those areas in a city that are undergoing significant gentrification or to those that have been "historically underserved" to address concerns that such preferences might have a disparate impact by race.[68] To show the dilemmas that poses, consider two other areas that are gentrifying—the Bushwick and Brownsville neighborhoods in Brooklyn. Figure 6.6 shows that Bushwick has been losing, or not gaining, people with extremely low and very low incomes and is seeing a shift toward households with moderate, middle, and higher incomes. The neighborhood's racial composition is also shifting, as Figure 6.7 shows: Bushwick either is losing, or failing to gain, African American and Latinx households, and the white population is growing.

On the one hand, those shifts may signal that anti-displacement tools intended to help existing residents to stay in the community as prices increase (such as a community preference for new affordable housing, homeowners' tax abatements or deferrals, rent regulation, or tenants' right-to-purchase acts) might be appropriate to prevent the neighborhood from becoming disproportionately white. On the other hand, perhaps those shifts are integrative because they are moving the neighborhood toward the average for the city as a whole (although that may depend upon whether the neighborhood becomes a stably integrated area or changes to a segregated, predominantly white community).

Brownsville, on the other hand, has not seen much change in household income or in its racial and ethnic composition, as Figures 6.8 and 6.9 reveal,

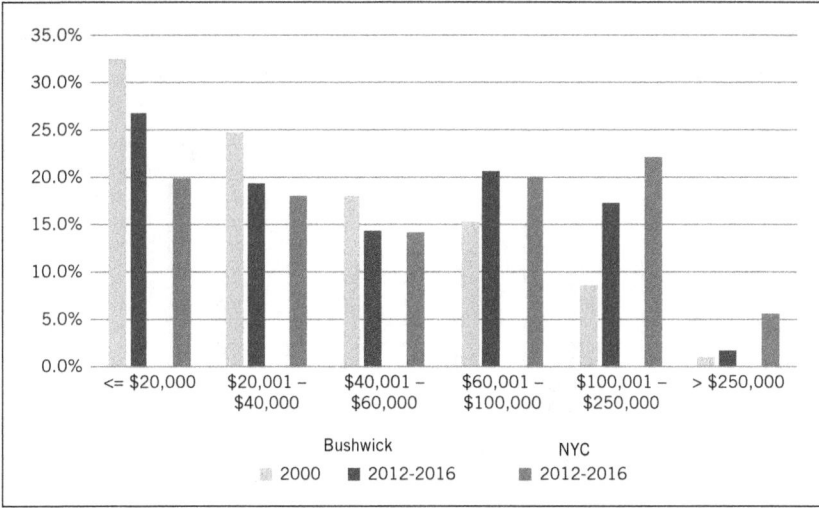

Figure 6.6. Bushwick household income distribution (2017$). *(Sources: American Community Survey; NYU Furman Center)*

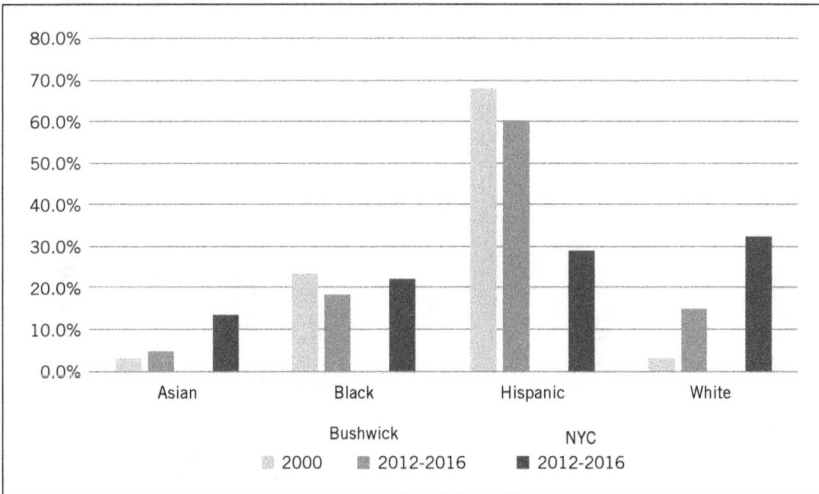

Figure 6.7. Bushwick racial and ethnic composition. *(Sources: American Community Survey; NYU Furman Center)*

even though it is gentrifying (again, defined as low income in 1990 and seeing sustained and above-average increases in housing costs since then).[69]

Does that mean that anti-displacement tools are unnecessary? Or does the fact that the neighborhood is made up almost entirely of African American and Latinx individuals mean that we should be particularly concerned about anti-displacement measures because any displacement that occurs is

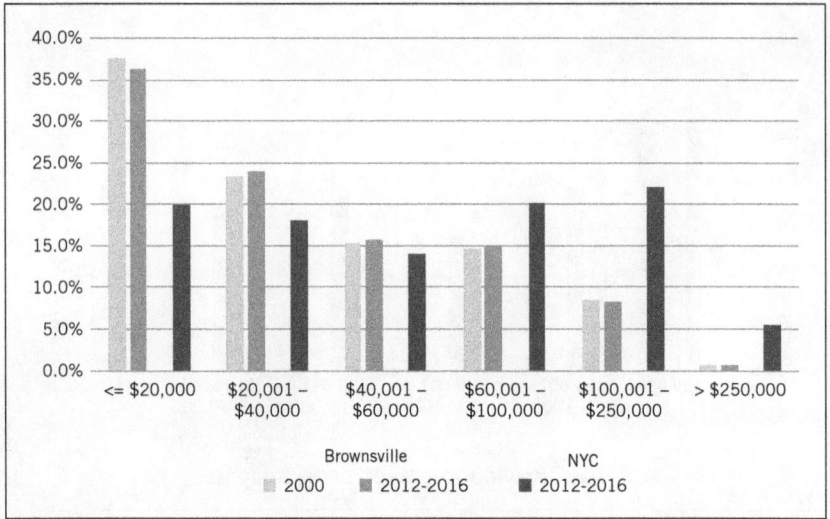

Figure 6.8. Brownsville household income distribution (2017$). *(Sources: American Community Survey; NYU Furman Center)*

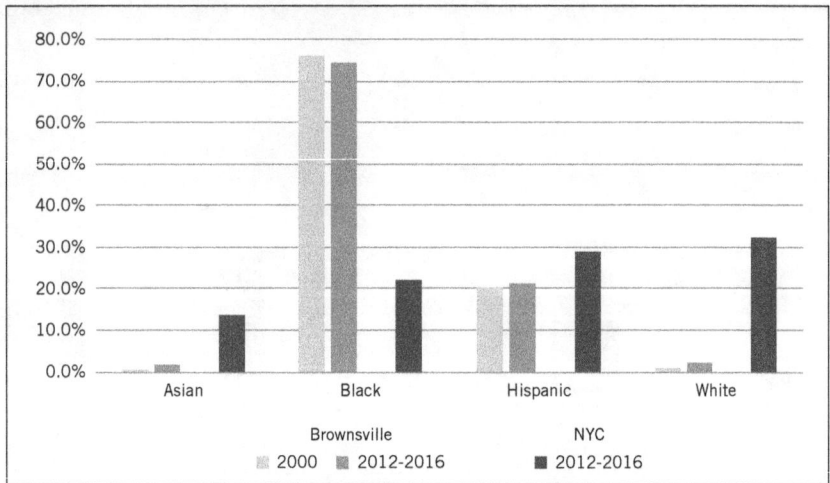

Figure 6.9. Brownsville racial and ethnic composition. *(Sources: American Community Survey; NYU Furman Center)*

going to disproportionately affect those groups? The contrast between Bushwick and Brownsville illustrates the difficulty of determining exactly how to structure anti-displacement policies. A policy that seeks to protect existing residents when the neighborhood is becoming more integrated (like Bushwick) might be seen as perpetuating segregation under some circumstances, but not protecting those residents may mean that more African American or Latinx individuals than whites suffer from displacement. Similarly, a policy that does not extend anti-displacement protections to a neighborhood because it is not (yet) seeing much demographic change (like Brownsville) may open the door to precisely that change (and result, at least for a time, in a more integrated neighborhood) through displacement that disproportionately affects African American and Latinx households.

Perhaps the answer to those questions depends upon what else the jurisdiction is doing to foster integration and to ensure that all households have access to neighborhoods with good schools, low crime, and other measures of opportunity. There are dangers in looking at issues one by one. The legitimacy of anti-displacement tools that allow people to stay in their current neighborhoods might be viewed differently if, for example, they were paired with the option of receiving a voucher that realistically could allow the household to move to a more integrated neighborhood. Or, anti-displacement tools that could be paired with affordable housing investments aimed at households making incomes that could help diversify the neighborhood's income mix might be better than either approach on its own.

Conclusion

The problems of how to grow fairly, especially when that growth may mean gentrification and therefore pose a risk or fear of displacement, present particularly difficult policy questions. Unfortunately, the heated debates over these issues have often failed to deal with the very concrete and practical issues that will have to be resolved if urban communities are to move beyond the anger and frustration that often accompany growth and change. Scholars and policy makers still do not agree about what is really meant by displacement, or about how often, or under what circumstances, it occurs. They disagree about what cities should do to protect against displacement and about who should bear the costs of anti-displacement tools. Similarly, they disagree about how to invest in communities that are left behind when those investments will change those neighborhoods (and perhaps other neighborhoods). Planners and policy makers have not thought enough about who is being asked to bear the burdens involved in integrating our neighborhoods or in accommodating growth or about what a fair distribution of those burdens would be. These are incredibly hard issues that require thoughtful soul searching and discussion among all the different stakeholders.

The assessments of fair housing that the 2015 AFFH Rule required provided an unusual opportunity to tackle these issues.[70] Those assessments could force local and state governments and public housing authorities to confront and address data about segregation, access to opportunity, and barriers to fair housing. The Rule demanded that the assessments be conducted with significant input from affected communities, including groups often left out of the discussion. The assessment process encouraged jurisdictions to adopt specific and measurable goals for which they could be held accountable in the years following the assessment. Those features of the assessment process provided a platform for determining, concretely, how each community in the United States should work to undo the legacy of residential segregation that still plagues our metropolitan areas. Unfortunately, HUD's subsequent actions to undermine the 2015 AFFH Rule have only delayed the thoughtful, specific, and concrete discussions about what fairness really requires that are so sorely needed across the country.

ENDNOTES

I would like to thank Ingrid Gould Ellen and Justin P. Steil for inviting me to participate in the MIT Department of Urban Studies and Planning Fair Housing Symposium, which provided the original impetus for this essay. Dylan Lonergan (Law '19), Caroline Peri (Wagner '18), and Lauren Richardson (Law '19) provided excellent research assistance, and Stephanie Rosoff and Maxwell Austensen, the Furman Center's director of data analytics and data manager, respectively, were fonts of wisdom about neighborhood data. I am grateful for the support provided by the Filomen D'Agostino and Max E. Greenberg Research Account. Although I completed the research for this essay in my role as a faculty director of the Furman Center, which is affiliated with NYU's School of Law and the Wagner Graduate School of Public Service, it does not purport to present the institutional views (if any) of NYU or any of its schools.

1. After decades of first ignoring the AFFH language in the Fair Housing Act and then inadequately enforcing the obligation, HUD finally promulgated a rule implementing the obligation during the Barack Obama administration. Affirmatively Furthering Fair Housing, Final Rule, 80 Fed. Reg. 42272 (July 16, 2015) (codified at 24 CFR § 5, 91, 92, 570, 574, 576, and 903 (2015)). On January 5, 2018, HUD effectively suspended the key requirements of the AFFH Rule, and in January 2020 issued a proposed rule eliminating many of the 2015 rule's key advances. Affirmatively Furthering Fair Housing, Proposed Rule, 85 Fed. Reg. 2041 (Jan. 14, 2020).

2. Richard Rothstein, *The Color of Law: A Forgotten History of How Our Government Segregated America* (New York: Liveright, 2017).

3. See, e.g., *NAACP v. Secretary of Housing and Urban Development*, 817 F.2d 149, 155 (1st Cir. 1987) (HUD's duty under the Fair Housing Act requires it to "do more than simply refrain from discriminating").

4. Rothstein, *The Color of Law*; Thomas M. Shapiro, *Toxic Inequality: How America's Wealth Gap Destroys Mobility, Deepens the Racial Divide, and Threatens Our Future* (New York: Basic Books, 2017); Justin P. Steil, Jorge De la Roca, and Ingrid Gould Ellen, "Desvinculado y Desigual: Is Segregation Harmful to Latinos?" *Annals of the American Academy of Political and Social Science* 660, no. 1 (2015): 57–76; Douglas S. Massey and Nancy A. Denton, *American Apartheid: Segregation and the Making of the Underclass* (Cambridge, MA: Harvard University Press, 1993).

5. Sheila Crowley, *Affordable Housing Dilemma: The Preservation vs. Mobility Debate* (Washington, DC: National Low Income Housing Coalition, 2012), available at http://nlihc.org/library/other/periodic/dilemma.

6. See Affirmatively Furthering Fair Housing, available at https://www.regulations.gov/document?D=HUD-2013-0066-0001. A number of simplistic, hateful, and reactionary comments were also submitted.

7. Implementation of the Fair Housing Act's Discriminatory Effects Standard, available at https://www.regulations.gov/document?D=HUD-2011-0138-0001. HUD has since issued a proposed rule dramatically changing its interpretation of disparate impact. Proposed Rule, HUD's Implementation of the Fair Housing Act's Disparate Impact Standard, 84 Fed. Reg. 42854 (Aug. 19, 2019).

8. See https://www.regulations.gov/docket?D=HUD-2016-0063.

9. I focus on New York City in part because I served as commissioner of the city's Housing Preservation and Development (HPD) agency between 2014 and 2017 and helped shape many of the strategies on affordable housing that I describe. In that role, I struggled with many of the issues discussed in this essay. I do not purport to speak for the city, however, and my reflections are not necessarily the views of HPD either currently or during my tenure as commissioner. In May 2019, I returned to New York City government to serve as the deputy mayor of Housing and Economic Development, but again, I am not speaking here on behalf of the city.

10. Affirmatively Furthering Fair Housing: Withdrawal of the Assessment Tool for Local Governments, 83 Fed. Reg. 23922 (May 23, 2018).

11. See, for example, the controversies over gentrification in Detroit, Michigan, in Peter Moskowitz, "The Two Detroits: A City Both Collapsing and Gentrifying at the Same Time," *Guardian*, February 5, 2017, sec. Cities, available at https://www.theguardian.com/cities/2015/feb/05/detroit-city-collapsing-gentrifying.

12. New York City Planning, "Current Estimates of New York City's Population for July 2019," 2019, available at https://www1.nyc.gov/site/planning/planning-level/nyc-population/nyc-population.page.

13. Ibid.

14. Vicki Been, Stephanie Rosoff, and Jessica Yager, "Focus: Changes in New York City's Housing Stock," in *State of New York City's Housing and Neighborhoods in 2017*, ed. Maxwell Austensen et al. (New York: NYU Furman Center, 2018), available at http://furmancenter.org/files/sotc/SOC_2017_FOCUS_Changes_in_NYC_Housing_Stock_1JUN2018.pdf.

15. Ibid.

16. NYC Planning, *The Geography of Jobs*, 2nd ed., 2019, available at https://www1.nyc.gov/assets/planning/download/pdf/planning-level/housing-economy/nyc-geography-jobs2-1019.pdf.

17. Emily Badger, "When the (Empty) Apartment Next Door Is Owned by an Oligarch," *New York Times*, July 21, 2017, sec. The Upshot, available at https://www.nytimes.com/2017/07/21/upshot/when-the-empty-apartment-next-door-is-owned-by-an-oligarch.html; Richard Florida, "The Foreign Buyers You Haven't Heard About," *CityLab*, August 10, 2017, available at https://www.citylab.com/life/2017/08/the-foreign-buyers-you-havent-heard-about/536490/; National Association of Realtors Research Department, "2017 Profile of International Activity in U.S. Residential Real Estate," 2017, available at https://www.nar.realtor/sites/default/files/documents/2017-Profile-of-International-Activity-in-US-Residential-Real-Estate.pdf.

18. Been, Rosoff, and Yager, "Focus: Changes in New York City's Housing Stock."

19. Jed Kolko, "Urban Revival? Not for Most Americans," *Jed Kolko*, March 30, 2016, available at http://jedkolko.com/2016/03/30/urban-revival-not-for-most-americans/.

20. U.S. Census Bureau, "American Factfinder, Selected Economic Characteristics," 2012–2016 American Community Survey 5-Year Estimates, available at https://fact finder.census.gov/faces/tableservices/jsf/pages/productview.xhtml?pid=ACS_16_5YR _DP03&src=pt.; U.S. Census Bureau, "Households and Families 2010 Census Summary File 1," 2010 Census, available at https://factfinder.census.gov/faces/tableservices/jsf /pages/productview.xhtml?src=bkmk.

21. Judith Evans, "The Gilded Glut: Falling Demand Hits Luxury Property Market," *Financial Times*, June 9, 2017, available at https://www.ft.com/content/c8bae1f4-3898 -11e7-821a-6027b8a20f23.

22. Been, Rosoff, and Yager, "Focus: Changes in New York City's Housing Stock."

23. NYU Furman Center, "CoreData.Nyc," available at http://app.coredata.nyc.

24. Maxwell Austensen, Vicki Been, Katherine M. O'Regan, Stephanie Rosoff, and Jessica Yager, "Focus: Poverty in New York City" in *State of New York City's Housing and Neighborhoods in 2016*, ed. Maxwell Austensen et al. (New York: NYU Furman Center, 2017), available at https://furmancenter.org/files/sotc/SOC_2016_FOCUS_Poverty_in _NYC.pdf.

25. U.S. Census Bureau, "American Factfinder, Selected Economic Characteristics."

26. Elyzabeth Gaumer, *Selected Initial Findings of the 2017 New York City Housing and Vacancy Survey* (New York: New York City Department of Housing Preservation and Development, 2018), available at https://www1.nyc.gov/assets/hpd/downloads/pdfs /about/2017-hvs-initial-findings.pdf.

27. Note that middle-income or even higher-income neighborhoods could experience rent increases faster than the citywide average or have other characteristics of gentrifying neighborhoods, such as demographic change. But the NYU Furman Center defined gentrification to require that the neighborhood be a low-income area in 1990. For the purposes of this chapter, I use this definition of gentrification, although, as noted earlier, even the definition of gentrification is sharply contested. Maxwell Austensen et al., *State of New York City's Housing and Neighborhoods in 2015* (New York: NYU Furman Center, 2016), available at https://furmancenter.org/research/sonychan /2015-report.

28. The City of New York, "Housing New York: A Five-Borough, Ten-Year Plan," 2014, available at http://www.nyc.gov/html/housing/assets/downloads/pdf/housing _plan.pdf; The City of New York, "Housing New York 2.0," 2017, available at https:// www1.nyc.gov/assets/hpd/downloads/pdf/about/hny-2.pdf.

29. The City of New York, "Housing New York 2.0."

30. New York City Housing Preservation and Development, "Housing New York By the Numbers" (Mar. 31, 2020), available at https://www1.nyc.gov/site/housing/action/by -the-numbers.page.

31. The percentage of affordability required varies with the level of incomes to be served by the housing. The city council must decide for each rezoning whether to require that 25 percent of the units be affordable at an average of 60 percent of AMI, with at least 10 percent of the units targeted to households making 40 percent of AMI or to require that 30 percent of the housing be affordable at an average of 80 percent of AMI. In addition, the city council can choose to offer two other options to developers: a deep affordability option requiring 20 percent of the housing to be affordable, with all 20 percent aimed at households making 40 percent of AMI, or a workforce housing option requiring 30 percent of the housing to be affordable at an average of 115 percent of AMI, with at least 5 percent targeted at 70 percent of AMI and another 5 percent targeted at 90 percent AMI. New York City Planning, "Mandatory Inclusionary Housing Text Amendment,"

March 22, 2016, available at https://www1.nyc.gov/assets/planning/download/pdf/plans
-studies/mih/approved-text-032216.pdf.

32. New York City Planning, "Zoning for Quality and Affordability Text Amendment," 2016, available at https://www1.nyc.gov/assets/planning/download/pdf/plans-studies
/zqa/approved-zoning-text-032216.pdf.

33. A more comprehensive look at the various policy and programmatic initiatives
underway to achieve Mayor de Blasio's housing goals can be found in The City of New
York, "Housing New York: Three Years of Progress," 2017, available at https://www1.nyc
.gov/assets/hpd/downloads/pdf/about/hny-three-years-of-progress.pdf. For review of
the progress made in East New York since the rezoning, see, e.g., Sadef Ali Kully, "Wor-
ries about the Pace of Progress Four Years after East New York's Rezoning," *City Limits*,
May 28, 2020, available at https://citylimits.org/2020/05/28/worries-about-the-pace-of
-progress-four-years-after-east-new-yorks-rezoning/

34. Tanay Warerkar, "East Harlem Rezoning Faces Mounting Public Opposition,"
Curbed NY, August 24, 2017, available at https://ny.curbed.com/2017/8/24/16199516/east
-harlem-rezoning-city-planning.

35. Ben Adler, "New Package of Bills Aims to Stop Tenant Harassment in NYC,"
Next City, June 9, 2017, available at https://nextcity.org/daily/entry/nyc-bills-stop-tenant
-harassment-bad-landlords; Rebecca Baird-Remba, "East Harlem Tenants Speak Out
against Planned Neighborhood Rezoning," *New York YIMBY*, December 20, 2016, available at https://newyorkyimby.com/2016/12/east-harlem-tenants-speak-out-against-the
-citys-planned-rezoning.html; Laurie Cumbo, Walter Mosley, and Eric Adams, "Crown
Heights Had Changed, and So Must Its Armory Project," *Crain's New York Business*,
June 6, 2017, available at https://www.crainsnewyork.com/article/20170606/OPINION
/170609951/crown-heights-has-changed-and-so-must-its-armory-project; "A Confusing
'No' Vote on East Harlem Rezoning," *Voices of NY*, June 22, 2017, available at https://
voicesofny.org/2017/06/a-confusing-no-vote-on-east-harlem-rezoning/.

36. New York City Office of the Mayor, "Press Release: Mayor Bill de Blasio and
City Council Speaker Melissa Mark-Viverito Announce Creation of Office of Civil Justice to Provide Legal Assistance to New Yorkers in Need," January 28, 2016, available
at http://office-of-the-mayor/news/108-16/mayor-bill-de-blasio-city-council-speaker
-melissa-mark-viverito-creation-office-of; New York City Housing Preservation and
Development, "Press Release: HPD Commissioner Torres-Springer and City Council
Member Espinal Announce the Launch of the East New York Homeowner Help Desk,"
February 8, 2017, available at https://www1.nyc.gov/site/hpd/about/press-releases/2017
/02/02-08-17.page.

37. Gale Brewer, "Recommendation on ULURP Application Nos. C 170358 ZMM,
N 170359 ZRM, and C 170360 HAM - East Harlem Rezoning by The New York City
Department of City Planning," 2017, available at https://www.scribd.com/document
/355410421/Final-Manhattan-B-P-Recommendation-Re-Nos-C-170358-ZMM-Et-Al-East
-Harlem-Rezoning.

38. Ibid.

39. Thomas Angotti and Sylvia Morse, eds., *Zoned Out! Race, Displacement, and
City Planning in New York City* (New York: Terreform, 2016); Michael Greenberg,
"Tenants under Siege: Inside New York City's Housing Crisis," *New York Review of
Books*, August 17, 2017, available at https://www.nybooks.com/articles/2017/08/17
/tenants-under-siege-inside-new-york-city-housing-crisis/.

40. Tom Angotti, "Zoned Out in the City: New York City's Tale of Race and Displacement," *Poverty and Race* 26, no. 1 (March 2017), available at https://prrac.org/newsletters

/janfebmar2017.pdf; Vicki Been, "The Clear and Present Danger of Supply Skepticism," *Poverty and Race* 26, no. 1 (March 2017), available at https://prrac.org/newsletters /janfebmar2017.pdf; Vicki Been, Ingrid Gould Ellen, and Katherine M. O'Regan, "Supply Skepticism: Housing Supply and Affordability," *Housing Policy Debate*, 2018, available at http://www.law.nyu.edu/sites/default/files/Been%20Ellen%20O%27Regan%20supply _affordability_Oct%2026%20 revision.pdf.

41. See https://www.regulations.gov/docket?D=HUD-2016-0063 (especially the comments of Enterprise Community Partners; National Fair Housing Alliance; Brian Knudsen on behalf of a coalition of fair housing and civil rights groups; Deb Niemeier and Matthew Palm, University of California, Davis; New York City Housing Preservation and Development and New York City Housing Authority; New York State Homes and Community Renewal).

42. Vicki Been and Leila Bozorg, "Spiraling: Evictions and Other Causes and Consequences of Housing Instability," *Harvard Law Review* 130 (2017): 1408–1433.

43. *Broadway Triangle Cmty. Coal. v. Bloomberg*, 941 N.Y.S.2d 831 (Sup. Ct. NY County 2011).

44. Henry Grabar, "Why Was California's Radical Housing Bill So Unpopular?" *Slate*, April 20, 2018, available at https://slate.com/business/2018/04/why-sb-827-cali fornias-radical-affordable-housing-bill-was-so-unpopular.html.

45. NYU Furman Center, "The Poor Door Debate," *The Dream Revisited*, 2015, available at http://furmancenter.org/research/iri/discussions/the-poor-door-debate.

46. See, for example, NY Multiple Dwelling Law § 26.3 (limiting density to a floor area ratio of 12).

47. Vicki Been. Ingrid Gould Ellen, Michael Gedal, Edward Glaeser, and Brian J. McCabe, "Preserving History or Hindering Growth? The Heterogeneous Effects of Historic Districts on Local Housing Markets in New York City," *Journal of Urban Economics*, NBER Working Papers, 92 (2016): 16–30.

48. See, for example, *Hawkins v. Town of Shaw*, 303 F. Supp. 1162 (N.D. Miss. 1969) (class action brought by Black residents against municipality seeking injunctive relief against discrimination in the provision of municipal services in violation of 42 U.S.C. §1983).

49. See for example, *R.I.S.E., Inc. v. Kay*, 768 F. Supp. 1144 (E.D. Va. 1991), aff'd, 977 F.2d 573 (4th Cir. 1992); *East Bibb Twiggs Neighborhood Ass'n v. Macon-Bibb County Planning and Zoning Comm'n*, 706 F. Supp. 880 (M.D. Ga. 1989), aff'd, 896 F.2d 1264 (11th Cir. 1989); *Bean v. Southwestern Waste Management Corp.*, 482 F. Supp. 673 (S.D. Tex. 1979), aff'd, 782 F.2d 1038 (5th Cir. 1986); Vicki Been, "What's Fairness Got to Do with It? Environmental Justice and the Siting of Locally Undesirable Land Uses," *Cornell Law Review* 78, no. 6 (1993): 1001.

50. Jon Dubin, "From Junkyards to Gentrification: Explicating a Right to Protective Zoning," *Minnesota Law Review* 77 (1993): 739–801.

51. Rothstein, *The Color of Law*.

52. Three of the five wealthiest neighborhoods in New York City also are among the city's densest, for example. Sean Capperis et al., *State of New York City's Housing and Neighborhoods in 2014, Focus on Density* (New York: NYU Furman Center, 2015), available at http://furmancenter.org/files/sotc/SOC2014_FocusOnDensity.pdf.

53. Vicki Been, Josiah Madar, and Simon McDonnell, "Urban Land-Use Regulation: Are Homevoters Overtaking the Growth Machine?" *Journal of Empirical Legal Studies* 11, no. 2 (2014): 227–265.

54. See, for example, *S. Burlington Cty. N.A.A.C.P. v. Mount Laurel Twp.*, 92 N.J. 158, 237–238, 456 A.2d 390, 430 (1983) (rejecting the notion that only "developing" munici-palities must provide affordable housing).

55. Abigail Savitch-Lew, "Huge Waterfront Towers Frame Debate over LES Re-zoning," *City Limits*, April 17, 2017, available at https://citylimits.org/2017/04/17/huge-waterfront-towers-frame-debate-over-les-rezoning/.

56. New York City Planning, "New York City Population Projections by Age/Sex & Borough, 2010–2040," 2013, available at http://www1.nyc.gov/assets/planning/download/pdf/data-maps/nyc-population/projections_report_2010_2040.pdf.

57. Sean Capperis et al., *State of New York City's Housing and Neighborhoods in 2014.*

58. Stacy E. Seicsnaydre, "The Fair Housing Choice Myth," *Journal of Affordable Housing and Community Development Law* 23, no. 2 (2015): 149–203.

59. New York City Planning, "Sustainable Communities: East New York," 2014, available at https://www1.nyc.gov/assets/planning/download/pdf/plans-studies=/sustainable-communities/eny/east_ny_report/east_ny_full.pdf.

60. Austensen et al., *State of New York City's Housing and Neighborhoods in 2016.*

61. Capperis et al., *State of New York City's Housing and Neighborhoods in 2014.*

62. Ibid.

63. New York City Economic Development Corporation, "Inwood NYC Planning Initiative," 2017, available at https://www.nycedc.com/project/inwood-nyc-neighborhood-study; Ameena Walker, "Inwood Rezoning Gets Approval from City Planning Commission," *Curbed NY*, June 26, 2018, available at https://ny.curbed.com/2018/6/26/17506598/inwood-rezoning-approval-city-planning-commission.

64. NYC Housing Connect, "What to Expect: Your Guide to Affordable Housing," New York City Housing Preservation and Development, 2017, available at https://www1.nyc.gov/assets/hpd/downloads/pdf/what-to-expect/English.pdf.

65. *Winfield v. City of N.Y.*, No. 15CV5236-LTS-DCF (S.D.N.Y. Oct. 24, 2016).

66. J. K. Dineen, "Feds Reject Housing Plan Meant to Help Minorities Stay in SF," *San Francisco Chronicle*, August 17, 2016, available at https://www.sfchronicle.com/politics/article/Feds-reject-housing-plan-meant-to-help-minorities-9146987.php; Henry Grabar, "Obama Administration to San Francisco: Your Anti-Gentrification Plan Promotes Segregation," *Slate*, August 17, 2016, available at http://www.slate.com/blogs/moneybox/2016/08/17/a_local_preference_affordable_housing_plan_in_san_francisco_might_violate.html; Caleb Pershan, "Feds Accept Version of Anti-Displacement Pref-erence Plan," *SFist*, September 22, 2016, available at http://sfist.com/2016/09/22/hud_breed_willie_kennedy.php.

67. Ethan Geringer-Sameth, "'Community Preference' Lawsuit at Center of Af-fordable Housing, Segregation Debates," *Gotham Gazette*, March 29, 2017, available at http://www.gothamgazette.com/city/6838-community-preference-lawsuit-at-center-of-affordable-housing-segregation-debates.

68. Austensen et al., *State of New York City's Housing and Neighborhoods in 2015.*

69. Affirmatively Furthering Fair Housing Rule, 24 C.F.R. § 5, §91, §92, §570, §574, § 903 (2015); see also U.S. Department of Housing and Urban Development, *AFFH Guidebook*, 2015.

70. See supra n1.

7

Incorporating Data on Crime and Violence into the Assessment of Fair Housing

MICHAEL C. LENS

Why Fair Housing and Exposure to Violence Matter

Fair housing remains vital to U.S. housing policy. Fifty years after the Fair Housing Act, disparate outcomes by race are persistent in the United States, and income and wealth inequality continue to grow. For example, while in 1983 the median white family had eight times the wealth as the median Black family, in 2017, that ratio was 10 to 1, and disparities in homeownership rates and home values are a central contributing factor to these dramatic disparities in wealth.[1]

Further, small but steady declines in segregation by race (particularly Black-white segregation) have been largely offset by increases in segregation by income. Since 1970, high-income households have increasingly segregated themselves into richer and richer enclaves, while the poor had just one decade—the 1990s—in which they became more integrated with other income groups.[2] In all other decades since 1970, concentrated poverty has been on the rise.

To bolster federal efforts to further fair housing and hold local governments accountable for fair housing outcomes, the U.S. Department of Housing and Urban Development (HUD) published its landmark Affirmatively Furthering Fair Housing (AFFH) Rule in 2015. A key part of the AFFH process, and the topic of this chapter, is the Assessment of Fair Housing (AFH), which was expected to be conducted every five years by jurisdictions receiving HUD funds. Reflecting what we now know about how segregation and neighborhoods affect life chances, particularly for low-income and minority households, the AFH process got a lot right. Specifically, the AFH guided jurisdictions to collect a wide range of data that go well beyond simplistic measures of segregation by race and income. Importantly, the AFH focused explicitly on disparities in access to neighborhood opportunities, such as quality schools, employment, and transit, in addition to concentrations of racial and ethnic groups and households in poverty.

However, while weighing such a wide range of attributes is virtually impossible to do perfectly, I argue that two problems exist with the guidance provided under the 2015 rule. In turn, these key areas need improvement if there is to be a more robust revival of the rule's aspirations. First, the AFH process largely treats all spatial concentrations equally, yet the literature on residential decision making and neighborhood effects suggests that these opportunities should not be weighed equally. In particular, neighborhood violence and school quality rise to the top in two strands of research that are vitally important to consider in evaluating the AFH process—the literature on residential location decisions (or preferences) and the literature on neighborhood effects. Second, and the explicit focus of this chapter, is the complete absence of data on crime and violence in the AFH process. Again, the research on residential location decisions and on neighborhood effects suggests that exposure to neighborhood violence frequently outweighs other neighborhood characteristics in terms of importance.

This chapter reviews the research on neighborhood preferences and neighborhood effects to identify the key attributes that low-income and minority households weigh most heavily when making residential location decisions and the neighborhood attributes that have the strongest effect on life outcomes. Although there is much uncertainty in each of these domains—our understanding of household preferences and specific neighborhood effects is imperfect and incomplete—each strand of literature points to neighborhood violence as being the neighborhood attribute that households care the most to avoid and the one that appears to have the greatest effect on life outcomes. Given this confluence of empirical research and household instinct, it is paramount that we find ways to incorporate data on crime and violence into the fair housing framework.

The Assessment of Fair Housing

In 2015, HUD published its new AFFH Rule. From a data and neighborhood opportunity standpoint, the key is that the Analysis of Impediments (AI), filed by all jurisdictions receiving HUD funding, was replaced with an AFH, to be conducted every five years.[3] HUD also produced the AFFH data tool to guide local governments and public housing authorities (PHAs) in conducting their fair housing analyses (for more detail, see the Introduction in this volume). The data tool and the AFH encourage jurisdictions to collect and report data in several domains. First, given that fair housing laws prohibit discrimination by race or ethnicity, the AFFH tool and the AFH are heavily focused on measuring the spatial distribution of a region's population by race and ethnicity—specifically, isolation and dissimilarity indices. Second, jurisdictions are to identify racially and/or ethnically concentrated areas of poverty (R/ECAPs), census tracts where at least 50 percent of the population identify as ethnic or racial minorities and the poverty rate is either 40 percent or more or greater than three times the poverty rate of the metropolitan area.[4] Third, localities are to assess the spatial distribution of population sorted by other demographic attributes, including national origin and limited English proficiency, disability status, sex/gender, families with children, and households living in publicly supported housing. There are also data on housing problems and disproportionate housing need, such as the distribution of high-rent burdens. Finally, the AFH focuses on the concentration of neighborhood attributes through the creation of several indices: the School Proficiency Index, the Jobs Proximity Index, the Labor Market Engagement Index, the Low Transportation Cost Index, the Transit Trips Index, and the Environmental Health Index. Notably missing are data on crime, about which HUD states:

> HUD realizes that there are other assets that are relevant, such as neighborhood crime or housing unit lead and radon levels. However, these lack consistent neighborhood-level data across all program participant geographies. As a consequence, HUD encourages program participants to supplement the data it provides with robust locally available data on these other assets so that the analysis is as all-encompassing as possible.[5]

Residential Preferences and Fair Housing

The initial impetus for the Fair Housing Act was to hold local governments accountable for reducing segregation by race and income, which was often explicitly encouraged at the local level. As segregation by race and income has persisted over time and continues to result in non-white and poor households disproportionately occupying low-amenity neighborhoods, the focus has slowly shifted from explicit segregation policies to disparate neighborhood outcomes. An important first step in assessing disparities in neighborhood outcomes is to identify the neighborhood attributes that households prioritize when making residential location decisions.

Several studies examine the motivations and preferences of low-income households with respect to residential location, and they provide important insights into what matters for these residents when choosing to locate in a neighborhood. We have two general sources of data on residential preferences. The most straightforward is data on *revealed preferences*, those that we observe based on the attributes of people's residential locations. These preferences are clearly constrained by household resources and housing market discrimination, at a minimum.[6] Moreover, there are also limits to conclusions we can make about neighborhood preferences from studies that speak directly to households and capture their *expressed preferences*, chiefly because of tradeoffs between dwelling and neighborhood quality that they are forced to make and the limited menu of options that these families often consider to be realistically attainable.[7]

With these caveats in mind, it is useful to summarize what we know about the neighborhood preferences of low-income families. Notably, crime and violence are often cited as a concern for those who wish to move out of distressed neighborhoods. In surveys of Moving to Opportunity for Fair Housing (MTO) participants, crime was consistently offered as a primary motivation for wanting to enroll in those programs and move out of their original neighborhoods, which were typically quite unsafe.[8] For participants in the other major housing voucher demonstration program—Gautreaux, in Chicago—we can surmise that the astonishingly high crime rates were among the reasons why participants were motivated to enter that program as well. In fact, drastic improvements in neighborhood safety can be highlighted as one of the clearest success stories in the MTO and Gautreaux programs. In the Gautreaux program, for example, participants starting out in the Robert Taylor Homes came from an environment that in 1980 comprised only 1 percent of Chicago's population yet experienced 10 percent of the city's murders, aggravated assaults, and rapes.[9] Before moving to the suburbs, nearly half of Gautreaux participants "told of dangerous and frightening incidents that occurred regularly on the streets of their inner-city neighborhoods."[10] Criminal victimization rates were twice as high among Chicago public housing tenants overall as in the city as a whole. Micere Keels, Greg J. Duncan, Stefanie Deluca, Ruby Mendenhall, and James Rosenbaum estimate that violent crime rates in Gautreaux participants' original neighborhoods were three times as high as those in Chicago.[11]

Unfortunately, Gautreaux participants who moved to other parts of the city continued to face higher crime rates than in the city overall, and the same outcomes were found for suburban movers. However, those crime rates were still significantly lower than what they left behind. Suburban movers had a violent crime rate about 5 times as high as the crime rate in the Chicago suburbs at that time, and those who moved to the city faced violent crime rates about 1.5 times as high as the Chicago crime rate at that time. More promisingly, many years after their initial move, the Gautreaux households tracked by Keels et al. lived in neighborhoods with very comparable violent and property crime rates to Cook County (which includes Chicago and surrounding suburbs) as a whole. Mark Votruba and Jeffrey Kling estimate that in a sample of 2,850 Gautreaux participants moving to better-educated, safer neighborhoods, program participation saved up to seventeen lives, with thirteen of those averted deaths due to homicide.[12]

In the MTO program, an astonishing 77 percent of household heads cited "moving away from crime and drugs" as their primary or secondary reason for wanting to move.[13] Similarly, 45 percent reported that a household member had been a crime victim in the previous six months, and 50 percent described their streets as very unsafe. Despite living in housing units and neighborhoods with multiple negative aspects (such as substandard housing conditions and neighborhoods with very high poverty rates and limited retail options), MTO participants overwhelmingly cited crime as the top motivation to move.

School quality is another neighborhood aspect that likely has clear ramifications for quality of life, and once again the Gautreaux and MTO programs provide insights on participants' preferences for better schools. Positive educational outcomes for Gautreaux participant children have been consistently cited as one of the main success stories of the program and an incentive to expand the housing voucher program.[14] James Rosenbaum, Marilyn Kulieke, and Leonard Rubinowitz examine the link between educational outcomes for youth Gautreaux participants and the quality of schools in suburban neighborhoods where participants moved. They find that educational standards were higher in suburban districts where the participants moved and that student-movers also received additional educational assistance.[15] However, they experienced significant obstacles to adjusting to these new school environments, including increased racial discrimination in their new schools, which were predominantly white. Ultimately, the students were able to rise to the higher standards in their new schools—their grades were equivalent to those received in their previous schools. Further, children's attitudes toward school were found to be higher in their new schools.

As with crime, MTO baseline surveys cite the search for school quality as a common motivation for entering the program. Lisa Sanbonmatsu et al. report that just under half (49.4 percent) of participants cited better schools as a primary or secondary reason for moving. Given that the study was limited to families with children, this is almost certainly an overestimate of the overall public housing population who seeks to move to neighborhoods with better schools, but it is telling that school quality is the second-highest priority (behind crime) among this population.[16]

Despite the strong evidence for preferences for neighborhoods with low crime and quality schools, even substantial interventions such as MTO have had limited success in placing families in neighborhoods with these attributes. Jens Ludwig et al. report clear gains for the experimental group in terms of reduced exposure to neighborhood crime. At follow-up four to seven years after moving, a gap of 30 percentage points was observed between the experimental and control groups in their response to whether they felt safe in their neighborhood at night. A 9 percent gap was found in the proportion of families who reported a member of their household being victimized in the previous six months. However, by the second follow-up ten to fifteen years after baseline, no statistically significant differences were found in recent criminal victimization history between the experimental and control groups. On the other hand, adults in the experimental and Section 8 groups were more likely to report feeling safe in their neighborhoods, were less likely to report that the police did not respond, and were less likely to report drug activity in their neighborhoods than the control group. While it is troubling that criminal victimization rates were equal across these groups in the long term, improved perceptions of neighborhood safety were persistent positive outcomes in the MTO study.[17]

It is telling that households so often point to crime as an impetus to participate in mobility programs designed to change neighborhood locations, but the fact remains that when we look at the revealed preferences of low-income households, they commonly occupy higher-crime neighborhoods than the average. Much of this circumstance has to do with the increased costs of living in lower-crime environments, but qualitative research suggests that these households face additional constraints.

In this vein, Peter Rosenblatt and Stefanie DeLuca provide a much-needed mixed-methods investigation into this phenomenon in an effort to explain the divergence between stated and revealed preferences of low-income renters. They use data on Baltimore MTO participants and extensive features on Baltimore neighborhoods to paint a fuller picture of the trade-offs, constraints, and priorities of these households that help determine their residential locations. In interviews, a desire to move to safer environments is consistently mentioned as a motivation for entering the program and a chief benefit of participant moves. Parents talk frequently of increased feelings of safety when their children left their homes to play. However, problems with the housing unit also surface as a reason why participants frequently made subsequent moves back to less-safe and/or higher-poverty neighborhoods. Often participating in the private-rental market for the first time, MTO movers sometimes find it difficult to identify landlords who would accept their voucher, and then when they do finally find one, sometimes they discover that those landlords are neglectful. Through this research, Rosenblatt and Deluca identify explanations in addition to limited financial resources that may explain why we observe households occupying high-crime areas, despite their stated preferences. Along with neglectful landlords and substandard housing units, they uncover a process of evaluating neighborhood crime conditions in potential destination neighborhoods that may subject low-income households to unsafe spaces. Specifically, they describe a process that they label "telescoping," in which the homeseekers look at the immediate block of their unit—which may be relatively safe—while discounting or ignoring high-crime conditions on neighboring streets. In quantitative research undertaken at the census-tract level, we would observe such households as being highly exposed to neighborhood crime, although the households—which unfortunately may have experience navigating even more dangerous conditions—are less likely to view their blocks as immediate threats.[18]

What Is It about Neighborhoods That Matters?

Research on residential preferences tells us that low-income households often value lower-crime neighborhoods and better schools first and foremost and that they make trade-offs between these and several other neighborhood attributes, including access to employment and green space and proximity to environmental toxins. What does the neighborhood effects literature tell us about which neighborhood attributes matter the most in affecting key household outcomes, such as employment, education, and health? A better understanding of the key mechanisms in neighborhood effects will allow us to better prioritize and assess neighborhood attributes in the fair housing context.

In *The Truly Disadvantaged*, published in 1987, William Julius Wilson focuses on the segregation of Black households into jobless ghettoes as a result of racial discrimination in housing, manufacturing decline, white flight, and the flight of the Black middle class. Wilson identifies this concentration of joblessness as the main factor for deteriorating social conditions among urban Black families, such as high school dropouts, criminal involvement, and a rise in poor single-parent families.[19] The neighborhood effects literature has largely consisted of efforts to test and extend Wilson's hypotheses using a variety of data sources and methods. Specifically, this work often seeks to evaluate the mechanisms through which concentrated poverty and race affect a host of other household outcomes. Although segregation scholars often debate whether segregation by income or by race is more harmful, it is likely that these two forces of spatial stratification interact in important ways, particularly with respect to inherited neighborhood disadvantage and exposure to neighborhood violence.

Ingrid Gould Ellen and Margery Turner, writing in 1997, take stock of the neighborhood effects literature in the first ten years following publication of *The Truly Disadvantaged*, a point when Gautreaux had given way to MTO as the policy lever designed to test the effect of neighborhood on household outcomes. Ellen and Turner conclude that empirical research generally confirms that neighborhood environment has an influence on important outcomes for children and adults, but they find that efforts to identify which characteristics matter most and to quantify their importance are inconclusive at that point. Further, they note that neighborhood effects are much less important than family characteristics, although there is typically a very high correlation between neighborhood and family characteristics.[20]

The results from MTO speak to how neighborhood poverty affects a variety of household outcomes, but it is difficult to connect MTO outcomes to specific neighborhood attributes other than poverty. In all, the impact of moving MTO households out of high-poverty, dangerous neighborhoods was less profound than many expected, particularly for adults. Adults in the experimental group were no more likely to be employed at the first or second follow-up than those in the control and comparison groups, and being in the experimental group had no positive effects on children's schooling or employment outcomes. Children were also no less likely to engage in risky or criminal behaviors. The experimental group did experience statistically significant declines in adult obesity relative to the comparison groups, as was the case with mental health problems for female adolescent participants. Raj Chetty, Nathaniel Hendren, and Lawrence Katz look at long-term outcomes by using tax returns to estimate earnings and identify current neighborhood locations and whether younger MTO recipients subsequently attended college between the ages of eighteen and twenty.

They continue to find no effects on adult outcomes, even when testing for a dosage effect (the length of time spent in low-poverty neighborhoods). However, they find substantial, positive effects on long-term outcomes for children who moved when they were young—specifically, an increased likelihood of college attendance and higher earnings.[21] We can conclude from the extensive research on MTO that neighborhood poverty rates matter, particularly for children who are exposed to these neighborhoods the longest. But many adult and youth outcomes do not respond to changes in neighborhood poverty. Further, several neighborhood attributes are highly correlated with poverty rates in these areas, including racial segregation, crime and violence, and low-quality schooling, meaning it is unclear whether escaping concentrated poverty is truly the driver of these outcomes.

A few studies have used MTO data to examine the effect of neighborhood attributes other than poverty rates to determine their effects. Ludwig and Kling isolate the effects of neighborhood crime rates to determine whether the presence of crime leads youth to engage in more crime themselves.[22] They find little evidence for such a contagion effect and instead find that racial segregation has a statistically significant impact on the propensity to commit crime. Evelyn Blumenberg and Gregory Pierce test whether access to public transit plays a role in employment outcomes for MTO participants and find that improved access to public transit is associated with the increased likelihood of keeping a job but not of finding and securing one.[23] Michael C. Lens and C. J. Gabbe test the spatial mismatch hypothesis by using MTO data and find that MTO did not improve spatial proximity to jobs for program participants, but that it would not likely have mattered anyway; they find no connection between job proximity and increased likelihood of employment or increased earnings at follow-up.[24]

The findings by Lens and Gabbe reaffirm the often-inconclusive findings regarding the role of employment accessibility in determining employment outcomes. This phenomenon is persistently studied and yet has a decidedly mixed record. Michael Stoll finds that Blacks and Latinxs live in areas of Los Angeles with poor job growth, which results in their spending more time and effort to find work.[25] Also in Los Angeles, Paul Ong and Evelyn Blumenberg find that the job-poor neighborhoods lived in by welfare recipients make it less likely that they will find work.[26] By contrast, Robert Cervero, Onésimo Sandoval, and John Landis find no relation between regional job accessibility and employment outcomes for welfare recipients in Alameda County, California—a finding echoed by Thomas Sanchez, Qing Shen, and Zhong-Ren Peng, who look at Temporary Assistance for Needy Families recipients in six U.S. cities.[27] Given this information, it is unclear whether employment accessibility should be a central feature in the fair housing discussion.

Some of the more groundbreaking work on the role of segregation by income and race examines the confluence of these two concentrations rather than isolating them, as has been past practice.

Patrick Sharkey focuses explicitly on the confluence of concentrated poverty and racial segregation to examine the role of what he terms "inherited neighborhood disadvantage." Using the Panel Study of Income Dynamics (PSID), Sharkey finds that many of the wealth and income disparities observed between whites and African Americans can be explained by the incredibly stark differences in neighborhoods that these different racial groups occupy.[28] Among the PSID cohort born between 1955 and 1970, only 4 percent of white households lived in relatively high-poverty neighborhoods, where the poverty rate was 20 percent or higher. For African Americans born at the same time, that number was fifteen times higher, or 62 percent. These differences barely changed in thirty years; among the 1985 to 2000 cohort, those numbers were 6 percent and 68 percent, respectively.

In other words, higher-poverty neighborhoods that are commonplace for African Americans are almost unheard of for white Americans. Importantly, these disparities hold when controlling for income differences between whites and Blacks.

Sharkey links living in a high-poverty neighborhood to two key outcomes—inherited neighborhood disadvantage and economic mobility. He finds that neighborhoods are largely inherited across generations: the correlation between the income level of parent and child neighborhoods is quite high (about 0.67). However, he also finds that when white families live in high-poverty neighborhoods, it tends to be for a single generation, and whites tend to live in affluent neighborhoods for multiple generations. The opposite pathways are typical for African-American families—multigenerational exposure to neighborhood poverty is common, and multigenerational exposure to affluent neighborhoods is rare.

The exposure to neighborhood disadvantage, Sharkey argues, contributes to the remarkably persistent gaps in income and wealth between Black and white families. Sharkey finds that the neighborhood poverty rate of a child explains a great deal of the income he or she earns as an adult and also explains much of the economic mobility gap. The latter fact reflects the reality that Black children are more likely than white ones to experience downward mobility (moving from a high-income category to a lower one) and that Black children are less likely to experience upward mobility (moving from a low family-income category to a higher one).

Sharkey's conclusions have been reaffirmed by Raj Chetty, Nathaniel Hendren, Patrick Kline, and Emmanuel Saez, who examine the geography of intergenerational mobility, looking at the regional scale rather than the neighborhood. They find that movement up and down the economic ladder across successive generations varies dramatically by metropolitan area. They describe the United States as "a collection of societies"—in some metro areas, economic mobility across generations is common, whereas elsewhere, movement out of poverty is a rare event.[29] Importantly, they find that the spatial concentration of particular demographic characteristics, such as college attendance and teenage birth rates, is strongly linked to rates of economic mobility.

Further, the persistence of racial and economic segregation is continuing to lead to substantial inequities in terms of public services that people consume and exposure to crime and violence. Higher-quality services and other amenities are concentrated in particular locations within metropolitan areas, and these concentrations map onto patterns of economic and racial segregation. Jorge De la Roca, Ingrid Ellen, and Katherine O'Regan use Census data, a unique tract-level dataset on crime in ninety-one U.S. cities, and geocoded school-zone data at the Census-block level to estimate the effects of racial segregation on the exposure of different racial groups to low-socioeconomic-status neighbors, crime, and low-quality schools.[30] They find substantial racial disparities in exposure to disadvantaged neighborhoods. Specifically, whites and Asians are much less likely to live in low-status neighborhoods or neighborhoods with high crime or low-quality schools than Blacks and Hispanics. Further, these disparities are not fully explained by differences in income; they find "that the average poor white person lived in a neighborhood with a lower violent crime rate than the average non-poor black person."[31] They also find that metropolitan-area segregation levels (i.e., dissimilarity and isolation indices between various racial groups and whites) are strong predictors of these racial gaps in exposure to all three domains of neighborhood disadvantage—neighborhood socioeconomic characteristics, quality of the zoned school, and violent crime.

Robert Sampson's Project on Human Development in Chicago Neighborhoods (PHDCN), which, like MTO, began in the early 1990s, has collected perhaps the most extensive set of neighborhood characteristics in the pursuit of identifying their effects on household outcomes. Sampson's book *Great American City: Chicago and the Enduring Neighborhood Effect* summarizes this work.[32]

PHDCN researchers combine field observations with data on housing, crime and violence, residential mobility between neighborhoods, contacts between public officials and leaders in different neighborhoods (to measure communication between neighborhoods), administrative records, and a letter-drop survey to measure social altruism and civic cooperation—key components of what Sampson and his colleagues term "collective efficacy."[33] This method is best suited to a project like the PHDCN that is able to collect data on a broad scope of variables, but more data are available at small levels of geography than ever before. Furthermore, some countries, such as Sweden, have better individual-level data available to tie neighborhood opportunity measures to individual outcomes.[34]

Using these extensive data on neighborhood domains and over multiple time periods, Sampson finds substantial overlap between various measures of disadvantage and also finds that neighborhood disadvantage is very persistent over time. Neighborhoods with high rates of violence also have low health indicators and poor collective efficacy. Further, disadvantaged neighborhoods tend to remain disadvantaged for decades—and neighborhood poverty is particularly persistent in neighborhoods with high proportions of African Americans—stressing again the interaction between race and poverty concentration. Sampson's data allow him to tie together the role of community social capital in protecting neighborhoods from becoming violent and disadvantaged.

Finally, research from Sharkey suggests that neighborhood violence is particularly influential on children's outcomes. Using data from the PHDCN, Sharkey finds strong evidence that local homicides affect children's performance on verbal and reading assessments taken shortly after the homicides occurred.[35] He exploits the exogenous variation in the timing of the homicides to strengthen the causal linkages between violence and assessments. In another paper, Patrick T. Sharkey, Nicole Tirado-Stayer, Andrew V. Papachristos, and C. Cybele Raver find more evidence that geographically proximate homicides have a negative impact on several youth outcomes, including pre-academic cognitive skills, such as impulse control, and vocabulary and math assessment scores.[36] Further, they find that parents' mental health conditions are negatively affected by local homicides. In Sharkey's recent book *Uneasy Peace,* he succinctly sums up the effects of violence: "Local violence does not make children less intelligent. Rather, it occupies their minds."[37]

Sharkey provides further evidence that the slow declines in the Black-white education achievement gap may be attributable to declining violence in urban America by linking data from the National Assessment of Educational Progress (NAEP) to local crime rates. Once more, in *Uneasy Peace,* Sharkey reports work with colleague Gerard Torrats-Espinosa that examines the link between crime and upward mobility, a key outcome that fair housing policy should try to influence. They find that in areas where violence declined faster, upward mobility became much more likely.[38]

Incorporating Crime and Violence Data into the Assessment of Fair Housing

Strong evidence shows that neighborhood matters, and persistent disparities in neighborhood quality are key justifications for why fair housing laws continue to be necessary. Segregation research, which has consistently summarized myriad justifications for fair housing law, has typically focused on the attributes of those who live around you rather than on the spatial sorting of structural characteristics that shape opportunities for individuals and families. Although the precise mechanisms through which neighborhoods affect people's lives are often unclear, I argue that we should emphasize the structural characteristics of neighborhoods that reflect spatial inequalities in the location of amenities and disadvantages, particularly neighborhood violence.

When MTO and Gautreaux participants discussed their motivations for leaving behind public housing for new housing locations, they did not talk much about there being too many Black or poor neighbors around them. Time and again, participants talked about neighborhood safety as a primary reason for neighborhood dissatisfaction. They also discussed school and housing-unit quality and a lack of jobs or retail options. In other words, people in high-poverty, racially segregated neighborhoods do not tend to talk about the people who live around them.

They talk about the structural, rather than demographic, characteristics of their neighborhoods. Research by Sharkey and others suggests that these motivations are particularly well justified—living in violent neighborhoods not only is dangerous and exposes you to risk of bodily harm or worse but affects your ability to function and excel in life.

The AFH process generally reflects what we know about neighborhood effects. Although considerable attention is paid to neighborhood demographic analyses, quite a few domains would also be considered structural: school proficiency, job indices, transportation costs, and environmental health indicators are all included. What is clearly necessary and missing is an emphasis on collecting and assessing the spatial distribution of crime and violence.

Importantly, we now often have the data to do this. Neighborhood crime data have been collected before on a large scale, suggesting that collecting data in a large number of cities is feasible. Two decades ago (1999–2001), Ruth Peterson and Lauren Krivo (2010) conducted the National Neighborhood Crime Study (NNCS), a nationally representative sample of crime data for 9,593 Census tracts in ninety-one U.S. cities.[39] The resulting public dataset includes an average of the major crime categories developed by the Federal Bureau of Investigation's Uniform Crime Report System over the entire three years for each Census tract.

More recently, tract-level crime data have been used with increasing frequency, covering a variety of years and cities. Lens, Ellen, and O'Regan, writing in 2011, collect neighborhood-level crime data for ten U.S. cities for a purpose closely related to assessing fair housing—measuring the neighborhood crime rates faced by housing subsidy recipients.[40] Brent Mast and Ronald Wilson investigate the relationship between vouchers and crime in Charlotte, North Carolina, by using data on property, violent, residential burglary, and street crimes from 2000 to 2009.[41] Elizabeth Griffiths and George Tita use tract-level data on homicides in Los Angeles to explore whether public housing is a "hotbed" for crime.[42] John MacDonald, John Hipp, and Charlotte Gill also use tract-level crime data in Los Angeles to investigate the effects of immigrant concentration on crime. Los Angeles, like many U.S. cities, has crime data available online for anyone to access.[43] John Hipp and Daniel Yates use tract-level data to study how returning parolees affect crime in Sacramento.[44] This breadth of research suggests that technology and a greater appreciation for data sharing among public agencies—including police—are helping foster an era in which crime data are increasingly available at small levels of geography, including Census tracts.

Some may suggest that neighborhood crime is so highly correlated with many of the other factors that are captured in the AFH process that it is unnecessary to exert extra effort to collect these data. However, many have shown, including Sampson, Raudenbush, and Earls, that demographic features of a neighborhood do not determine violent crime rates.[45] Hipp finds that the association between poverty and murder rates becomes insignificant when neighborhood inequality is accounted for, suggesting that the relationship between poverty and violent crime is much more complicated than people think.[46] It is likely that concentrated disadvantage coupled with racial segregation explain much of the variation in neighborhood crime, but these urban features do not map perfectly onto one another.[47] Specifically, Robert Sampson, Jeffrey Morenoff, and Stephen Raudenbush find that although the proportion of a neighborhood's population who identifies as Black is highly correlated with violent crime in neighborhoods, particular neighborhood characteristics, such as immigrant concentration, percentage of professional/managerial occupations, concentrated disadvantage, and residential stability, wash out the link between race and crime.[48]

Fair housing protections target low-income and minority households. These populations are deeply concerned with crime and violence in their communities. The research on neighborhood effects consistently points to neighborhood violence as a key mechanism through which neighborhood affects life chances. Given this significance of exposure to violence for individual outcomes and the fact that the neighborhood characteristics identified in the 2015 version of AFH process are inadequate proxies for neighborhood violence, we need to find ways to make crime data accessible to more jurisdictions undertaking these assessments. As noted, crime data on several cities and years have already been collected and utilized for research purposes, suggesting that collecting neighborhood crime data on a wide scale is feasible. Further, given that municipalities conduct the AFH, they are particularly well positioned to obtain data from local police agencies.

An important limitation may always be the lack of neighborhood crime data in most suburban areas. Thousands of suburban jurisdictions and police departments exist across the country, and it is simply not feasible to collect crime data from all those areas. To conduct assessments of entire metropolitan areas will inevitably be difficult. However, in some cases, police agencies cross city boundaries. For example, there are eighty-eight cities in Los Angeles County, most of which are suburban. Many of these jurisdictions are policed by one agency—the L.A. County Sheriff's Department. Scholars doing work on the AFH process can help assess the feasibility of collecting neighborhood crime data across metropolitan areas and begin the task of overseeing data-collection efforts.

Further, the lack of availability of crime data is reflective of a lack of transparency and accountability in U.S. municipal police departments, a problem laid bare by countless instances of police brutality, which have received heightened attention in recent years. Housing and segregation scholars should join the chorus of voices seeking increased police transparency, specifically through the dissemination of accessible data. Housing segregation means that not only violence is concentrated in communities of color but also oppressive policing practices ranging from everyday harassment to murder.

Looking forward to a future, more progressive, HUD effort to revise the AFFH Rule and the accompanying AFH, it will be important to pay more attention to crime data. Extensive research has made clear that one of the neighborhood characteristics that has the most significant effect on the educational performance and socioeconomic mobility of individuals is their childhood exposure to neighborhood violence. The ability of the AFFH Rule to reduce socioeconomic disparities and enhance the well-being of young people could be improved, therefore, by adding data regarding disparities in exposure to crime to the existing measures that HUD is already providing, where such data are publicly available. Where such data on crime are not already publicly available, HUD could encourage municipalities to make them public or, at a minimum, to analyze the spatial patterning of the crime data that municipalities should be able to obtain from their own police departments. The lack of attention to crime and violence in the current AFFH Rule is arguably its most significant shortcoming. Remedying that absence by including analyses of disparities in exposure to violence should be a priority for HUD, for block grant recipients, and for civil rights advocates.

ENDNOTES

1. Signe-Mary McKernan, Caroline Ratcliffe, and C. Eugene Steuerle, "Nine Charts about Wealth Inequality in America," October 5, 2017, https://apps.urban.org/features/wealth-inequality-charts/.

2. Kendra Bischoff and Sean F. Reardon, "Residential Segregation by Income, 1970–2009," *US2010* (Russell Sage Foundation, October 16, 2013), available at https://s4.ad.brown.edu/Projects/Diversity/Data/Report/report10162013.pdf; Paul A. Jargowsky, *Stunning Progress, Hidden Problems: The Dramatic Decline of Concentrated Poverty in the 1990s* (Washington, DC: Brookings Institution, May 1, 2003), available at https://www.brookings.edu/research/stunning-progress-hidden-problems-the-dramatic-decline-of-concentrated-poverty-in-the-1990s/.

3. Robert Mark Silverman, Li Yin, and Kelly L. Patterson, "Siting Affordable Housing in Opportunity Neighborhoods: An Assessment of HUD's Affirmatively Furthering Fair Housing Mapping Tool," *Journal of Community Practice* 25, no. 2 (April 2017): 143–158.

4. U.S. Department of Housing and Urban Development (HUD), "AFFH-T Data Documentation - HUD Exchange," September 2017, available at https://www.hudex change.info/resource/4848/affh-data-documentation/.

5. Ibid.

6. S. J. South, K. Crowder, and E. Chavez, "Exiting and Entering High-Poverty Neighborhoods: Latinos, Blacks and Anglos Compared," *Social Forces* 84, no. 2 (December 2005): 873–900.

7. Peter Rosenblatt and Stefanie DeLuca, "'We Don't Live Outside, We Live in Here': Neighborhood and Residential Mobility Decisions among Low-Income Families," *City and Community* 11, no. 3 (September 2012): 254–284.

8. Maria Hanratty, Sarah McLanahan, and Becky Pettit, "The Impact of the Los Angeles Moving to Opportunity Program on Residential Mobility, Neighborhood Characteristics, and Early Child and Parent Outcomes," Working Paper (Bendheim-Thoman Center for Research on Child Wellbeing, Princeton University, 1998); Lisa Sanbonmatsu et al., *Moving to Opportunity for Fair Housing Demonstration Program—Final Impacts Evaluation* (Washington, DC: HUD, 2011), available at http://www.huduser.org/portal /publications/pubasst/MTOFHD.html.

9. Leonard S. Rubinowitz and James E. Rosenbaum, *Crossing the Class and Color Lines: From Public Housing to White Suburbia* (Chicago: University of Chicago Press, 2000).

10. Ibid., 83–84.

11. Micere Keels, Greg J. Duncan, Stefanie Deluca, Ruby Mendenhall, James Rosenbaum. "Fifteen Years Later: Can Residential Mobility Programs Provide a Long-Term Escape from Neighborhood Segregation, Crime, and Poverty?" *Demography* 42, no. 1 (2005): 51–73.

12. Mark Edward Votruba and Jeffrey R. Kling, "Effects of Neighborhood Characteristics on the Mortality of Black Male Youth: Evidence from Gautreaux, Chicago," *Social Science and Medicine* 68, no. 5 (March 2009): 814–823.

13. Sanbonmatsu et al., *Moving to Opportunity for Fair Housing Demonstration Program*.

14. Ibid.; James E. Rosenbaum, Marilyn J. Kulieke, and Leonard S. Rubinowitz, "White Suburban Schools' Responses to Low-Income Black Children: Sources of Successes and Problems," *Urban Review* 20, no. 1 (March 1988): 28–41.

15. Rosenbaum, Kulieke, and Rubinowitz, "White Suburban Schools' Responses to Low-Income Black Children."

16. Sanbonmatsu et al., *Moving to Opportunity for Fair Housing Demonstration Program*.

17. Jens Ludwig et al., "What Can We Learn about Neighborhood Effects from the Moving to Opportunity Experiment?" *American Journal of Sociology* 114, no. 1 (July 2008): 144–188; Sanbonmatsu et al., *Moving to Opportunity for Fair Housing Demonstration Program*.

18. Rosenblatt and DeLuca, "'We Don't Live Outside, We Live in Here.'"

19. William Julius Wilson, *The Truly Disadvantaged* (Chicago: University of Chicago Press, 1987).

20. Ingrid Gould Ellen and Margery Austin Turner, "Does Neighborhood Matter? Assessing Recent Evidence," *Housing Policy Debate* 8, no. 4 (January 1997): 833–866.

21. Raj Chetty, Nathaniel Hendren, and Lawrence Katz, *The Effects of Exposure to Better Neighborhoods on Children: New Evidence from the Moving to Opportunity Experiment* (Cambridge, MA: National Bureau of Economic Research, May 2015).

22. Jens Ludwig and Jeffrey R. Kling, "Is Crime Contagious?" *Journal of Law and Economics* 50, no. 3 (August 2007): 491–518.

23. Evelyn Blumenberg and Gregory Pierce, "A Driving Factor in Mobility? Transportation's Role in Connecting Subsidized Housing and Employment Outcomes in the Moving to Opportunity (MTO) Program," *Journal of the American Planning Association* 80, no. 1 (January 2014): 52–66.

24. Michael C. Lens and C. J. Gabbe, "Employment Proximity and Outcomes for Moving to Opportunity Families," *Journal of Urban Affairs* 39, no. 4 (May 2017): 547–562.

25. Michael A. Stoll, "Spatial Job Search, Spatial Mismatch, and the Employment and Wages of Racial and Ethnic Groups in Los Angeles," *Journal of Urban Economics* 46, no. 1 (July 1999): 129–155.

26. Paul Ong and Evelyn Blumenberg, "Job Access, Commute and Travel Burden among Welfare Recipients," *Urban Studies* 35, no. 1 (January 1998): 77–93.

27. Robert Cervero, Onésimo Sandoval, and John Landis, "Transportation as a Stimulus of Welfare-to-Work: Private versus Public Mobility," *Journal of Planning Education and Research* 22, no. 1 (September 2002): 50–63; Thomas W. Sanchez, Qing Shen, and Zhong-Ren Peng, "Transit Mobility, Jobs Access and Low-Income Labour Participation in US Metropolitan Areas," *Urban Studies* 41, no. 7 (June 2004): 1313–1331.

28. Patrick Sharkey, *Stuck in Place: Urban Neighborhoods and the End of Progress toward Racial Equality*, 1st ed. (Chicago: University of Chicago Press, 2013).

29. Raj Chetty, Nathaniel Hendren, Patrick Kline, and Emmanuel Saez, *Where Is the Land of Opportunity? The Geography of Intergenerational Mobility in the United States* (Cambridge, MA: National Bureau of Economic Research, January 2014).

30. Jorge De la Roca, Ingrid Gould Ellen, and Katherine M. O'Regan, "Race and Neighborhoods in the 21st Century: What Does Segregation Mean Today?" *Regional Science and Urban Economics* 47 (July 2014): 138–151; Ruth D. Peterson and Lauren J. Krivo, "National Neighborhood Crime Study (NNCS), 2000: Version 1," May 5, 2010, available at http://www.icpsr.umich.edu/icpsrweb/RCMD/studies/27501.

31. De la Roca, Ellen, and O'Regan, "Race and Neighborhoods in the 21st Century," 143.

32. Robert J. Sampson, *Great American City: Chicago and the Enduring Neighborhood Effect* (Chicago: University of Chicago Press, 2012).

33. Robert J. Sampson, Stephen W. Raudenbush, and Felton Earls, "Neighborhoods and Violent Crime: A Multilevel Study of Collective Efficacy," *Science* 277, no. 5328 (August 15, 1997): 918–924.

34. George Galster, Roger Andersson, Sako Musterd, and Timo M. Kauppinen, "Does Neighborhood Income Mix Affect Earnings of Adults? New Evidence from Sweden," *Journal of Urban Economics* 63, no. 3 (May 2008): 858–870.

35. Patrick Sharkey, "The Acute Effect of Local Homicides on Children's Cognitive Performance," *Proceedings of the National Academy of Sciences* 107, no. 26 (June 29, 2010): 11733–11738.

36. Patrick T. Sharkey, Nicole Tirado-Stayer, Andrew V. Papachristos, and C. Cybele Raver, "The Effect of Local Violence on Children's Attention and Impulse Control," *American Journal of Public Health* 102, no. 12 (December 2012): 2287–2293.

37. Patrick Sharkey, *Uneasy Peace: The Great Crime Decline, the Renewal of City Life, and the Next War on Violence*, 1st ed. (New York: Norton, 2018), 87.

38. Ibid.

39. Peterson and Krivo, "National Neighborhood Crime Study (NNCS), 2000."

40. Michael C. Lens, Ingrid Gould Ellen, and Katherine O'Regan, "Do Vouchers Help Low-Income Households Live in Safer Neighborhoods? Evidence on the Housing Choice Voucher Program," *Cityscape* 13, no. 3 (2011): 135–159.

41. Brent D. Mast and Ronald E. Wilson, "Housing Choice Vouchers and Crime in Charlotte, NC," *Housing Policy Debate* 23, no. 3 (July 2013): 559–596.

42. Elizabeth Griffiths and George Tita, "Homicide in and around Public Housing: Is Public Housing a Hotbed, a Magnet, or a Generator of Violence for the Surrounding Community?" *Social Problems* 56, no. 3 (August 2009): 474–493.

43. Office of Mayor Eric Garcetti, "Los Angeles Open Data: Information, Insights, and Analysis from the City of Los Angeles," *A Safe City: Crime Data from 2010 to Present*, available at https://data.lacity.org/A-Safe-City/Crime-Data-from-2010-to-Present /63jg-8b9z; John M. MacDonald, John R. Hipp, and Charlotte Gill, "The Effects of Immigrant Concentration on Changes in Neighborhood Crime Rates," *Journal of Quantitative Criminology* 29, no. 2 (June 2013): 191–215.

44. John R. Hipp and Daniel K. Yates, "Do Returning Parolees Affect Neighborhood Crime? A Case Study of Sacramento," *Criminology* 47, no. 3 (August 2009): 619–656.

45. Sampson, Raudenbush, and Earls, "Neighborhoods and Violent Crime."

46. John R. Hipp, "Income Inequality, Race, and Place: Does the Distribution of Race and Class Within Neighborhoods Affect Crime Rates?" *Criminology* 45, no. 3 (August 2007): 665–697.

47. Lauren J. Krivo, Ruth D. Peterson, and Danielle C. Kuhl, "Segregation, Racial Structure, and Neighborhood Violent Crime," *American Journal of Sociology* 114, no. 6 (May 2009): 1765–1802.

48. Robert J. Sampson, Jeffrey D. Morenoff, and Stephen Raudenbush, "Social Anatomy of Racial and Ethnic Disparities in Violence," *American Journal of Public Health* 95, no. 2 (February 2005): 224–232.

8

Furthering Fair Housing

Lessons for the Road Ahead

MEGAN HABERLE

T he contours of the Fair Housing Act's obligation to affirmatively further fair housing have evolved over the five decades since its enactment. These contours are sometimes murky, due to a lack of political
will to prompt the U.S. Department of Housing and Urban Development
(HUD) to firmly define performance standards or outcomes across the
breadth of the statutory obligation to affirmatively further fair housing. Yet
a new surge of interest in federal housing policy—catalyzed by advocates demanding a response to the growing shortage of affordable housing—means
that there may be revitalized potential for a wave of reforms that could more
concretely further fair housing within future, progressive administrations.
To understand this potential, it is instructive to look back at the groundwork
laid by the Barack Obama administration and the lessons it can provide.

Building on the Groundwork of the Affirmatively
Furthering Fair Housing Rule

Although the systemic barriers to residential racial integration are significant, efforts at reforming them advanced in meaningful ways during the
Obama years. For HUD, the obligation to affirmatively further fair housing
has two overlapping components: it applies to the agency's oversight of its
grantees and to its direct administration and design of its own affordable
housing programs. In addition, HUD's oversight function clarifies for its

grant recipients the parameters of their own, independent obligation to affirmatively further fair housing.[1] In the Obama administration, HUD began to institute progressive new policies across these interrelating aspects of the affirmatively furthering obligation. The department took steps aimed at improving the design and administration of its own programs (such as housing vouchers), strengthening its enforcement and oversight over its grant recipients, and using guidance and enforcement examples to propel recipients to fulfill their own fair housing obligations.

The most notable accomplishment was the issuance in 2015 of the Affirmatively Furthering Fair Housing (AFFH) Rule requiring HUD block grant program participants—localities and states, in addition to public housing authorities (PHAs)—to document step-by-step fair housing analyses and commit to specific goals to address fair housing in their regions. Civil rights and housing policy communities heralded the rule's release: at long last, HUD was meaningfully implementing the directive to affirmatively further fair housing in its block grant programs and holding its recipients accountable.[2] HUD also embarked on a number of incremental reforms to housing voucher administration and other housing programs. Across a range of program areas, HUD issued a series of funding notices and guidance documents intended to help recipients improve their fair housing practices by enabling residential mobility and taking care not to cluster subsidized housing into high-poverty areas.[3] These measures were partial and largely relied on recipients' initiative but were still important steps toward institutionalizing fair housing as a real consideration across HUD programs. They also built a foundation of research that might support future fair housing policies. The notices and guidance were a start at undoing the ways in which federal housing program administration, in its design, perpetuates the legacy of government-backed residential segregation by concentrating subsidized housing.

Without understating the losses created by the post-Obama regime of deregulation and hostility toward civil rights, advocates and progressive policy makers can build upon the momentum of these earlier efforts. Local and state governments and PHAs can remain places to incubate and test ideas; but in the longer term, there is still a need for an improved, firmer federal commitment to civil rights, so that residents of all areas—not only the pioneering ones—may benefit accordingly. This requirement means looking ahead to a restoration of fair housing at HUD and to the next wave of reforms that are needed in federal program administration and funding oversight.

What can be learned from the progress made at HUD before the 2016 election, specifically with regard to the AFFH Rule? And how do those lessons inform what remains to be done? This chapter explores those questions, with a focus on two particular characteristics of the 2015 rule: its requirement for a planning process as well as a mechanism for accountability and its potential to influence other federal housing programs as they are administered on the ground. The chapter identifies and discusses three important sets of lessons that can be gained from the initial implementation of the AFFH Rule: (1) the advantages of the rule's approach to balancing local flexibility with federal accountability; (2) the benefits of the rule's design as a framework for local or regional, cross-departmental planning efforts; and (3) the importance of extending the rule's priorities across other federal programs.

One initial lesson is that the particular federalism balance of the 2015 AFFH Rule undergirded much of its early success. As discussed by Raphael W. Bostic, Katherine O'Regan, Patrick Pontius, and Nicholas F. Kelly in Chapter 2, in designing the 2015 rule, HUD allowed its recipients significant flexibility and discretion, ostensibly to accommodate local variability in housing markets and conditions but also to avoid unsettling the status quo of local and state authority over specific housing policies. However, the rule also contains strong standards with regard to the required analysis and documentation and facilitates the formulation of meaningful goals that would be responsive to significant local housing issues. It engages funding recipients in actively working through their own means of civil rights compliance but ultimately holds them accountable to HUD—and HUD, crucially, provided thorough reviews of the analyses and their key components, such as the sufficiency of fair housing goals and inclusion of input from fair housing groups.

A second set of lessons relates to the design of the AFFH Rule as a framework for planning. The rule conveys important process benefits by enlisting grant recipients to draw up their own fair housing goals. These benefits include, for example, increased public participation in the fair housing assessment process and increased public and government investment in fair housing issues. The rule was also designed to catalyze collaboration among local entities—such as planning departments, PHAs, and others—that serve common populations and face shared fair housing problems, but whose domains have been splintered by divergent funding streams and administrative requirements. Similarly, the structure and oversight features of the 2015 rule have the potential to guide funding recipients toward meaningful regional collaborations, which can seek to overcome the imbalance of affordable housing and resource distribution among cities and suburbs.

At the same time that the rule conveys those process benefits, it also achieved specific fair housing outcomes due to the rigor of federal supervision. HUD's deep oversight of the initial cohort of participants following the new requirement was necessary in helping them break from long-standing inertia around fair housing and take concrete steps toward addressing seg-regation and other issues. Reviving HUD's fair housing review capacity, but also going further to build and strengthen HUD's historically under-resourced Office of Fair Housing and Equal Opportunity (FHEO), should be a priority of the next progressive administration.

A third set of lessons revolves around the need for further reforms to other HUD programs (such as the voucher program) in line with the AFFH Rule. As discussed below, the Donald Trump administration's suspension of the rule and overall curtailment of fair housing progress at HUD left unanswered questions about how the suspended rule might affect the op-eration of those other housing programs that must also be administered so as to "affirmatively further fair housing." Continued application of the AFFH Rule onto local housing plans (even without HUD review) could, re-gion by region, help funnel the operation of housing programs with diffuse and competing priorities into better fair housing outcomes. Strong HUD review capacity, as well as a restoration of the AFFH Rule or equivalent as applied to public housing agencies, is necessary for long-term fair housing progress. But, as discussed below, widespread improvement will occur only if significant changes are also made within the architecture of federal hous-ing programs themselves, disrupting the ways in which program design still drives segregation.

Federal Programs, but Local Discretion: The Context of Affirmatively Furthering Fair Housing

Despite the potential reach of the affirmatively furthering fair housing pro-vision, it has not so far enabled the U.S. government to make a clean break from its history of sponsoring residential segregation.[4] Discrimination still concentrates its effects within segregated communities, impeding access to quality schools, employment, health, economic development, stable hous-ing, and other aspects of life opportunity. Although more than fifty years have passed since the enactment of the Fair Housing Act, fair housing (espe-cially in the structural sense) has yet to take hold as a moral norm for most American communities. Real estate industry interests and institutional in-ertia have been countervailing forces impeding systemic change. Today, just as persistent discrimination by landlords, real estate agents, lenders, and potential neighbors continues to impose a barrier to open housing choice and integration, federal, state, and local housing policies still contribute to segregation or fail to prioritize its redress.[5] This institutional inertia across levels of government and among different public agencies contributes to segregation, often in interlocking ways.

For example, federal funding incentives, overlaid on local zoning decisions, act on a systemic level to shape the locational patterns of subsidized and other affordable housing. Bureaucratic structures within public housing administration, set by the federal government, reinforce jurisdictional fragmentation among local housing authorities and focus them on short-term needs and efficiencies rather than on fair housing goals (such as tenants' mobility beyond segregated areas).

In legal terms, the AFFH Rule and other fair housing regulations respond to the need for an effective "institutionalized method"[6] through which HUD, and its grant recipients, further the Fair Housing Act's aims and redress this complex, continuing legacy. The "affirmatively furthering" directive requires proactive measures to undo the patterns of segregation and exclusion,[7] and it requires a regional approach, in which cities and their suburbs work together to heal the legacies of redlining and white flight.[8] Although the affirmatively furthering directive is fundamental to the Fair Housing Act's intended broad remediation of our country's residential divides, its scope and application have evolved over the years, in fitful response to litigation and other advocacy pushes and government trends. The Fair Housing Act itself does not define the content of the obligation to further fair housing (see 42 U.S.C. §3608(d), providing in simple terms that the HUD secretary shall "administer the programs and activities relating to housing and urban development in a manner affirmatively to further the policies of [the act]"). Instead, what it means to "affirmatively further fair housing" has been fleshed out episodically through judicial interpretation and on occasion systematized in agency regulations and guidance governing siting, tenant selection, and other policies.

Stretching over several decades of history, the story of the affirmatively furthering mandate is one of unfulfilled potential, reflecting themes of political will and access and institutional dynamics (and of how race and class can drive the government's priorities in overt and subtle ways). One contributing problem has been agency reticence to engage in rigorous oversight or create accountability for local policies, even among federal funding recipients. In addition, municipal fragmentation and insufficient political will to support fair housing policies pose enduring challenges to advocates working for change in this field from the grass roots up, as does the general absence of cross-issue policy infrastructure (such that housing segregation and reciprocal problems, such as school segregation or neighborhood environmental health, could be addressed in coordination).

A further challenge is that HUD historically has declined to use its spending leverage to prompt states and localities to redress their broad range of segregative policies, such as exclusionary zoning and siting policies for affordable housing. With regard to its grant administration, prior to the 2015 AFFH Rule, HUD traditionally did little to direct recipients away from segregative practices or condition its funds on their furtherance of fair housing. Recipients were required to certify that they were meeting their affirmatively furthering obligation, but oversight was vastly inadequate. Severe, widespread deficiencies and delays characterized HUD's pre-2015 Analysis of Impediments (AI) process, which lacked a template or any HUD review mechanism.[9] Testimony and reports from multiple experts, previous HUD officials, and civil rights groups abundantly documented the inadequacy of AIs to further fair housing or provide accountability;[10] meanwhile, impediments to fair housing remained in many places unexamined and deeply ingrained.

Although HUD is charged with the interpretation of the Fair Housing Act and the implementation and oversight of its AFFH provision, the agency has been reticent to exert its full authority to advance civil rights. This reticence holds true within HUD's program design and its block grant administration. Much of federal housing policy operates in a form of cooperative federalism, with federal, state, and local actors each playing a role in shaping program design and operation and in making decisions that can either advance or deflect fair housing mandates. Thus, housing voucher administration is funded and regulated by HUD but administered by PHAs—sometimes dozens throughout a metropolitan region—that set their own policies on rent structures, admissions and billing practices, local site selection, and other aspects of operation of great practical import in molding residential choice and options and, therefore, fair housing outcomes. Block grant spending is relatively loosely governed by HUD, although it is subject to civil rights laws and AFFH certification requirements for recipients. Another major program, the Low-Income Housing Tax Credit (LIHTC; administered by the Department of the Treasury), involves siting priorities and standards that are rooted in overlapping sources of authority: legislative, regulatory, and state agency directives. Local zoning, other land use, and anti-discrimination policies overlay each of these programs and help drive their outcomes (subject again to civil rights oversight).

On the one hand, the local flexibility inherent in this system has allowed for progressive experimentation and for some jurisdictions to undertake new and effective fair housing techniques. On the other hand, these overlapping roles have, at times, functioned as a way for any one actor to elude accountability, in ways that can impede progress toward systemic reforms.[11] Furthermore, because of practical concerns about accommodating varying local needs and political concerns about preserving local autonomy, federal housing policy has shied away from imparting to recipients clear performance goals or standards for desegregation. This is in contrast to other regulatory fields—such as environmental regulation—that similarly operate in a cooperative federalism model in which state or local actors are charged with implementation but which come with federally prescribed performance metrics. Within fair housing, this absence of performance metrics has been particularly problematic because it combines with other institutional forces that inhibit progress on civil rights (as described further in the section on federal housing program design, below). In addition, HUD has traditionally lacked the resources—or has failed to find them—for the kind of individualized, immersive oversight that is called for to further fair housing across such a localized system. For local actors, this lack of oversight has been a loss: localities benefit from federal priority setting in the interest of civil rights and from the synergies and political cover created when local advocates or progressive administrators can point to progressive federal directives.

While these federal-local dynamics are long-standing in housing administration, they are not inevitable. For example, the 2015 AFFH Rule responded to the widespread criticism around the lack of accountability for block grant recipients by mandating the completion of an Assessment of Fair Housing (AFH), which created a standardized process for recipients to document local fair housing issues and commit to "meaningful goals" to further fair housing. The AFH must also inform the recipient's subsequent Consolidated Plan, which describes how the recipient will use the block grant allocation, as well as the PHA's planning documents—thereby attaching HUD's AFFH mandate more firmly to its grant spending.

For the most part, the Obama administration worked along the grain of cooperative federalism and local discretion, even when building in new incentives and openings for fair housing (as discussed further below). But with the AFFH Rule, it also took an important step to more actively bind local discretion within fair housing parameters and to hold its block grant recipients accountable for their affirmatively furthering responsibilities as a condition of receiving HUD funds. With the issuance of the rule, HUD embarked on a period of detailed reviews of local fair housing issues and goal setting; the rule's implementation was also intended to begin a cycle of accountability during which jurisdictions would later need to answer for their progress.

Fair housing advocates noted during the rule's formulation that, while the regulation provided content and clarity for recipients, it adopted a collaborative tenor. It was not intended to be an intrusive leap into a vigorous new enforcement regime.[12] Much about the rule was process-oriented, in the sense that it helped localities draw up appropriate goals but stopped short of having HUD itself set forth metrics or standards. Moreover, because the rule leaves goal identification to the program participants, its degree of success in creating real change in any given location rests significantly on local consensus building and initiative. Yet, as Chapter 3 makes clear, the early results of the AFH process showed that, in fact, HUD had assertively propelled many recipients to create sharper, more meaningful goals.[13] This was significantly thanks to the diligence of HUD's fair housing staff, who thoroughly reviewed each submitted AFH, provided individualized feedback, and declined to accept AFHs that did not contain appropriate or sufficient goals. The goals generated by the early cohort of participants completing the AFH process included production of affordable housing units in low-poverty areas; zoning revisions to accommodate mixed-use, mixed-income development; landlord outreach programs to support moves by housing choice voucher (HCV) holders; adoption of new voucher payment standards to cover rents in higher-opportunity areas; and more.[14]

At the same time, the planning process itself also engendered new collaborations and public involvement, as participants worked to meet those requirements. Part of the Obama administration's legacy was to show that local flexibility can offer opportunities for civil rights not just continuing challenges.[15] That is, the process in itself—designed to accommodate local priorities and needs—conveyed important benefits to participating communities by enlisting them in the active design of their fair housing goals.

Process Benefits: Collaboration and Public Engagement

In comparison with many other fields of advocacy, fair housing has long had a collective action challenge.[16] In contemporary times, individuals who seek to live in less-segregated neighborhoods have not traditionally formed a political bloc, and public officials have too rarely been proactive in responding to their needs or the aspirations of a diverse society. Fair housing has largely been protected and advanced through litigation and a rights-enforcement model, rather than a political-mobilization model. There are positive exceptions, such as state AFFH legislation in California and Connecticut and inclusionary regional strategies such as that formed in the Twin Cities,[17] but most locations have been locked by inertia when it comes to developing measures to address segregation.

While the AFFH Rule lacks the power to change all these underlying dynamics, the rule's process in itself may be a driver of change if taken as a serious opportunity by advocates. The 2015 rule constitutes a shift to a truer vein of cooperative federalism, away from the empty formalism and lack of accountability represented by the previous AI process.

This sort of collaborative governance not only enables local flexibility but also actively enlists recipients in such a way that may spark new coalition building and public understanding of civil rights.[18] The 2015 AFFH Rule, for example, requires public participation in the creation of the AFH, urges interagency consultation, and encourages the use of local data provided by such entities as advocates and universities. Through these provisions, it offers a framework for documentation and coalition building around residential segregation, including segregation's reciprocal relationship with other issues, such as environmental health, school segregation, and other land-use policies. Problems that are factually and causally linked, such as economic development and housing development, are frequently the purviews of different local agencies. The AFH can potentially provide a coordinating framework for collaboration around these issues as well as related advocacy and planning.

Additionally, the 2015 rule requires a regional analysis and encouraged regional collaborations (among adjacent entities, such as cities, their suburbs, and their PHAs). This requirement can help promote regional strategies that aim to overcome the fragmentation of resources and services throughout metropolitan areas. This fragmentation was driven, at the outset, by federal and state regimes that enabled boundary drawing around services and tax bases and by the capacious sprawl that aligned development interests and government support.[19] Local autonomy was secured by state and federal court decisions that rejected equal protection arguments seeking a broader conception of rights and accountability.[20] As David Troutt observes, a series of Supreme Court cases during the prime era of white flight, including *Village of Belle Terre v. Boraas, Warth v. Seldin, Village of Arlington Heights v. Metropolitan Housing Development Corp., San Antonio Independent School District v. Rodriguez*, and *Milliken v. Bradley,* "put the Court's imprimatur on the critical aspects of local autonomy. . . . Without them, the twin pillars of local autonomy and land use and school finance would not have been secure in the jurisprudential edifice succeeding racial segregation."[21] These protective theories of federalism and localism were reinforced by the development of limiting theories of causation, and therefore accountability, for regional actors.[22] Such court decisions not only encouraged such boundary-drawing behavior but also helped elide the ways in which institutional mechanisms were creating segregation.[23]

Such scholars as Sheryll Cashin, Richard Briffault, and others have noted that fragmentation is closely linked to resource hoarding by historically advantaged groups and to segregation.[24] This process is part of an enduring American "ideology of localism," as Cashin puts it. Over time, as it comes to mimic an ingrained natural order, boundary drawing and racial distance have a self-reinforcing effect.[25] What is fundamentally driven by self-interest, among exclusionary areas, enfolds itself in notions of "community." The long-term hope of civil rights advocates is that the majority notions of self-interest are fluid and can be redefined to a less narrow and short-sighted conception. Realism dictates that, more immediately, self-interest must be redirected by the tools available, which in civil rights often entail federal oversight, funding incentives, and regulatory design.

Advocates hope that public engagement efforts around fair housing may help the broader communities of metropolitan regions perceive that they share a collective identity and fate, even as this shared identity is hidden by geographic distance and municipal boundary lines.[26] These communities may also come to understand better the ways in which housing policy perpetuates racial distance and can serve as a form of corrective justice for past wrongs.[27] As well as pulling the mask off local segregative histories and connecting them to continuing discrimination, public education efforts around fair housing may help expose the extent of private discrimination, which is drastically underreported and thus underenforced.[28] The rule provided for richer documentation of Fair Housing Act violations, such as affordable housing distribution, exclusionary zoning, or inadequate anti-discrimination enforcement. Civil rights advocates remain hopeful that this platform will drive increased public understanding about fair housing as well as spur specific policy change through federal oversight.[29]

With concerted involvement by advocates and progressive policy makers, a revived AFFH process could, as the early results already suggest, yield models of dialogue and action. For example, the Greater New Orleans Fair Housing Action Center, which partnered with the city of New Orleans to conduct its AFH, engaged in extensive stakeholder outreach, in particular to maximize the participation of "those that have been historically underrepresented in the planning process," including public housing residents.[30] Together with the AFH's analytical framework, this process resulted in a series of strong, specific goals in housing voucher administration and other areas. In Philadelphia, advocates leveraged the AFH's requirements to engage the city in formulating strong goals responsive to pressing local fair housing issues. In Seattle and New York, city staff convened ongoing cross-agency and cross-issue working groups to focus on the intersections of such issues as environmental health and education with fair housing. Overall, the initial AFHs yielded rich gains in public participation, including in "the number of opportunities for public engagement; the inclusiveness of those opportunities; the provision of data for assessing public engagement; documentation and consideration of the public input; and existence of cross-jurisdictional or cross-sector engagement."[31]

What Difference Could the Affirmatively Furthering Fair Housing Rule Make to Other Federal Housing Programs?

Because of the overall halt in momentum of initiatives to affirmatively further fair housing at HUD that occurred during the Trump administration, the potential of the AFFH Rule has yet to be realized. At the same time, its initial rollout also posed significant questions about the next steps needed at HUD and other agencies responsible for affirmatively furthering fair housing. In particular, the overlay of the rule onto subsidized housing program implementation has intriguing potential. An updated version of the 2015 AFFH Rule could make a real difference in improving the fair housing performance of such programs as HCVs, the LIHTC program (administered by the Department of the Treasury), and other aspects of federal housing administration—but it should also be accompanied by serious changes to the design of those programs themselves. With regard to HUD's own programs, fair housing has been treated as a subsidiary concern, peripheral rather than fundamental to program design and operation. That is, although the AFFH mandate is designed to shape the administration of all federal housing program from the outset, in actuality it tends to be applied inconsistently and *post hoc* alongside other civil rights compliance. The history of federal housing programs and the current state of segregation show how deep the need is for corrective direction within such programs. Cumulatively, HUD's own housing program designs fail to affirmatively lead local administrators to further fair housing—and in numerous respects have even counter-incentivized such moves.

Although the most egregious policies that historically confined low-income households to segregated areas are now curtailed, the administration of subsidized housing nonetheless continues to reproduce patterns of racial and ethnic segregation and concentrated poverty, especially for people of color.[32] This contribution to continuing segregation by race, ethnicity, and class is in part because federal housing administration, by and large, fails to sufficiently prioritize policies that could disrupt the "cycle of segregation"[33] embedded by racial information gaps, market forces (often shaped by racism), and the institutional inertia of a variety of actors. Federal housing programs also contribute to segregation due to the persistence of program design elements that are strikingly inconsistent with civil rights aims. For instance, in the HCV program, PHA budgeting structures and administrative incentives impede agencies from focusing on residential mobility.[34] HCV administration is by default deeply fragmented within geographic regions, such that separate apartment listings, resident applications, and billing hurdles impede residents' ease of movement, and PHAs lose administrative fees when residents depart their jurisdictions (even when those moves better serve families and improve distribution). Similarly, in LIHTC administration, unit production in high-poverty areas remains the primary program focus.[35]

More positively, during the same period in which it issued the AFFH regulation for block grant recipients, HUD ventured down a parallel path toward affirmatively furthering fair housing within many of its own programs.

Most of these fair housing advances were exploratory or incentive-based, with housing desegregation one of multiple, competing incentives. For instance, HUD's Strategic Plans included a focus on "housing as a platform for quality of life" and referenced the need to expand housing options but did not make a strong overarching commitment to break from the past reinforcement of segregation and prioritize housing choice.[36] HUD's general Notices of Funding Availability, providing guidance for grant applicants, did contain a new, explicit focus on affirmatively furthering fair housing starting in 2010, with points awarded for poverty and racial deconcentration and related strategies.[37] Specific HUD programs that were designed or expanded during the Obama administration—such as the Choice Neighborhoods Initiative, the Sustainable Communities Initiative, Moving to Work Demonstration (MTW), and Rental Assistance Demonstration (RAD)—similarly provided new opportunities, but not ground-breaking new requirements, for localities and PHAs to use federal programs to pursue housing mobility and desegregation.[38] One exception was the 2016 Small Area Fair Market Rent Rule, which required twenty-four designated metropolitan areas, with especially concentrated housing voucher use, to calculate voucher payments by zip code rather than (as generally prescribed) by metropolitan region. As discussed in the Introduction, this new range of payment standards enables voucher holders to access rental units in areas that are traditionally foreclosed to them because of relatively high rents but that offer lower neighborhood poverty levels, better-performing schools, and other amenities.

From a fair housing perspective, the majority of the new fair housing incentives were influential largely by enabling progressive PHAs and localities to pursue their own fair housing agendas and by signaling to recipients that affirmatively furthering fair housing should be a serious aspect of their missions. When it came to its own federal housing policies, in other words, the Obama administration's predominant approach in program design was one of expanding the opportunities for program participants to voluntarily advance equality. This conception of civil rights is an elastic one, in the sense of being flexible to accommodate individualized circumstances, but also reliant on the motivation of local actors, federal officials, and advocates. Furthermore, because such programs as MTW lack sufficiently strong internal fair housing standards, it has become increasingly clear in the Trump era that their inherent flexibility can also enable localities to shirk their fair housing responsibilities.

The AFFH Rule offered potential synergy with these other Obama-era HUD initiatives, which on their own gently guided PHAs toward better fair housing policies. The 2015 rule covered HUD block grant recipients and applied to all their housing activities and their PHAs, and it encouraged local entities to collaborate with each other in the analysis and development of goals. It was also meant to apply directly to PHAs, although this provision did not take effect before the rule's suspension. Still, many city and county AFH filers had already collaborated with their PHAs, including Philadelphia, New Orleans, Seattle, Albuquerque, Los Angeles, entities throughout Delaware, and Contra Costa County in California. Many of the early AFH goals entailed local improvements to subsidized housing administration, and if HUD were to engage in rigorous oversight, more such goals would follow. The AFFH planning process was a serious opportunity to place a fair housing overlay on PHA policy decisions, including regional initiatives, and should guide PHA (as well as local) discretion on housing policies. For example, the AFFH platform could serve as a mechanism for communities to push forward discretionary fair housing advances within federal programs, such as adjustments to voucher payment standards to allow for access to high-opportunity communities, incorporation of civil rights best practices into tax-credit allocation plans, and others. Advocates may be able to draw upon the AFH or AI process as well as the positive fair housing models incubated in progressive areas as ways to advance such change. However, the fact remains that while the cooperative federalism model of civil rights oversight can convey important benefits, it requires strong reviews and incentives to succeed with regard to PHAs, just as with other local entities.

In addition, the AFFH Rule should be seen as a complement—not a substitute—for reforms needed more broadly within the architecture of federal housing programs themselves. Absent the combination of restored AFFH oversight with more comprehensive fair housing reforms at the federal level, federal housing programs such as the LIHTC, HCVs, and others will continue to support the spatial concentration of housing and lack of choices for low-income people. Unless those facets of federal housing policy are directly addressed, they will act as a headwind—again preventing the AFFH Rule, or any successor, from achieving its full potential.

Conclusion

Along with other areas of civil rights, Obama-era progress toward desegregation underwent significant reversals during the Trump administration. Political directives at HUD impaired the agency's ability to provide fair housing oversight,[39] and the administration almost immediately targeted the newer civil rights requirements, to which jurisdictions were still adapting, as the low-hanging fruit of its deregulatory agenda—notably, in its suspension of the AFFH Rule.[40] Nonetheless, the Obama administration's regulatory initiatives have catalyzed positive transformations. For example, the AFFH Rule's initial rollout year yielded successes in jurisdictions' new commitments to meaningful fair housing goals, generated with the participation of advocates and protected groups.[41] And even after the rule's suspension, a number of cities, regions, and collaborating PHAs chose to follow the AFFH Rule's instructions and conduct rigorous fair housing analyses.

Although much of the work of fair housing assumed a defensive posture during the Trump administration, with increased attention paid to local policies and organizing strategies, federal reforms are still fundamental to advancing change. The federal role is essential to incentivize (or require) regional solutions and to sustain and "scale up" local progress. In addition, as noted above, HUD's own housing program structures still constrain open housing choice in many locations. Institutional inertia and resource constraints continue to impede fair housing reforms among a significant number of PHAs and localities, even as others engage in important, entrepreneurial fair housing endeavors. If a reawakened AFFH Rule is to fulfill its future potential for concrete change, stronger federal enforcement capacity will be needed, as will action by Congress, HUD, and the Treasury Department (and housing advocates) to improve upon federal housing program design. For local fair housing efforts to thrive and be sustained in more of the places where they are needed, and for us to break from the segregative patterns of the past, the next generation of progressive policies should build on past lessons but also more assertively push for change.

ENDNOTES

The author thanks Philip Tegeler and the editors for their insightful comments on earlier drafts.

1. See 42 U.S.C. § 3608(d) (requiring all executive branch departments and agencies administering housing and urban development programs and activities to administer these programs in a manner that affirmatively furthers fair housing); 42 U.S.C. § 3608(e) (5) (requiring HUD to "administer the programs and activities relating to housing and urban development in a manner affirmatively to further the policies of [the act]"). See also the Quality Housing and Work Responsibility Act of 1998, 42 U.S.C. § 1437v (2015); the Housing and Community Development Act, 42 U.S.C. § 5304; the United States Housing Act, 42 U.S.C. § 1437c-1(d) (15) (requiring that HUD recipients certify that they are affirmatively furthering fair housing).

2. See 24 C.F.R. § 5.152. See also Affirmatively Furthering Fair Housing Rule Preamble, 80 Fed. Reg. 42275 et seq., discussing legal authorities and policy background.

3. See Philip Tegeler, Megan Haberle, and Ebony Gayles, "Affirmatively Furthering Fair Housing in HUD Housing Programs: A First Term Report Card," *Journal of Affordable Housing and Community Development Law* 22 (2013): 27–60.

4. For fuller discussions of the AFFH Rule's potential and the structural reasons it has so far failed to achieve it, see, e.g., Olatunde Johnson, "The Last Plank: Rethinking Public and Private Power to Advance Fair Housing," *Journal of Constitutional Law* 13 (2011): 1191; Stacy E. Seicshnaydre, "The Fair Housing Choice Myth," *Cardozo Law Review* 33 (2012): 967.

5. See Megan Haberle, Ebony Gayles, and Philip Tegeler, "Accessing Opportunity: Affirmative Marketing and Tenant Selection in the LIHTC and Other Housing Programs" (Poverty and Race Research Action Council, 2012).

6. *Shannon v. United States Department of Housing & Urban Development*, 436 F.2d 809, 819 (3d Cir. 1970).

7. See, e.g., *N.A.A.C.P., Boston Chapter v. Secretary of Housing and Urban Development*, 817 F.2d 149, 154 (1st Cir. 1987); *County of Westchester v. United States Department of Housing and Urban Development*, 802 F.3d 413 (2nd Cir. 2015).

8. *Thompson v. United States Department of Housing and Urban Development*, 348 F.Supp.2d 398 (D. Md. 2005); *Gautreaux v. Romney*, 448 F.2d 731 (7th Cir. 1971).

9. U.S. Government Accountability Office, "HUD Needs to Enhance Its Requirements and Oversight of Jurisdictions' Fair Housing," GAO-10-905, September 2010, available at www.gao.gov/products/GAO-10-905. See also Affirmatively Furthering Fair Housing Rule Preamble, 80 Fed. Reg. 42275.

10. The Opportunity Agenda, "Reforming HUD's Regulations to Affirmatively Further Fair Housing," 2010, available at https://opportunityagenda.org/sites/default/files/2017-03/2010.03ReformingHUDRegulations.pdf (stating that "[a] range of housing experts, civil rights groups, and former HUD officials have documented the inadequacy of the current AI process" and detailing that testimony).

11. For example, government agency defendants in Fair Housing Act cases have successfully argued that plaintiffs failed to show sufficient causality because the policies at issue were not shaped solely or primarily by the agency; see *The Inclusive Communities Project Inc v. Department of Treasury*, No. 3:14-CV-3013-D (N.D. Tex. October 28, 2016).

12. See, e.g., Michael Allen, "HUD's New AFFH Rule: The Importance of the Ground Game," *The Dream Revisited*, September 2015, available at http://furmancenter.org/research/iri/essay/huds-new-affh-rule-the-importance-of-the-ground-game. See also Eloise Pasachoff, "Agency Enforcement of Spending Clause Statutes: A Defense of the Funding Cut-Off," *Georgetown Law Faculty Publications and Other Works* 124, no. 2 (2014), available at https://scholarship.law.georgetown.edu/facpub/1394.

13. See Justin P. Steil and Nicholas F. Kelly, *The Fairest of Them All: Analyzing Affirmatively Furthering Fair Housing Compliance* (Future of Housing Policy in the U.S., University of Pennsylvania, 2017), available at http://web.mit.edu/afs/athena.mit.edu/org/f/fairhousing/research/Steil_Kelly_Fairest_of_them_All.pdf.

14. Ibid.

15. Olatunde Johnson has written about this as part of a broader theme in governance, noting that "moving beyond traditional bureaucratic forms of regulation, civil rights agencies in recent years have experimented with new forms of regulation to advance inclusion. This new 'inclusive regulation' can be described as more open ended, less coercive, and more reliant on rewards, collaboration, flexibility, and interactive assessment than traditional modes of civil rights regulation." Olatunde C. A. Johnson, "Overreach and Innovation in Equality Regulation," *Duke Law Journal* 66, no. 8 (2017): 1771.

16. Sheryll Cashin has also discussed the "collective action" problem that local fragmentation poses to regional equity. See Sheryll Cashin, "Localism, Self-Interest, and the Tyranny of the Favored Quarter: Addressing the Barriers to New Regionalism," *Georgetown Law Journal* 88 (2000): 1985–1988.

17. See David Rusk, *Inside Game/Outside Game: Winning Strategies for Saving Urban America* (Washington, DC: Brookings Institution, 1999), 228.

18. For a comparative view, discussing a similar dynamic in the environmental context, see Gabriel Pacyniak, "Making the Most of Cooperative Federalism: What the

Clean Power Plan Has Already Achieved," *Georgetown Environmental Law Review* 29 (2017): 301.

19. See, e.g., Rusk, *Inside Game/Outside Game*; Kenneth T. Jackson, *Crabgrass Frontier: The Suburbanization of the United States* (New York: Oxford University Press, 2006), 26; Andrew Ross, *Bird on Fire: Lessons from the World's Least Sustainable City* (New York: Oxford University Press, 2011).

20. David D. Troutt, "Localism and Segregation," *Journal of Affordable Housing and Community Development Law* 16, no. 4 (2007): 323–347.

21. Ibid., 323.

22. See Michelle Adams, "Causation, Constitutional Principles, and the Jurisprudential Legacy of the Warren Court," *Washington and Lee Law Review* 59 (2002): 1173.

23. Ibid., at 1183: "The Court . . . paid insufficient attention to the roles of the State, local officials, and the Board in creating what are now self-perpetuating patterns of residential segregation. The Court was all too willing to accept a narrative which presumed that the school district did not cause residential segregation and that the cause or causes of such segregation were due to 'personal preferences,' safely outside the purview of constitutional requirements and federal judicial authority."

24. See, e.g., Richard Briffault, "Localism and Regionalism," *Buffalo Law Review* 48 (2000): 1–30; Cashin, "Localism, Self-Interest, and the Tyranny of the Favored Quarter."

25. See Troutt, "Localism and Segregation," 333–334. In accordance with the concept of "binary capitalism," Troutt writes, "If spatial separations among people, however unequal, are rationally and legally justified, the resource imbalance created by those relationships will fulfill certain instrumental cultural prophecies. The first is that in the absence of overt racial discrimination in housing, education, and employment, something must be inherently wrong with the segregated poor. . . . Conversely, in the absence of overt racism or privilege taking, something must be inherently right about the separated middle class."

26. See, e.g., Cashin, "Localism, Self-Interest, and the Tyranny of the Favored Quarter." As Cashin writes, "Viewed from a regional perspective, this dominance of the favored quarter is decidedly anti-majoritarian. But the fact of fragmented metropolitan governance, coupled with society's strong cultural preference for local powers, may be blinding us to these realities. In particular, the degree of influence and subsidization of the favored quarter is completely hidden from public view. This invisibility of the favored quarter's systematic advantage occurs in part because fragmented governance reduces the ability of citizens to learn what is going on regionally. But more specifically, it occurs because information about the geographic allocation of public investments is not systematically collected or disclosed to the public" (ibid., 1988).

27. See Ira Katznelson, *When Affirmative Action Was White: An Untold History of Racial Inequality in Twentieth-Century America* (New York: Norton, 2005), 149 (discussing the role of affirmative action as corrective justice).

28. Kelly L. Patterson and Robert Mark Silverman, "How Local Public Administrators, Nonprofit Providers, and Elected Officials Perceive Impediments to Fair Housing in the Suburbs: An Analysis of Erie County, New York," *Housing Policy Debate* 21, no. 1 (January 2011): 173. ("Underreporting of housing discrimination is the product of limited fair housing education, a lack of confidence in the fair housing enforcement system, time and resource constraints experienced by victims of discrimination, and other factors.")

29. Johnson, "The Last Plank."

30. See Declaration of Maxwell Ciardullo in support of Plaintiff's Motion for a Preliminary Injunction, *National Fair Housing Alliance et al. v. Carson*, available at http://prrac.org/pdf/2-2_Declaration_of_Maxwell_Ciardullo.pdf.

31. See Declaration of Daniel Urevick-Ackelsberg in support of Plaintiff's Motion for a Preliminary Injunction, *National Fair Housing Alliance et al. v. Carson*, available at http://prrac.org/pdf/2-9_Declaration_of_Daniel_Urevick-Ackelsberg.pdf.

32. See, e.g., Stacy E. Seicshnaydre, "How Government Housing Perpetuates Racial Segregation: Lessons from Post-Katrina New Orleans," *Catholic University Law Review* 60, no. 3 (2011): 661–665; Florence Roisman, "Keeping the Promise: Ending Racial Discrimination and Segregation in Federally Financed Housing," *Howard Law Journal* 48, no. 3 (2005): 913; Richard Rothstein, *The Color of Law: A Forgotten History of How Our Government Segregated America* (New York: Liveright, 2017); Paul Jargowsky, *The Architecture of Segregation* (Century Foundation, August 7, 2015), available at https://tcf.org/content/report/architecture-of-segregation/.

33. Maria Krysan and Kyle Crowder employ this term as the title of their book discussing a number of these dynamics. Maria Krysan and Kyle Crowder, *Cycle of Segregation: Social Processes and Residential Stratification* (New York: Russell Sage Foundation, 2017).

34. See, e.g., Deborah Thrope, "Achieving Housing Choice and Mobility in the Voucher Program: Recommendations for the Administration," *ABA Journal of Affordable Housing and Community Development Law* 27, no. 1 (2018): 145–160.

35. See, e.g., Florence Roisman, "Mandates Unsatisfied: The Low-Income Housing Tax Credit Program and the Civil Rights Laws," *University of Miami Law Review* 52, no. 4 (1998): 1011.

36. See Tegeler, Haberle, and Gayles, "Affirmatively Furthering Fair Housing in HUD Housing Programs."

37. Ibid.; see also, e.g., U.S. Department of Housing and Urban Development, "General Section to HUD's Fiscal Year 2016 Notice[s] of Funding Availability for Discretionary Programs," 2015, available at https://www.hud.gov/program_offices/administration/grants/fundsavail/nofa16/gensec.

38. Tegeler, Haberle, and Gayles, "Affirmatively Furthering Fair Housing in HUD Housing Programs."

39. See, e.g., Glenn Thrush, "Under Ben Carson, HUD Scales Back Fair Housing Enforcement," *New York Times*, March 28, 2018, available at https://www.nytimes.com/2018/03/28/us/ben-carson-hud-fair-housing-discrimination.html.

40. *Open Communities Alliance v. Carson*, No. 1:17-cv–02192 (D.D.C. 2017); *National Fair Housing Alliance v. Carson*, No. 1:18-CV–01076 (n.d.).

41. See Steil and Kelly, "The Fairest of Them All."

Conclusion

Conclusion

From Suspension to Renewal

Regaining Momentum for Fair Housing

JUSTIN P. STEIL AND NICHOLAS F. KELLY

This volume illustrates the promises of, protests against, and prospects for affirmatively furthering fair housing in the twenty-first century. From its nineteenth-century roots in Reconstruction through the civil rights movement and extending to recent battles within and beyond the U.S. Department of Housing and Urban Development (HUD) to rigorously enforce it, fair housing has changed not only in its meaning but in its implementation. For the last half century, the very concept of "affirmatively furthering fair housing" has existed in a kind of suspended animation. How can we move from suspension to revival and renewal?

As Nicholas Kelly, Maia Woluchem, Reed Jordan, and Justin Steil show in Chapter 3, the 2015 Affirmatively Furthering Fair Housing (AFFH) Rule was a substantial improvement over the previous regulations that so weakly supported past efforts at advancing fair housing. It led to a dramatic increase in the number of goals that municipalities set regarding fair housing and, even more importantly, enhanced the robustness of those goals—measured in terms of the concrete metrics that municipalities put forward to evaluate progress and in terms of the policies or programs that municipalities created to realize the goals. Second, contrary to expectations, it was not only large, coastal cities or liberal or left-leaning local governments that engaged deeply with the AFFH Rule. Instead, local governments across the country, from cities, to suburbs, counties, and metropolitan regions, with a range of political ideologies, set out thoughtful and ambitious goals regarding fair housing. Indeed, one of the strongest predictors of goal strength was a *high* level of racial segregation in the municipality, suggesting that localities may see segregation as a salient challenge and regard the AFFH Rule as an opportunity to address the disparities to which that segregation contributes. Third, the approaches that localities were proposing to advance fair housing were not solely mobility solutions, as some critics feared. The solutions certainly included supporting the mobility of low-income households, but they also embraced investing in low-income communities, improving public housing, creating new affordable housing in gentrifying neighborhoods, enhancing transportation options, channeling resources to local schools, and more. The initial results suggest that the AFFH Rule at the outset managed to chart a productive path through the complicated federalist balance of power, encouraging meaningful local innovation through required community engagement, robust technical assistance, and the threat of HUD review and rejection. The preliminary results from the forty-nine Assessments of Fair Housing (AFHs) that were submitted before the rule was suspended point in promising directions and suggest that the AFFH Rule is worth continued public attention and engagement. Indeed, cities engaged in the fair housing assessment process submitted comments to HUD opposing the suspension and proposed changes. For instance, New York City wrote that "we believe that the AFFH rule and its associated tools present significant progress in providing clear guidance and helping local governments shift operations toward a more meaningful fair housing approach," adding that "the City has already benefited from the process conceived in the AFFH rule, particularly its thorough and comprehensive community engagement requirements."[1]

At the same time, despite setbacks, potential future revisions to the rule present opportunities to strengthen and enhance it. Improving the quality of the data provided to HUD program participants is one important place to start. As Michael C. Lens points out in Chapter 7, it would be particularly valuable to invest in improving the data about neighborhood characteristics that have been shown to be most salient in affecting life outcomes, especially school performance and crime. Relatedly, Lens as well as Howard Husock (in Chapter 4) highlight the importance of continuing research about how neighborhoods influence the lives of their residents, analyzing with care exactly how concentrated poverty and racial segregation come to be correlated with negative socioeconomic outcomes across generations and which policy tools can most effectively improve socioeconomic mobility. As changes to the AFFH Rule are considered or altogether new policies are created, it is essential to continue to ask who is bearing the burden of these housing and neighborhood policies and whether they are actually improving the lives of their intended beneficiaries, as Husock, Vicki Been (in Chapter 6), Edward Goetz (in Chapter 5), and Alexander von Hoffman (in Chapter 1) all note. It is also essential to continually interrogate the balance between attempts to increase access to resources in low-income communities and parallel efforts to give low-income households the ability to choose homes and neighborhoods freely.

Since the AFFH Rule was finalized, concerns over gentrification and the implications of these neighborhood changes for racial equity have only grown. Been highlights how the relationships among racial equity, economic justice, and housing and neighborhood policy have shifted since the Fair Housing Act's passage in 1968. Conceptions of fair housing as defined primarily by the fight to access high-income suburban neighborhoods are already outdated as investments and jobs flow again into many central cities. In low-income communities of color within high-cost cities enmeshed in fights for the right to the city and struggles over access to space, displacement and resegregation are often the most salient concerns. In addition to isolating low-income households from growing central-city resources, displacement caused by gentrification may exacerbate cultural dispossession, again marking African American individuals as the "displaced persons" of American democracy.[2] Many of the AFHs already submitted explicitly mention concerns about gentrification and put forward concrete anti-displacement strategies. In high-cost cities, anti-displacement strategies are likely to be a growing focus of fair housing efforts. Been's chapter highlights many of the complex questions that policy makers must ask as they consider the fair housing and racial equity implications of new urban investments.

Many of the early AFHs set out plans to rewrite specific zoning policies to prevent displacement, to enable more affordable and multifamily developments in neighborhoods with substantial resources, to ease the construction of homes for individuals with disabilities, and others. This renewed attention to the details of land-use policy is particularly important because of what von Hoffman describes as the "web of land-use regulations" that enables exclusionary suburbs and because, as Been describes, land-use policy determines where growth goes and who benefits or is burdened by that growth. Attention to land use brings with it a focus on the regional nature of housing markets and the need for regional collaboration when creating AFHs. In Chapter 8, Megan Haberle articulates the importance of greater incentives for regional collaboration in future versions of the rule. Stronger incentives for regional efforts are a crucial starting point, and so too are greater resources for HUD to continue to meaningfully enforce the rule. One of the largest surprises of its initial implementation was the close attention that most HUD regional offices and the Office of Fair Housing and Equal Opportunity paid to the details of the AFHs—including their willingness not to accept seventeen initial submissions and insistence that they be sent back for revision. The combination of technical assistance, support, and, ultimately, enforcement was a crucial part of the rule's initial success but will, as HUD has noted, require more resources to continue and to expand.

In Chapter 2, reflecting on their time as federal policy makers, Raphael Bostic, Katherine O'Regan, and Patrick Pontius (with assistance from Nicholas Kelly) set out the blueprint for how difficult conversations can happen within HUD as future revisions are considered. They describe in detail best practices of governance and community engagement in the initial drafting of the rule. The level of dialogue that HUD leadership developed among agency employees who disagreed on various aspects of the rule was essential to finding a meaningful path forward and creating an effective final rule. The methods they detail suggest not only what the obstacles may be but, even more importantly, what is possible as the rule is revised or as other related efforts are undertaken.

Indeed, Kelly and colleagues found support for the utility of the cooperative planning process outlined by Bostic, O'Regan, and Pontius, since grantees whose plans were initially rejected by HUD worked collaboratively with the agency to improve their submissions. This research suggests that despite HUD's post-2017 claims about its ineffectiveness, if the AFFH Rule were reinstated, it could have a powerful impact on encouraging cities to develop plans to reduce segregation in their communities.

The issuance of the AFFH Rule in 2015 seemed like a sea change in the long effort to finally address the significant disparities in access to place-based opportunities that still characterize U.S. metropolitan areas. Crafted with careful input from civil rights advocates, state and local government officials, public housing authorities (PHAs), and others, it provided valuable tools to state and local governments and PHAs to help them identify and address harmful patterns of discrimination, disinvestment, and inequality in access to transportation, jobs, schools, and healthy environments. The revisions that HUD proposed in 2019 eliminated any requirements to analyze segregation or identify or redress place-based disparities in access to resources, substituting a focus on housing supply. These 2019 revisions proposed transforming the AFFH Rule into a platform for state and local deregulation, potentially threatening important environmental protections, subsidized housing production, and tenants' rights. As this book went to press, HUD abruptly repealed the rule altogether. But does this mean that the broad promises of the 2015 AFFH Rule have irreversibly met a premature end?

As in the Reconstruction era and in the civil rights era, promises for racial equity in America's neighborhoods provoke strong resistance. Resistance to fair housing policies that call into question white supremacist norms and that challenge wealthy, white opportunity hoarding have set back movements for racial equity in housing before, but each time, new plans and new policies are made to push equality forward again. Recent state and local policy developments, such as California's Affirmatively Furthering Fair Housing Law (A.B. 686) or New York City's Assessment of Fair Housing (Where We Live NYC), suggest that the 2015 issuance of the AFFH Rule may have just been the next step in the ongoing journey to address the intersection of housing, neighborhoods, and racial equity. Many municipalities have continued to work on AFHs despite the suspension of the rule, and future research could examine how these municipalities' efforts have been shaped by regulatory uncertainty.

The expansion of the Black Lives Matter movement in 2020 further highlighted the need to directly confront and uproot white supremacy to create a truly multiracial democracy. Addressing the wide racial disparities in wealth, health, and other outcomes in the United States will require dramatic changes to housing and land-use policies. Advancing racial and economic justice will require reimagining local government structures and the functioning of U.S. regions and reconceptualizing the funding of public services and the relationships among local governments. The AFFH Rule is an important catalyst for these conversations.

As this volume demonstrates, efforts continue to envision how future federal policy makers could more effectively work with state and local governments to reshape our metropolitan areas in ways that can improve socioeconomic mobility for all and advance racial justice in America's neighborhoods. This book provides a starting point for these discussions and for a future generation of efforts to realize the Reconstruction-era hopes for a truly multiracial democracy, one that might finally support Black liberation and be politically, socially, and economically inclusive of all residents.

ENDNOTES

1. City of New York, comment re: Affirmatively Furthering Fair Housing: Streamlining and Enhancements, Docket No. FR-6123-A-01, October 11, 2018.

2. Ralph Ellison, "Harlem Is Nowhere" in *Shadow and Act* (New York: Random House, 1964), 294–302; Sharifa Rhodes-Pitts, *Harlem Is Nowhere: A Journey to the Mecca of Black America* (New York: Little, Brown, 2011), 117.

About the Contributors

Vicki Been is the Deputy Mayor for Housing and Economic Development for the city of New York. She was previously the New York City commissioner of housing preservation and development. Prior to her public service, she was the Boxer Family Professor of Law at the New York University (NYU) School of Law, an affiliated Professor of Public Policy at the NYU Wagner Graduate School of Public Service, and the Faculty Director of the NYU Furman Center for Real Estate and Urban Policy.

Raphael W. Bostic is the fifteenth President and Chief Executive Officer of the Federal Reserve Bank of Atlanta. From 2012 to 2017, Bostic was the Judith and John Bedrosian Chair in Governance and the Public Enterprise at the Sol Price School of Public Policy at the University of Southern California (USC), following a three-year stint as the Assistant Secretary for Policy Development and Research at the U.S. Department of Housing and Urban Development (HUD).

Edward G. Goetz is the Director of the Center for Urban and Regional Affairs at the University of Minnesota and the Codirector of the University-Metropolitan Consortium. He has served as an Associate Dean and as the Director of the Master of Urban and Regional Planning program at the Humphrey School. His research focuses on issues of race and poverty and how they affect housing policy planning and implementation.

Megan Haberle is the Deputy Director of the Poverty & Race Research Action Council, where she has worked since 2012. She specializes in policy designs, public education, and technical assistance relating to government programs and civil rights, with a focus on advancing fair housing and environmental justice.

Howard Husock is the Vice President for Research and Publications at the Manhattan Institute. From 1987 through 2006, Husock was the Director of Case Studies in Public Policy and Management at Harvard University's Kennedy School of Government, where he was also a Fellow at the Hauser Center on Nonprofit Organizations and an Adjunct Lecturer in Public Management.

Reed Jordan is an urban planner and policy analyst. He is currently the project manager for Where We Live NYC, the city of New York's comprehensive fair housing plan to fight discrimination, confront segregation, and increase access to opportunity. He previously was a housing and community development policy researcher at the Urban Institute. He received his master's degree in city planning at the Massachusetts Institute of Technology (MIT).

Nicholas F. Kelly is a Ph.D. candidate in Urban Studies and Planning at the Massachusetts Institute of Technology. His research focuses on affordable housing and public policy, with a particular focus on segregation and urban politics. His current work develops tools to increase access to opportunity neighborhoods for low-income families and examines how political institutions shape efforts to promote equity in housing. He has worked at the Boston Housing Authority, at the New York City Economic Development Corporation, and as an aide for Senator Chuck Schumer.

Michael C. Lens is the Associate Faculty Director of the University of California, Los Angeles (UCLA) Lewis Center for Regional Policy Studies and an Associate Professor of Urban Planning and Public Policy at UCLA Luskin. In recent research, Professor Lens is studying the effect of the housing bust on housing subsidy demand and local government finances, the role of public investments in gentrification processes, and the spatial concentration of evictions.

Katherine O'Regan is a Professor of Public Policy and Planning at NYU Wagner, the Faculty Director of the Master of Science in Public Policy program, and the Faculty Director of the Furman Center for Real Estate and Urban Policy. She spent April 2014 to January 2017 in the Barack Obama administration, serving as the Assistant Secretary for Policy Development and Research at HUD.

Patrick Pontius serves as a principal adviser at the Federal Reserve Bank of Atlanta, providing leadership to the bank's outreach strategy and working closely with bank president Raphael W. Bostic and the Management Committee to advance the bank's strategic plan. Before relocating to Atlanta, he served for six years in the federal government in several roles, including as a senior policy adviser at HUD.

Justin P. Steil is an Associate Professor of Law and Urban Planning at the Massachusetts Institute of Technology. Broadly interested in social stratification and spatial dimensions of inequality, Steil is a leading scholar of causes, consequences, and policy responses to residential segregation, particularly the intersection of urban policy with land use and civil rights law. He is also the coeditor of *The Dream Revisited: Contemporary Debates about Housing, Segregation, and Opportunity* (Columbia University Press, 2019) and *Searching for the Just City: Debates in Urban Theory and Practice* (Routledge, 2009).

Lawrence J. Vale is an Associate Dean and Ford Professor of Urban Design and Planning at the Massachusetts Institute of Technology. His eleven books include four prize-winning volumes about low-income housing in the United States (*From the Puritans to the Projects* [Harvard University Press, 2000]; *Reclaiming Public Housing* [Harvard University Press, 2002]; *Purging the Poorest* [University of Chicago Press, 2013]; and the coedited compilation, *Public Housing Myths: Perception, Reality, and Social Policy*

[Cornell University Press, 2015], as well as the recently published book *After the Projects* [Oxford University Press, 2019]).

Alexander von Hoffman is a Senior Research Fellow at the Joint Center and a Lecturer in Urban Planning and Design at the Harvard Graduate School of Design. A historian by training, he is the author of *House by House, Block by Block: The Rebirth of America's Urban Neighborhoods* (2003), which chronicles the rise of the community development movement in New York, Boston, Chicago, Atlanta, and Los Angeles; and *Fuel Lines for the Urban Revival Engine: Neighborhoods, Community Development Corporations, and Financial Intermediaries* (Fannie Mae Foundation, 2001), which examines the relationship between funding organizations, community development corporations, and others.

Maia S. Woluchem is a Technology Fellow at the Ford Foundation in New York City. She received a master's degree in city planning from the Massachusetts Institute of Technology, working on issues of housing, socioeconomic and racial equity, and social marginality. She previously served as a Harvard Rappaport Public Policy Fellow, dually housed at the Department of Innovation and Technology and the Office of Fair Housing and Equity in the city of Boston.

Index

www.ingramcontent.com/pod-product-compliance
Lightning Source LLC
Chambersburg PA
CBHW030359270326
41926CB00009B/1179